This

... is an authorized facsimile made from the master copy of the original book. Further unauthorized copying is prohibited.

Books on Demand® is a publishing service of UMI®. The program offers digitally scanned, xerographic reprints of more than 152,000 books that are no longer in print.

The primary focus of Books on Demand is academic and professional resource materials originally published by university presses, academic societies, and trade book publishers worldwide.

CHRISTIAN EDUCATION IN A
PLURALIST SOCIETY

Christian Education in a Pluralist Society

Edited by
V. ALAN McCLELLAND

ROUTLEDGE
London and New York

First published in 1988 by
Routledge
a division of Routledge, Chapman and Hall
11 New Fetter Lane, London EC4P 4EE

Published in the USA by
Routledge
a division of Routledge, Chapman and Hall, Inc.
29 West 35th Street, New York NY 10001

© 1988 V.A. McClelland

Printed in Great Britain by Billing & Sons Ltd, Worcester

British Library Cataloguing in Publication Data

Christian education in a pluralist society.
    1. Great Britain. Christian religious
    education
    I. McClelland, V. Alan
    207'.41
    ISBN 0-415-00540-X

Library of Congress Cataloging-in-Publication Data

    ISBN 0-415-00540-X

CONTENTS

Introduction

PART I

Contents

INTRODUCTION

It is recorded that when the artist Eric Gill experienced final religious conversion, he suddenly began to think of everything in terms of religion, including sex. This is a not altogether surprising consequence of religious conversion, effecting as it does a complete <u>bouleversement</u> of attitude based upon strength and depth of commitment. Religious conversion has always had the uncomfortable implication associated with it that the whole of human life and existence, as well as all human relationship, be re-evaluated in the light of eternal truth. Edward Hulmes delineated religious commitment in terms of synthesis, integration and wholeness. The committed Christian cannot be the possessor of a ready-made checklist of solutions to every problem likely to be encountered in life. He must not allow himself to suffer from the arrogance associated with the man of closed mind. Commitment is but a starting point, an initiation into a lifetime of struggle, renewal and readjustment. Two recent writers have analysed the process graphically:

> Christian identity is important in itself. It is also important as a basis for responding to the situation in which individually and corporately, Christians now find themselves. This situation has many dimensions. It includes the personal situations of the lonely individual, the tensions that are tearing apart so many families, the Church's struggle to understand itself and win the loyalty of others, the economic problems of every local community, the difficulty of making sense of traditional Christian ideas in a changed intellectual and

cultural climate, and the problem of adapting traditional Christian mores and ethical teaching to new social conditions (J.C. Hough and J.B. Cobb: Christian Identity and Theological Education, Scholars Press, Chicago, 1985).

This is not a new claim. On the eve of the passing of the 1944 Education Act which enshrined religious education as the only compulsory subject in the English school curriculum, Spencer Leeson was preparing to deliver the Bampton Lectures at Oxford. The underlying theme of those lectures was that Christian education is much more than a matter of theology or of pedagogics. It is concerned with quality of life, with the fulfilment and integration of human personality, with individual freedom and social service. Parents, state, school and church, he declared, must regard themselves as co-operative agents in a child's education, not as agents balanced against each other 'in a precarious and mutually suspicious tension.' But tension there has always been! Agreed syllabuses and joint statements, as Leeson noted, could never be an adequate substitute 'for living membership in a worshipping community.' The fullness of the Christian life demands fertile soil in human wholeness and only finds its growth in human integrity. That growth leads to perfection; we call it holiness.

The essays in this book are concerned with synthesis, with integration, with wholeness; they confront the challenges presented to these concepts when Christians contemplate the education of their children in an age of shifting beliefs and situational ethics. The contributions in Part I of the book re-examine the relationship of family, church and school in the educative process today and consider the challenges posed to that interconnected and interactive relationship by the changing nature of modern society and its demands. They look at the condition of the Christian presence in both denominational and state schools and consider the connection between it and current forms of religious, moral, social and political education. The essays in Part II are somewhat different in approach, being governed by Telhard de Chardin's view that nothing is comprehensible except through its past. In order that we truly understand the challenges of today and those likely to be posed in the immediate future, it is necessary to retrace the steps that have led up to the need for reappraisal. Each contributor to the book is a specialist in his field and has enjoyed freedom

Introduction

to approach the task in his own way.

V.A. McClelland
Anatole von Hügel Fellow
St. Edmund's College, Cambridge

PART I

Chapter One

CHURCH, FAMILY AND SCHOOL

Philip R. May

The two most crucial statements ever made so far as the Church, the family and education are concerned, can both be found in the first chapter of the Bible. In Genesis 1, verse 1, we read: 'In the beginning, God created the heavens and the earth'. Twenty-five verses later come the following words:

> Then God said, 'Let us make man in our image, in our likeness, and let them rule over the fish of the sea and the birds of the air, over the livestock, over all the earth, and over all the creatures that move along the ground'.
> So God created man in his own image, in the image of God he created him, male and female he created them. (Genesis 1:26-27, NIV)

Buried in these statements, and developed in more detail throughout the rest of Holy Scripture, are central truths concerning the nature and needs of children, the aims of education, and the role of Church, family and school in the care and nurture of the young.

It has been the Church's privilege and duty down the centuries to expound and apply those parts of the Bible that bear on every child's family life and schooling. The task has been undertaken with varying degrees of success, but has probably been more effectively performed on behalf of the family than of the school. Christian teaching about the role and duties of parents and children and the place of the family in society has, generally speaking, been fairly precise. When the subject of education has been considered

3

at all, Christian writing, especially denominational formulations, has tended to be rather more diffuse and woolly. Only in the present century, with writers like Spencer Leeson, M.V.C. Jeffreys, Fred Clarke, W.R. Niblett, and documents like 'The Fourth R' and 'Growing into Citizenship', has education from a Christian standpoint been examined with both academic authority and detailed insight.

Formerly, the Church tended to take it for granted that its role and influence in children's education was central and did not need to be defended. Most societies in the Western world accepted this view. After all, the Christian church from its earliest times had recognised the importance of giving children at least an elementary education, and had taken the lead in educational provision. In many countries it was both initiator and innovator. As is well known, this is no longer the case.

Consequently, the Church now faces a situation of formidable difficulty. It still wishes its voice and influence to be acknowledged. Yet it is widely regarded by both governments and ordinary people as irrelevant in the education of children both in the home and at school. For this state of affairs it must itself bear the principal blame. It has allowed the Western world at least, to think that human thought and action can be compartmentalised into the religious and the mundane. Some ideas and activities are sacred, and others - and these include the business of learning and teaching - are secular.

From the educational standpoint this has come about for a reason already mentioned - the lack of rigorous educational thinking. The Church had not thought it obligatory to develop a detailed educational philosophy. With a few notable exceptions, it has only been in recent years that Christian writers have felt the need to expound their educational ideas in any detail. Too often that need has been because of outside attack rather than from inner conviction. Hence the impact of Christian truth on family and educational theory and practice has been too slight to be really influential. The field has been too much left to the secularists. This is still the case today.

Individual Christians in education at all levels must share some of this blame. They too have for the most part not thought it necessary to apply their beliefs to their professional practice. They look automatically to secular experts for their guidelines about what to teach, how to teach, and why. They too generally seem to accept that

Christian doctrine is for Sundays and religious activities only. Impassioned and well argued pleas for the Christian mind to be applied to all areas of life, such as that of Harry Blamires' excellent book The Christian Mind (SPCK, 1960) have had nothing like the response they deserved. Yet, as O.R. Barclay has more recently commented, 'it is not enough, either biblically or practically, to think only about the basic issues of the gospel ... In the Bible (and in daily life) we are faced with the need to build on that foundation a Christian way of life and thought that can cope with the whole range of practical questions that come before us' (Developing A Christian Mind, IVP, 1984, p. 12).

But there is a deeper reason for the Church's failure here. Why does so much Christian writing and speaking about the family and schooling pass unnoticed or have too blunt a cutting edge when it is read and heard? Sadly, it is because it is too often based on inadequate theology, theology which gives too much place to man-made rationalising and too little to the unequivocal teaching of the Bible. It is too acquiescent and accommodating to the unbelief and the pluralism which surrounds it. This criticism may well apply more to certain Protestant writing of the last hundred years. The Roman Catholic church has held on more firmly to its central doctrines, and refused to compromise to anything like the same extent. Even so, only when all three parts of the Christian church, Protestant, Roman Catholic and Orthodox unequivocally proclaim via pupilt, pen and practice, the central Biblical truths about the nature of God and man and the purpose of life will a lasting impact be made on the thought and actions of the world.

However, it must also be said that another factor, outside the Church's control, has exacerbated the problem it now faces. This is the rise of state educational theory and provision to a level which now makes it, in most countries, the determinant in philosophy, supply and practice of schooling for most boys and girls. Allied to its vast resources, which the Church has never been able to match, the state has increasingly espoused secular assumptions and theories. The main disciplines, philosophy, psychology and sociology of education, take for granted a world view in which God and the Church, if acknowledged at all, are allotted a small curricular part in religious studies or humanities programmes. Hence to suggest that the teachings of the Bible and the Church have a central place in what we teach our children and why, is nowadays to receive from most quarters at best raised eyebrows and at worst ridicule. The secular humanist view of the nature of man and the purpose of life, in which materialist and rationalist thinking predominate, appears to prevail at all levels of educational theory and practice. This is despite the fact that trust in its too often unexamined presuppositions - for instance that man is the measure of all things, and that his creeds must all rest on observable facts, empirically grounded - is as much, if not more, an act of faith as that demanded by most religions. Certain it is that the impact of Christian truth on the current educational scene is slight. Yet it is still the case that no other world view so accords with all the evidence available, or provides the practical help to deal with every person's total situation, let alone educational needs.

Most people accept the centrality of family and school in every child's upbringing. Without the family, there is likely to be a lack of intimate knowledge of the self as loved, accepted, nurtured. With such personal identification missing, deep inner healing will be necessary for the children fully to cope with their lives. Without some formal training in school, there will be inadequate instruction in the main subject areas, along with serious lack of peer group contact, help and stimulus. Christians insist that the Church also has a central role to play. Without the Church and its teaching, children will acquire a deformed, secular world view which misses the whole purpose and meaning of life. No matter how wise and knowledgeable a child may become in human terms, he or she will never be able by secular means and insights alone to arrive at the real truth about life, about self, even about wisdom and knowledge.

All of which brings us back to Genesis 1. The fact that the universe was created by a loving and holy God, who continues to uphold and maintain it by His providential care, has radical implications for the family and the school as well as for every individual human being. So has the fact that man is made in the image of God - rational, moral and personal. The whole basis of man's responsibility to God and for his fellow creatures is grounded upon them. The Church has always emphasised the importance of this personal relationship between man and God, and also man's relationship to the rest of the created order in the commission given him to rule over it on God's behalf. This rule must be in accordance with the laws of creation, respecting both the Creator and the integrity and worth of all other created things.

Inevitably and rightly, therefore, the Church has underlined the need for education both in the home and elsewhere. Each new generation must be equipped to carry out God's command to rule and have dominion. This means transmitting the knowledge and skills of one generation to the next. It also means helping all children and young people to understand something of the nature of God, and His laws for His creation. Just as the universe is based on certain scientific laws and principles, so God, as the Bible stresses, also gave man certain moral and spiritual laws which are equally absolute and inescapable. Hence, for example, just as in physics for every action there is an equal and opposite reaction, so in daily life, whatsoever a person sows, that shall he also reap - in relationships and personal development as well as in farming.

In a sentence, all learning has a religious basis. Because man is not, as Julian Huxley described him, a chance collection of metabolising protoplasm, but the dependent creation of a holy and gracious God to whom he owes everything, the whole human enterprise derives its meaning and purpose from this religious foundation. It must flow from and be guided by the will of the Creator as revealed in Holy Scripture. In this way it will take proper account of all the facts of life, and of the nature and needs of every individual. The role of the Church, therefore, in education, is threefold. First it must expound and explain Christian teaching about God, man and his world, and its relevance to the upbringing of children. Second, it must offer as much practical help as possible to assist parents, teachers and the young in the daily tasks of education and family life. Third, it must, where necessary, protect the family and individual children. The family, as an institution, needs protection from the devaluing of its role caused by state - and school - encroachment, and children need protection from schooling dominated by secularist world view assumptions and values.

To scrutinise with any thoroughness all aspects of this role is beyond the scope of this chapter. There is also no intention to consider all the various combinations which count in relation to Church, family and school. Some families are Christian; others are not. Most schools in the UK are secular establishments but there are specifically Christian schools also. Some families and schools see the Church as a partner. Others don't.

What follows therefore, will first of all examine the obligations which Holy Scripture puts upon the family in relation to schooling and the Church, and then consider some of the implications for all three institutions. For it is the family that has the most important role to play. And on the subject of education, it is what the Bible says about parents and children that should significantly determine what both Church and school should contribute to the process.

THE BIBLE AND THE FAMILY

The human family is the basic unit in any society or culture, although David Watson used to point out that the Bible emphasises households rather than the nuclear family. Whether family or household, it is the primary social group, established well before both the development of the Church and the giving of the law of Moses. The Biblical norm for marriage is monogamy, and the Adam and Eve story in Genesis 2 suggests that the principal purpose of marriage is companionship. There, God is recorded as commenting that 'it is not good for man to live alone', so He creates a 'helper' for Adam. Interestingly, the same word ('ezer') is used by Moses when he described the Lord as Israel's shield and helper, and by David in Psalm 121 when he says that his help comes from the Lord. It is perhaps also worth noting that it was to both male and female, husband and wife, that the command to rule and have dominion was given.

The Bible in many places makes it clear that, as the psalmist puts it, children are a heritage and a reward from the Lord (Psalm 127:3). In a very real sense this means that although my two daughters belong to me and my wife - they are 'ours' - we, like all other parents, are nevertheless stewards on God's behalf for them. Ultimately they belong to Him. This fact helps to put all the functions of the family unit into proper perspective.

Briefly, the Old and New Testaments underline four main functions for the family. Firstly, parents are to protect and nurture, through love and proper provision for basic needs. Secondly, they are there to discipline and control. Thirdly, to instruct and educate. Lastly, to send children out into the community to make their own contribution to the life of the Church and society. All four are family functions whether or not particular parents

8

recognise them as related to God. But for those parents (and their children) who overlook or reject their accountability to their Creator in these matters, the consequence is very serious.

What exactly do these duties involve for parents? 'Train up a child in the way he should go', says the Book of Proverbs (22:6). This is an interesting instruction because it does not merely imply that there is a right path to follow. It also emphasises the individuality of each child. The 'way' must be the right way for each particular person. But as the first function underlines, the setting must be one of love.

God Himself provides the pattern for all parenting. As Paul reminded the Corinthians, He promised that 'I will be a Father to you' (2 Corinthians 6:18). A father's compassion for his children is likened to God's compassion for His people (Psalm 103:13). And as God is also both shield and defender and place of refuge, so should parents be for their children. Home should be not simply a place where bodily needs are catered for, but a place where joy, encouragement, appreciation and protection from evil are part of the normal daily experience for all who live there. Above all it should be a place where love is given unconditionally. Love consistently given without any strings attached is the ground of security in the family, as it is for all Christians' security with their Father in heaven.

To a certain degree, the Bible takes for granted that parents will cherish and nurture their children. It makes more of the second and third functions of the family, discipline and education. Discipline first. This is never something negative but includes the idea of guidance as well as punishment. What son is not disciplined by his father?, asks the writer to the Hebrews. Both Old and New Testaments stress the importance of parental government. Proverbs 19:18 comments: Discipline your son for in that there is hope. Paul told the Ephesians to 'bring up your children in the training (discipline) and instruction of the Lord' (6:4). Anyone who aspires to leadership in the Church must be one who can 'manage his own family and see that his children obey him with proper respect' (1 Timothy 3:4).

Once again God provides the example as the risen Christ reminded the exiled John when He stated that: 'Those whom I love, I rebuke and discipline' (Revelation 3:19). These words are also a reminder that control and reprimand are necessary, and that they stem from and illustrate love. Correction is an important aspect of loving children. This

9

truth is a prominent part of the Church's witness to society as well as family and school. Another positive truth about discipline, as the passage in Hebrews 13 indicates, is that it identifies a child as a member of the family. It will therefore not be vindictive, harsh, spiteful, or carpingly critical, but firm and consistent, helping children to recognise that life has boundaries and limits. Justice that is based on love will also be tempered with mercy and forgiveness.

All children need teaching, and the Bible places the responsibility once again firmly on the parents, especially fathers. The verse from Ephesians 6, quoted above, is one example of this. The Book of Proverbs supplies many more. According to Scripture, instruction in the home should centre on the Word, works and worship of God, along with direct moral training, a task in which the Church also shares. There is an interesting use of words on this subject in Deuteronomy 6:7-9, where parents are instructed to teach their children the commandments of God. The word translated 'teach' (shaman) literally means to whet or sharpen. This teaching will hone as well as inform children's spiritual and intellectual understanding. For it is 'training and instruction in the Lord' that is commanded.

John and Paula Sandford, in their fascinating book The Transformation of the Inner Man (Bridge Publications, 1982), have an interesting comment on this quotation from Ephesians 6. They argue that

> the task of fathers and mothers is to evoke humanity in their children. In the beginning, to call forth the spirit to embrace. Then to build 'truth', the ability of heart and mind to interpret meanings and to cherish others' interests ... In the command '... bring them up in the nurture and admonition of the Lord' (Ephesians 6:4, KJV), it is those last words which tell. Only nurture in the Lord brings forth children who have learned to contribute their 'I' in love to another's 'Thou' without overriding or being themselves dominated. (p. 214)

A page further on, they write that 'we are to produce children who then as adults persistently choose never to treat another "Thou" as a usable, discardable, destructible "it" '.

This remark leads naturally into the fourth Scriptural function of the family, to send out children into the community and the Church, in their own right. Obviously, the ways in which parents relate, or do not relate, to each other and to God have a profound influence on their children's attitudes, standards and values, as has what they teach or fail to teach their offspring. With school first, but also society in mind, six factors are worth stressing, all of them consistently taught throughout the Bible.

First of all, children should learn about belonging. Every child is a unique creation, of supreme worth and importance. As man is dependent on God, so children belong to and depend on their family. The love, respect, protection, concern, acceptance and sense of personal identity they experience in the home delivers them from the sense of isolation and enables them to relate to themselves and to others in positive, wholesome ways.

Second, they learn about living together. This involves sharing, learning about and respecting the needs and rights of others, and accepting the responsibilities that each individual has towards others, especially the weak, the handicapped, the less able, and 'the poor, widows, orphans' met with outside the immediate family circle.

Third, they should learn what it means to submit to one another out of reverence for Christ (Ephesians 5:21), and also to respect the law. The word translated 'submit', 'hupotasso', literally means 'to arrange under', and is usually used in a military connection. Confusion and error have surrounded its meaning in contexts like that of Ephesians 5, where, for instance, the command 'Wives submit to your husbands' is wrongly interpreted by some to imply servile obedience. If it is remembered that we are all to submit to one another, and that husbands are commanded (in the next verse) to love their wives in the same self-sacrificing way that Christ loved the Church, then a proper perspective is possible. In homes where these attitudes prevail, children quickly learn the respect for persons and the consideration for others which are essential to all social intercourse. Similarly it is the home primarily where the young learn genuine respect for law, and the educative and character-building values of obedience based on love.

Fourth, children are specifically commanded to honour their parents. To do so has tremendous benefits in addition to the promise of long life which goes with the command. It is excellent preparation for the time when they in turn become parents. And this honouring of those over them extends to respect for the elderly, and for all in positions of

11

legitimate authority in school or society, to whom also honour is due, whatever one may think of their policies and practice.

Fifth, the home is the place where children can best learn effective communication with others by both word and deed. Through the teaching of parents, through explanation, information, discussion, considerate listening to one another, and through mutual help in action, children acquire the attitudes and standards which they can then apply in their relationships outside the family circle. Lastly, it is in the Christian home where children first hear about God and His word and learn to worship, thank and praise. This is something the Bible indicates that they are capable of from very early years, and experience bears this out. Of course, their experience of worship will be extended in Church and Sunday School, but as always it is at home that the main learning takes place.

Blessed indeed are those children who take up their adult responsibilities having learned the important skills of belonging, living together, submitting, honouring, communicating and praising. It is perhaps worth adding that none of this describes an impossible ideal which at best can only be aimed at. The Bible makes it abundantly clear that all this is achievable for any family, not in their own strength and wisdom, but by the grace and power of the Lord.

SOME IMPLICATIONS FOR CHURCH AND SCHOOL

The fact remains, of course, that families, including Christian families, are by no means perfect. They need the help which Church and school can give in the upbringing of children. This help becomes particularly urgent for those children who come from families where discord and neglect prevail, where homes are broken for whatever reason, and where parents are under stress through their own inadequate upbringing and difficult social circumstances. Many parents today are unsure of their role and the Church can provide models and the guidance they need. Christ, who is described more than once in the New Testament as the husband of the Church, is the supreme model. But as was hinted earlier, Church leaders also can, in their family life, offer illustrations of good parenting. And the Church family itself, as the body of Christ, can be a model to help families to learn how to operate. All this is in addition to the Church's teaching role on the subject.

This teaching role, as the Scriptural guidance on parents and children clearly shows, is even more crucial at a time when other social institutions have such an influence on the upbringing of children. This increased assumption of tasks once rightly thought to be primarily that of parents has weakened the place and value of the family in society, not least in the eyes of parents themselves. It is the Church's task to defend the family in this situation and to correct current assumptions by insisting on the Biblical principles for true family - household - life and influence. Allied to this, it should be part of the programme of every local church to provide training in marriage relationships and parenting. For there is so much generally agreed wisdom in the Church on these subjects, following Scriptural guidelines. Such training is a fundamental responsibility of both the family and the Church. Since many parents fail or need help themselves, the Church's duty in the matter is all the greater.

The sphere of education is perhaps the most important area where the Church needs to protect the family and children. As Western society has become increasingly secularised, so has the assumption that education means whatever is provided in the schools, colleges and universities of the state. As this chapter has already demonstrated, the assumption is false. It is true that few if any parents are now able by themselves to give their children an adequate grounding in all the subjects and skills needed for a rounded education. Nevertheless the part they play in the education process is more significant than that of any other source. And that is true of every family whatever its background and limitations.

John H. Westerhoff has written helpfully on this matter, as on the subjects of Christian and religious education. In his book Will our Children Have Faith (Seabury Press, 1976) he rightly attacks the current attitude that as any new 'need' or 'lack' is felt in society, so the state schools should teach about it. He cites sex education, political education, peace studies and moral education as recent examples. He will not accept either that education merely means going to school or that formal instruction is the means to achieve it. And he is highly critical of the Church in the West for adopting so readily, what he calls 'the schooling/instruction paradigm' of the secular schools. He is especially concerned about religious education in this context and comments that 'the context or place of religious education needs to be changed from an emphasis on schooling to a community of faith' (p. 51). In the light of the Scriptural teaching noted earlier, his words apply to much more than religious education.

Hence the imperative need for the Church collectively and individually to apply Christian truth to educational theory and practice. The doctrines of creation and providence have implications for what children should learn. The doctrine of man makes clear the true nature and needs of children and young people, and also should influence how they are treated and taught. Issues like authority and responsibility, the nature and purpose of rules and discipline, wisdom and knowledge, morality and moral development, creativity, and spiritual education all form part of a distinctively Christian approach. Along with teaching about marriage and the family already mentioned, all these subjects need to be seen in the light of Christian revelation for the benefit of all who teach and learn. This is part of the Church's ongoing responsibility to each new generation. It is part of its witness to the world of the claims of Christ on every aspect of every person's life.

What the Church and individual Christians have to do therefore, with Biblical guidelines to point the way, is to present a clear exposition of the Christian approaches to all these issues and to insist on their being taken into account by the state and the schools. This also involves exposing the inadequacies and reinforcing the strengths of secular theory and practice. The question which then follows is: how do these Christian beliefs actually apply in practice?

To mention two examples. Firstly, the Christian view of creation and providence undergirds a particular view of world history and of the nature and purpose of science. Curriculum theory and context ought to take these views into account, as should those who teach these subjects. Pupils should not be allowed to go through their school life believing there is only one - a secular - standpoint on which to base their understanding and interpretation of these areas. Secondly, the Christian doctrine of man has practical implications for every teacher's approach to every child. For instance, the supreme worth of every pupil should be acknowledged in day to day relationships and all activities in the life of every school. It is the Christian teachers in all our schools who must give a lead to demonstrate the value of all students whatever their intelligence, background, handicap or potential.

Few if any writers on education would equate it solely with what goes on in school even though most seem to believe that what really matters goes on there. But the idea has a firm hold on the popular mind. Here again the Church as a faith community and the Christian home as a faith community also, can both demonstrate by practice as well as precept the rightness of the wider Biblical perspective. And by setting schooling along with all other aspects of life in, to borrow a striking phrase of Harry Blamires, 'the eternal perspectives of heaven and hell', the value and purpose of what is taught there is more likely to be realised by both those who teach and those who learn.

It was with this sort of reason that the different denominations of the Church set up schools of their own. They not unreasonably saw these schools as an extension of both family and Church. The decline of Church schools and denominational teacher training is well known. Lack of Christian educational conviction is again probably the main explanation, rather than lack of resources, though that was a problem too. But interestingly enough the present day is again witnessing to the old adage that where there is a will, there's a way. More and more Christian parents are working to send their children to Christian schools and there is a new and growing Christian schools movement both in the UK and the USA. Examples are the Accelerated Christian Education approach to teaching founded in 1964, the Christian Parent Teacher League, begun in 1966, and the Christian Schools International Organisation started in 1919 and enjoying a resurgence at the present time. And there are small but growing numbers of new independent Christian schools such as those run by Charles Oxley in the Liverpool area. Their purpose is not just to educate children in the faith. Rather it is to set their formal schooling firmly in the context of Christian doctrine and community where what they experience in the formal classroom is a continuation of their experience at home and in the Church. So their upbringing has a wholeness and consistency which allows for judgements to be made which take all factors into account.

In its defence of the faith and of the family, the Church must continue wholeheartedly to support such endeavours. This will involve much sacrifice, particularly financial, especially where state education becomes more thoroughly secularised and even anti-religious. Thankfully in countries like the United Kingdom and the USA, Christian parents can still send their children to state schools with some confidence. At the very least, they will learn important moral values like respect for persons, consideration for others, justice, co-operation and truth-telling. But even in these countries there are problems, despite open sympathy and support for Christianity. As any democratic society becomes more pluralist, so, perhaps inevitably, the state takes an increasingly lowest common denominator approach. It tries to help all, and to offend no-one. Hence distinctive emphases, like that of Christianity, are blurred or overlooked.

An excellent example of this has been uncovered by Dr Paul Vitz of New York University's department of psychology. In a recently completed research study of school textbooks, full details of which have only just gone to press, he found very strong bias against any mention, for or against, of religion and what he calls traditional family values. He concluded that basal readers, like the social studies texts, are so written as to present a systematic denial of the history, heritage, beliefs and values of a very large segment of the American people (Religion and Traditional Values in Public School Textbooks, The Public Interest, No. 84, Summer 1986, p. 90). Understandably, more and more Christians in the USA are sending their children to private Christian schools. This trend could develop in the UK also.

C. Ellis Nelson once wrote in his article: Is Church Education Something Particular? (Religious Education LXVII, Jan/Feb 1972, pp. 5-15) that 'the particular role of education in the church is to foster deliberate efforts to help persons in the Church develop a Christian mentality'. His main concern was 'to help people make sense of their experience in the perspective of the Christian faith'. He was thinking mainly about the education people receive in Church itself. But his comments, especially the second one quoted, exactly express the intentions of these new and revived Christian schools. Such schools along with the older established denominational schools and the denominational teacher training establishments represent another vital response of the Church to its Scriptural obligations, a response which may need to grow stronger in the future.

Yet most children will continue to attend state rather than denominational schools, and Christians can hardly expect secular establishments to adopt Christian

16

perspectives in toto. Even so, by the grace of God, the Church in its own educational theory and practice, and individual Christian teachers in their personal, professional witness, can still have a real influence on state education. For example, most teachers still accept that the school is in part an extension of the home, and that teachers have therefore a role in loco parentis. By argument, and by example, it is still possible to encourage the practice of Christian family values in school. All children everywhere need affection, acceptance and understanding. They all need order and authority, a chance to belong, and a sense of purpose. They all need opportunities to achieve, to be recognised, to be respected, and to contribute to something of lasting worth. Every one of these needs is recognised by all good teachers even when they are unaware of the Christian teaching which helps to explain them. It is up to the Church and its members to promote greater understanding of these things.

How should society as a whole, and its schools respond to Church teaching about education? A just society will openly acknowledge its debt to the Church for the educational initiatives it has taken down the years, and still takes today. It will continue to allow denominational schools and colleges to flourish. It should aim to work closely with both the family and the Church for the good of all children. Practice has shown that shared concern for the young often produces approaches in which divergence about the details is slight. It should be open enough to take proper account of the educational principles and values taught by the Church, some of which have in any case been adopted and taken for granted for years. And there is no doubt that we learn better how to operate in school because of what we know about the family and the Church.

On one issue, however, it is not certain how the state and its schools would respond. This is the question of the power of education itself to provide the answers to the needs of children and society. Many people, distinguished and unknown, continue to believe that man's future is secure and that all will be well if children can truly be provided with a good all round education. Every Christian knows that this is a vain hope. Education, no matter how effectively presented, in the most ideal conditions and with every necessary resource available, will never save man. It can provide many right and true values, excellent knowledge, skills and understanding, and splendid training for life, all of which may well have a positive influence on the young. But it cannot deliver man from himself. It cannot create the new birth which only comes from faith in Christ.

And so we return to the role of the Church, the Christian family and the Christian school. It is there and only there that the rest of the world will find the outworking of that new life in the upbringing of the young. It is only in the community of faith, where training in personal and community living takes place, that full education of body, mind and spirit will be wholly acknowledged. A remark of John Westerhoff's is relevant here. In his book <u>Bringing Up Children in the Christian Faith</u> (Winston Press, 1980) he wrote: 'What the Church needs to model is a way of life that demonstrates that children, like adults, have equal rights before God and all humanity' (p. 29).

It would be foolish to deny that the task of the Church at the present time is very difficult. Getting a fair hearing becomes more and more of a problem. But if the trumpet does not sound a clear call who will get ready for battle? The faithful will be confused and the opposition indifferent and unafraid of the challenge. It may be that in recent days, the Church has suffered a failure of nerve where education is concerned. It has been too accommodating to other views and too tentative about its own authority. That it has real authority to speak out on these issues is unquestionable. But with authority everywhere under attack since the 1960s, maybe the fear of being labelled over dogmatic, indoctrinatory or authoritarian has muted the approach unnecessarily. Again Harry Blamires has a valuable point to make. In his book <u>Where Do We Stand?</u> (SPCK 1980), he stated:

> Authority attaches essentially to the impersonal, the collective tradition, while <u>authoritarianism</u> attaches essentially to the personal, individual will ... The Public mind in our generation has been confused and misled precisely by concealment of the fact that in religion, in education, in the life of society generally, it is authority that saves us from authoritarianism ... Thus, to say 'The Bible says' or 'the Church teaches' is of compelling weight for the very reason that the speaker is <u>not</u> being authoritarian. He is not even saying that he, as an individual, necessarily fully understands, fully agrees. He is presenting the truly authoritative voice of

the Scriptures as heeded and reverenced by intelligent Christians for 2000 years, or of the Church as summing up in its teaching the collective wisdom of learned and simple men alike over the same period (pp. 72-3).

Perhaps the Church along with Christian families and schools needs to heed some words St. Paul once wrote to his young colleague Timothy. He reminded him that 'God did not give us a spirit of timidity, but a spirit of power, of love, and of self-discipline. So do not be ashamed to testify ...' (2 Timothy 1:7-8). The law of sowing and reaping applies as fully to Christians and the Church as to anyone else. Commitment to the truth is there. So is commitment to children, to the family and to schooling. So let the Church once again speak out by word and by example. This is no mere academic exercise. The destiny of countless children and young people is at stake.

Chapter Two

CHRISTIAN EDUCATION AND THE DENOMINATIONAL SCHOOL

Vincent A. McClelland

If we wish to encapsulate in one brief sentence the scope and purpose of the denominational school, its raison d'être, we cannot do better than refer to Pius XI's encyclical on the Christian education of youth:

> ... Christian education takes in the whole aggregate of human life, physical and spiritual, intellectual and moral, individual, domestic and social, not with a view of reducing it in any way, but in order to elevate, regulate and perfect it, in accordance with the example and teaching of Christ. (1)

Christian education is concerned with concepts of oneness and totality, with unity and purpose, with wholeness and uniqueness, with regeneration and ultimate perfection, with endurance in a world alternately buffeted and beguiled by conflicting pressures and seductions. Christianity witnesses to internal essence, to that innermost reality of man that cannot become subservient to external sense or material need if he is to remain true to his being and to the commitment of Christian baptism. (2)

Opposition to denominational education arises not only from an incapacity or reluctance to acknowledge the need for a unifying cohesion in the construction of an objective ideal for the educative process but from what Harry Blamires once described as 'the closed and vicious subjectivist circle' (3) that has assumed the mantle of its substitute. The intention of education, it is commonly advanced, is to develop each child to the maximum of innate capacity, the aim, extent and ulterior purpose of the process

20

being left deliberately vague. Such uncertainty is able to prevail because modern English society is no longer capable of identifying itself with a clear philosophy of life and thus cannot adhere to a commonly accepted intellectual basis for the development of a coherent philosophy of education. Teachers, schools and, sadly, teacher-trainers are as little concerned with posing and answering fundamental questions relating to the ultimate goal of human life and the steps man must take to reach it than they are with constructing an educational programme that leads to the fulfilment of a clearly defensible objective. It is, of course, always easier to be concerned with second-order matters in teaching - the methodology of this or that academic discipline, the development of this or that technique, the study of this or that aspect of child psychology or moral relationship, and the delineation of designated acceptable skills of classroom interaction and performance. All too often, however, teachers and teacher-trainers are men and women who have never come to grips with the meaning and goal of their own lives and, as a consequence, it is not remarkable if they set little store by such objectives in the training of others. Efficiency in classroom processes is of the greatest importance, but it is a vain concentration if it replaces the need to meet the challenges and questions that lie at the very root of man's reality: 'What is the meaning and goal of life? What kind of life is it most worthwhile to live and what constitutes the best preparation for it?' (4) These are the only questions worth posing and they are the only problems to which every man must seek an answer if he is not to become somewhat less than human.

For the Christian, the search for answers to such questions in relation to the education his children are undergoing is of paramount importance. All things have their origin, growth and sustentation in God, the overseer of all Creation, the Life-Giver in and for all created things. In God and through God all creatures have their rightful place. To understand creation, and man's co-operative role and enplacement therein, is to understand the love and power of God. He is the perfection of all order, dynamism and renewal in the universe; God alone adds meaning and intent to human growth. It follows that, insofar as man acts in conformity with God's purposes, his being exudes harmony and relationship and, insofar as he fails to live his life in conformity with those purposes, man is disoriented and at odds with his own welfare.

For the committed Christian, therefore, it is inconceivable that his children should be educated in a secular métier that takes no account of their ultimate spiritual destiny or of the harmony manifest in God's design for man and for the world in which he is fleetingly at home. He finds it equally unacceptable that his children should be educated by teachers who often have no knowledge of the Christian way of life or code of behaviour or by those who have ceased to believe that such things have relevance or validity. To place his children into such an ambience in their formative years would be tantamount to exposing them to noxious influences working counter to their ultimate good. Contrary to Richard Pring's view, furthermore, the convinced Christian cannot accept that religion and morality should be separated as if they were incommensurate with each other, providing what Pring calls 'two quite distinct angles upon this highly complex world to which the uninitiated pupil is being introduced'. Pring's assertion that 'education is not a means to anything' or that education 'has no aims' would also be rejected. (5) Such an outlook would necessitate the abandonment of 'wholeness', 'totality' and 'harmony' in the educative process and would have nothing to say about the interconnection of all things. A Christian cannot accept that the way a child lives in the world - his moral subscription - can be treated in a school as if it had no connection with the way in which that same child conceives of the meaning and purpose of his existence. Indeed, it is certain that the depth of understanding of the Christian faith will only be strengthened by the living out of its moral precepts, just as the moral life of the Christian emerges from, and is permeated by, his innate faith. There can be no dichotomy between moral education and religious commitment for, as B.H. Hosegood has pointed out 'the faith has this double aspect of something given and, in addition, a very large area which is very much our doing, and our choosing'. (6) The question: 'What am I as a being?' cannot be divorced from its correlate: 'How can I live my life in accordance with the purpose for which I have been created?' Edward Hulmes underscored the connection when he wrote in another context that the aim of religious education is 'to provide children with knowledge and skills which will enable them as they grow up into maturity not only to see how varied are the manifestations of religious experience but also how their experience constrains them to consider the implications of a personal commitment'. (7) Personal commitment in faith and personal morality arising out of and in conformity with that commitment are the identifying features of Christian harmony.

Religious education in general and a knowledge of the Christian way of life in particular must always find a significant place in the life of a non-denominational school within our Western culture; to contemplate otherwise would be to envisage a severance of children from all the roots of Western civilisation and its cultural heritage. In his seminal study, The Crisis of Western Education, Christopher Dawson once argued the point forcibly that 'the educated person cannot play his full part in modern life unless he has a clear sense of the nature and achievements of Christian culture: how Western civilisation became Christian, and how far it is Christian today and in what ways it has ceased to be Christian: in short, a knowledge of our Christian roots and of the abiding Christian elements in Western culture.' (8) Some, while subscribing to this view, would argue that the aim can be achieved in the appropriate teaching of the secular subjects of the modern school curriculum - English and history, for example. But such teaching may pay little regard to the need for man to rediscover the spiritual dimension of his human existence or to the role that Christian teaching may play in that process of rediscovery and reaffirmation. The development of technological society needs to be located within the cultural context that has made Western man the complex individual he is, those particular moral, social and religious values acquired from a history dependent upon a recognition of Christian mores. Again to quote Dawson:

> a system of education like that of the modern secular state which almost totally ignores the spiritual component in human culture and in the human psyche is a blunder so enormous that no advance in scientific method or educational technique is sufficient to compensate for it. (9)

In the process of correcting this 'blunder', religious education not only has a significant role to perform but, indeed, a central one in the unifying of the school curriculum and the adding of understanding and meaning to its apparently disparate elements. Religious education is concerned with the constituents of the life of a free man in a free society, with his physical integrity, his personal problems, his origin and ultimate destiny, his relationship to his fellow-men and to those that cannot share his beliefs and attitudes. (10) It is a sensitising ergon, as Raymond Holley would have it, a process of developing in the young an awareness of the things of the Spirit manifest, not only in themselves, but also in the whole community of human beings, the cultivation of a luminous viscosity to the world at large.

In the process of self-integration, of course, the Christian denominational school has a clear focus and a purposeful methodology. In many cases - but perhaps increasingly less so than formerly! - it is able to construct its educative programme upon a supporting, cohesive structure of home, family and church. Pupils are thus introduced to a form of Christian living in a community in which Christian values are paramount and recognised as the norm to be followed in the daily moral and social life of the school. Within such a métier, religious education is concerned with cultivating and spiritual awareness that reinforces acceptable norms of personal Christian living and pre-supposes an alignment of community, behaviour and heritage. A subscription to concepts of unity, oneness and integration provide the conditions, in the words of Rosemary Haughton, 'for the Spirit to act in the exchange of knowledge and love between teacher and taught, parents and children'. (11) It is the peculiar function of the denominational school, then, to create, in its ethos, curriculum, social structure, and moral and religious life, conditions needed for the Spirit to function, for 'in order that the spark may in the end set fire to the whole man there must be fuel that is inflammable, there must be a person formed for loving, and that is the task of Christian education'. (12) For the spark to ignite, however, the denominational school must be a community of love, not an inward-looking, protective kind of love, but an out-going exhalation of love that reaches beyond the confines of the school and the school-day into the family, the Church, the pluralistic community at large. Love is thwarted when it is merely a form of self-gratification, influenced either by fear and suspicion (as seems to be characteristic of certain manifestations of denominational schooling in Ulster) or by social exclusiveness or snobbery (as may perhaps be the case in some financially lucrative denominational Public Schools in England). Love is not narrow or confined, rather it is the ambience within which the Spirit proceeds to make sense and unity of what otherwise appears to be difficult or discordant.

The chief function of the denominational school must be to provide an atmosphere in which its pupils are receptive to loving - an atmosphere it quite often fails to create through a too-close adherence to the mores of the secular system of education that encircles it with the characteristics of class-streaming and ability-segregation, with the mindless use of retaliatory punishment, with the headlong eagerness to be competitive in sport and in work. Denominational schools, if they are to survive critical scrutiny, must be seen to be fulfilling their ultimate purpose by not losing view of the fact that the daily practical life of the school, based upon Christian love in action, rather that any peculiar manner of studying or any specific religious customs, is of paramount importance for the development of the human psyche. As Holley points out 'it is personal transcendence which is holiness' (13) and it is life in a loving community, in harmony with home and church and at peace with the wider community of which it is itself but a part, that will achieve it. 'Lapsation' and 'leakage' (rather 'old-fashioned' concepts these days!) are but the fruits of the mistaken identity of a denominational school that has failed to reflect a recognisably Christian ethic in its daily life and organisation and, in so doing, has prevented the full development of the life of love into one of personal commitment. Hulmes has defined that commitment as essentially dynamic, a quality 'associated with growth, vulnerability, decision and change'; (14) where love is absent from the organisation and conduct of a denominational school, commitment and integration are lost.

Pring, as we have seen, has written forcibly against the linking of moral and religious education, arguing that the two are 'quite distinct angles upon this highly complex world to which the uninitiated pupil is being introduced', (15) and more recently Holley has pronounced that 'moral attitudes and religious attitudes must not be confused'. (16) Both writers would admit, however, that religious attitudes may be influenced by moral concerns and that each may provocate insight into the other. Similarly, both writers maintain that moral behaviour necessitates acting from principle and that man's innate freedom is protected by his acting in relation to moral issues in accorance with 'conscience'. The 'forming' of 'principle' and the 'informing' of 'conscience', it is admitted, may well be a function of religion but need not necessarily be so. It is in regard to the caveat that the thoughtful Christian must take a different view.

To the Christian, education is little else than the unfolding of the human personality in accordance with the Divine plan for man's life in the world and for man's ultimate destiny with God, a view resting upon counsels of consistency and wholeness. No form of moral education can be engaged in which does not convey a view of life or which does not adopt some methodology in responding to societal and personal pressures. We are today witnessing this in microcosm in the public continuing debate about A.I.D.S. and sex education. The Christian requires that the educational ambit within which the processes of response are located be consistent with a true view of the meaning and purpose of life. To imagine other would be, for him, an irrational act. After all, for the Christian it must be argued that the adoption of the ethical code of his faith is a major means of personal dedication and sanctification, the one essential commitment, inspired by faith and by love, by which he binds himself securely to Christ and to the achieving of his counsels of perfection. Conscience is certainly paramount, but it is a conscience informed by the Divine Spirit in harmony with the precepts of Divine Law. Man's essential freedom and liberty is always carefully preserved in following the promptings of an informed conscience; a rational and free act cannot be sensibly based upon ignorance or misinformation.

Jacques Maritain considered the fundamental hindrance to the adoption of an acceptable moral code to lie in man's basic egoism. The prerequisite for the moral life is liberation from self. Only love, upon which the Christian faith is grounded, is capable of rescuing man from himself. Maritain went further: 'God is the only Person whom human love can fly to and settle in, so as to embrace also all other persons and be freed from egotistic self-love.' (17) Christian love embraces pain and death, humility and penitence, right-living and happiness; it places sin and suffering in the perspective of eternity in a way in which a moral code not rooted in religion would ignore. In Christianity, all things and all behaviour have their rightful place within the all-pervading love of God. A moral code, divorced from religious commitment, can have no permanence or eternal sanction; it can have nothing to say to the need for self-conquest in personal dedication to a loving and loved

Creator. Mary Warnock is not far from this position when she writes 'to be morally good is to have a certain sort of character, not a certain sort of ability, nor a certain sort of knowledge ...' (18) That 'character' is more likely to be strongly developed when the values and beliefs of home, church and school are in harmony and capable of reinforcing each other, for an education in virtue, as distinct from a knowledge of moral issues and their implications, can only be effected by living example and by experiencing the fullness of life as an integral member of a community that is itself perpetually struggling to maintain and develop its spiritual and moral integrity. As Harry Blamires once put it: 'Christian morality is not a list of duties; not a catalogue of do's and don't's, but a positive and personal directing and nourishing of God-given faculties'. (19) The Christian Church has a central task in that process of the enrichment of human life. Ivan Illich states it perfectly:

> The Church teaches us to discover the transcendental meaning of this experience of life. She teaches us in liturgical celebration to recognize the presence of Christ in the growing mutual relatedness which results from the complexity and specialization of development. And she reveals to us the personal responsibility for our sins: our growing dependence, solitude and cravings which result from our self-alienation in things and systems and heroes. She challenges us to deeper poverty instead of security in achievements; personalizations of love (chastity) instead of depersonalization by idolatry; faith in the other rather than prediction ... All men experience life - the Christian believes he has discovered its meaning. (20)

One of the major criticisms often asserted of the denominational school relates to its exclusiveness. In the desire for harmony between the religious and moral commitment of home, church and school, there is the risk that a distrust of one's fellow citizens educated in a different style and métier may be inculcated in such a school or that a child may become an alien in his generation. Paul Tillich, too, sees a deeper issue: 'The problem of the church schools is more than the problem of a particular educational aim. It is the problem of the relation of Christianity and culture generally and Christianity and education especially. The problem is infinite and must be solved again in every generation.' (21) A Christian, however, is not a man, <u>qua man</u>, set apart from his fellows but he is, in the words of Sebastian Moore, 'what man in the divine plan <u>is</u>'. (22) The inherent relationship between the Christian faith and the living of that faith must have affinity with the State educational system if only because the latter has grown out of Christian culture; its moral code, insofar as it still has an identifiable one, has emerged from that same culture. In that respect, the Christian school, driven by true Christian principles, can be no threat to social harmony. Indeed, it can be argued that the best way to promote racial and cultural harmony in modern society is to understand more fully our own lives, their purpose and their direction for, as Christopher Dawson once put it, 'without this full cultural awareness it is impossible either to interpret one's culture to others or to understand the problems of intercultural relations, problems which are of such incalculable importance for the future of the modern world'. (23) This can only be satisfactorily achieved by a child seeing the Christian way of life 'not as a number of isolated precepts imposed by ecclesiastical authority, but as a cosmos of spiritual relations embracing heaven and earth and uniting the order of social and moral life with the order of divine peace'. (24) The problem of 'exclusiveness', therefore, resolves itself in the hands of skilled and perceptive teachers. And, of course, none of this ought to be a one-sided response. The non-denominational school must itself become more closely aware of its Christian heritage if it is to appreciate why it is still transmitting the essential values of Western culture. Moral education cannot flourish in a cultural vacuum and the secular system has yet to re-discover that unitive factor which will become the essential catalyst in the integration of its life and work. It was the organic relationship between culture, philosophy and theology that Dawson saw as providing 'the integrative principle' in denominational schools. Even more so today than when he was writing a quarter of a century ago, society is in need of 'some higher spiritual principle of co-ordination to overcome the conflicts between power and morality, between reason and appetite, between technology and humanity and between self-interest and the common good'. (25)

It is sometimes argued that because our society is made up of a congeries of conflicting ideas, standards of behaviour and modes of belief, attendance at a denominational school merely delays that process whereby children come to see themselves as an integral part of a wider community, capable of relating in a mature way to the conflicting views and attitudes they must inevitably encounter. Children in a denominational school, however, cannot be considered as if they were a single homogeneous social grouping. They constitute a community reflecting varying levels of religious and social awareness, with a variety of family backgrounds, a range of intellectual ability and a diverse degree of exposure to material influences and media formation. The Christian school forms a special community in only three ways - its acknowledgement of the importance of the psyche in the educative process, its attempt to synthesise the religious and moral teaching of home, church and school and, above all, its commitment to the teachings of Jesus Christ with all that commitment implies in terms of spiritual and moral growth and community awareness. A child exposed to the pervasive ethos of a good denominational school will be fitted not only to cope with the pressures, strains, joys and pleasures of secular society but will also be fitted, in a spirit of tolerance and understanding, to contribute himself to the further enrichment and development of that society. Indeed, it is essential that such a catalytic process be initiated. What is taught in a Christian school must be presented as a part of living and must entail working at the forging of relationships with schools of a different nature - in academic programmes and charitable ventures, in social, sporting and cultural events, and in all forms of corporate endeavour. The Christian view, after all, is not an alternative view of the world, one among many, but a view that is greater than the world view, embracing the whole of life and existence in its cosmic awareness and dedication. The true Christian must therefore respond to the life of grace with faith and love, not only within a congenial Christian community, but also within the whole human family. (26) Dawson, indeed, saw the central role of Christianity, and hence of the denominational school, as helping to break down 'the closed, self-centred world of secularist culture' and to give 'human society a new spiritual purpose which transcends the conflicting interests of individual class and race'. (27) Central to the denominational school's role of cultivating a spirit of fellowship and brotherly love, which radiates from the Christian community into a pluralist society, is the school's daily act of worship, whether this takes the form of a properly-conducted and well-considered morning assembly or of a School Mass. It is in that act of worship that all things are placed in perspective and a sense of the harmony of creation made manifest. (28)

To achieve all this, of course, presupposes a specially trained and dedicated teacher. In recent years there has been a renewed emphasis upon the vocational commitment of teachers and tighter, more prescriptive, training programmes. For the Christian teacher, however, an increased emphasis upon his role as an agent in the formation of persons is still necessary. If a teacher hopes to work in a denominational ambience, he must be prepared to ensure that his personal attitudes to children, to teaching, and to the organisation of school life reflect Christian values and concern for others. The Plowden Report emphasised the community aspects of school life when it declared 'a school is not merely a teaching shop, it must transmit values and attitudes'. (29) A denominational school, in particular, will fail in its objectives if it compromises with the spirit of relativism, if it segregates its children into parcels of acceptability by formal streaming or rigid forms of academic classification, if it uses unchristian or unjust methods of punishment or deprivation, if it rewards success but ignores meritorious effort, if it uses religious privileges as a form of reward for good behaviour, if it fails to work with parents and the churches in the formation of a truly Christian polity. It is all too easy for a Christian school to become a caricature of itself. Christianity can only be taught in one way - by living in the light of faith and in conformity with that Faith's clearly enunciated precepts. A consciousness of dependence upon God in the light of which all activities of teaching, learning and living are subsumed must always remain, not only the characteristic of the Christian school, but also the sole true measure of its achievement and success.

NOTES

1.   G. Treacy (ed.) Five Great Encyclicals (The Paulist Press, N.Y., 1945), pp. 65 seq.
2.   A point at the heart of Professor W.R. Niblett's thesis in 'Church, Community and Higher Education' (Education in Church and Society, the Congregational Union

of England and Wales, 1965), p. 36.

3.   Harry Blamires, Repair the Ruins (Geoffrey Bles, 1950), p. 116.

4.   Howard H. Brinton, Quaker Education: In Theory and Practice (Pendle Hill Pamphlet, 1949), pp. 1-2.

5.   Richard Pring in Bernard Tucker (ed.), Catholic Education in a Secular Society (Sheed and Ward, 1968), p. 115.

6.   B.H. Hosegood in Tucker, ibidem, p. 171.

7.   Edward Hulmes, Commitment and Neutrality in Religious Education (Geoffrey Chapman, 1979), p. 11.

8.   Christopher Dawson, The Crisis of Western Education (Sheed and Ward, 1967) p. 135.

9.   Ibid., p. 203.

10.   For an interesting discussion of the role of literature, history, and religion in the education of free men in a free society, see Alex Molnar and John A. Zahorik (eds.), Curriculum Theory (A.S.C.D., Washington, 1977), pp. 67 et seq.

11.   Rosemary Haughton 'The Foundations of Religious Teaching' in Dom Philip Jebb (ed.), Religious Education (Darton, Longman and Todd, 1968), p. 225.

12.   Ibid.

13.   Raymond Holley, Religious Education and Religious Understanding (Routledge and Kegan Paul, 1978), p. 56.

14.   Hulmes, op. cit., p. 87.

15.   Richard Pring in Tucker, op. cit., p. 115.

16.   Holley, op. cit., p. 158.

17.   D. and I. Gallagher (eds.), The Education of Man: The Educational Philosophy of Jacques Maritain (University of Notre Dame Press, U.S.A., 1967), pp. 114-15.

18.   Mary Warnock, Education: A Way Ahead (Blackwell, 1979), p. 79.

19.   Blamires, op. cit., p. 161.

20.   Ivan D. Illich, Celebration of Awareness (Penguin Education, 1973), pp. 84-5.

21.   Paul Tillich, 'A Theology of Education' in The Theology of Culture (Oxford University Press, 1964), p. 157.

22.   Sebastian Moore, 'The Teaching Role of the Church' in Philip Jebb: Religious Education (Darton, Longman and Todd, 1968), pp. 249-50.

23.   Dawson, op. cit., p. 138.

24.   Ibid., p. 150.

25.   Ibid., p. 159.

26.   Faith   to   Life   (Augsburg   Publishing   Co.,
Minneapolis, U.S.A.), passim.
27.   Dawson, op. cit., p. 150.
28.   Rupert E. Davies (ed.), An Approach to Christian
Education (Epworth Press, 1957), p. 15.
29.   Children and Their Primary Schools (The Plowden
Report), p. 187.

Chapter Three

CHURCH, SCHOOL AND ECUMENISM

Alan S. Brown

> The story starts with the Education Act of 1944 which
> drew the many church schools into the 'voluntary-aided'
> sector of the state system. That process in itself was a
> trial for the political establishment: according to
> Correlli Barnett in 'The Audit of War', the politicians
> and civil servants were distracted from considering the
> real needs of British education by 'skull-emptying
> sessions with gentlemen of the cloth (of various
> persuasions) on the topic of how they could continue to
> run a large proportion of the nation's schooling thanks
> to the taxpayers' subsidy! The gentlemen of the cloth
> won the day ... (1)

Challenging words but ones which set the scene for any
reflection on Church, school and ecumenism. None of these
three areas can be disassociated from the political arena
and the politics of education. Piers Paul Read, in the above
quotation, pays due attention to the clergy and their
influence, correctly in the view of this writer, for the
legacy of the battle (or the 'deal' if one wishes to continue
the metaphor of 'skull-emptying sessions') has resulted in
each church doing its own thing. The Free Churches opted to
throw their lot in with the county schools; generally they
were fiercely opposed to the voluntary aided system that
encouraged church schools and that opposition still exists
though possibly less fiercely. The Church of England and the
Roman Catholic Church continued with their own schools
but neither of them were particularly concerned with any
ecumenical objectives.

In fact one of the most remarkable aspects of this topic

33

is how little literature appears to be available. This may be accounted for when one realises that there are no ecumenical schools in the maintained system as such; there are six Anglican/Roman Catholic schools (1 primary, 5 secondary) and 23 Anglican/Methodist schools (all primary or middle-deemed-primary) i.e. joint schools not ecumenical schools. So in the forty-three years since the 1944 Education Act there has hardly been a thunderous charge to break down the barriers of denominationalism!

Why this reluctance? We may find a clue in an excellent address given by the Very Revd Canon Edwin Regan at Lampeter in 1986 on 'The Catholic School - Past and Present':

> In September 1940, at the age of five, I began my formal religious and secular education by making my acquaintance with the local Catholic school in Port Talbot. Built at the side of the Church, it was an all-age school, designed to provide a Catholic atmosphere so that Catholic school children could grow and develop, free from the heresy that all religions were equal ...
>
> The aim of the school was simple - to produce Good Practising Catholics. The school saw itself as an extension of the Catholic home from which the children had come. The whole system was presided over by the parish priests: parents were largely excluded from the process. (2)

But then that was 1940, surely time will have eroded that singleminded aim of producing 'Good Practising Catholics'? But later in the same essay we read:

> What then is the purpose of the Catholic school today? In two words - to evangelise. I do not use the word in a crude narrow fashion, but the purpose of the school is to offer a vision of life based on Gospel values. (3)

So there has been a deepening of that single aim but is it effectively the same aim couched in the theological and educational language of the 1980s? Certainly at its face value it is an aim, or more correctly the interpretation of an aim, that would be acceptable to many Anglicans and members of other religious denominations, but is that 'vision of life' still an essentially Roman Catholic vision?

34

Richard Cunningham, Secretary of the Catholic Education Council, notes that in 1977 the Sacred Congregation for Catholic Education issued a statement stressing that a school must be a community whose values are communicated through the relationships between its members and their fidelity to its outlook on life:

> Since the educative mission of the Catholic school is so wide, the teacher is in an excellent position to guide the pupil to a deepening of his faith and to enrich and enlighten his human knowledge with the data of the faith ... The teacher can form the mind and heart of his pupils, guide them to develop a total commitment to Christ with their whole personality enriched by human culture. (4)

The unity of Catholic parish, Catholic home and Catholic school, in principle at least, makes any partnership with another Christian denomination one of great sensitivity if not nigh impossible. There are few non-Roman Catholic pupils in Roman Catholic schools - nationally the number is under 10% with the majority of teachers in primary schools being Roman Catholic, while in secondary schools perhaps 50% of the teachers will share the Roman Catholic faith. This creates a tension of itself, for the intensive concerns of the Roman Catholic Church to provide a Catholic education for Catholic children has to limit ecumenical opportunities. One may, however, admire its singleminded concern and its drive to fulfil its major aim.

The established Church has its own problems in defining and carrying out its educational vision. Robert Waddington, now Dean of Manchester, when General Secretary of The National Society summed up the Anglican dilemma in a most imaginative and thoughtful book 'A Future in Partnership' (National Society, 1984). He writes there that the Church of England, through the efforts of The National Society, set itself twin objectives in the nineteenth century when the National Society was a leader and innovator in the creation of Church schools:

> First, it wished to contribute to a programme which would enable the children of the nation, especially the poorer classes, to become literate and numerate and to develop skills which they required for work. Second, it had a duty to provide education in the Christian religion

35

Church, School and Ecumenism

in all its schools. (5)

These aims were taken up and developed in a publication of
the National Society, 'Positive Partnership' (6) and by the
General Synod of the Church of England in 1985. They
create no less a tension than the Roman Catholic aim and it
is necessary to dwell on them a little if we are to explore
the place ecumenism may hope to have in the Anglican
model of Church-school education.

The voluntary schools in England and Wales are part of
the maintained system - the total state provision. This is
not always recognised by some people who claim that
Church of England schools are 'for' Church people; on the
other hand some believe that Church of England schools
should have no distinctive features which might distinguish
them from County schools. As 'Positive Partnership' puts it:

> The Church needs to hold in the right balance the twin
> necessities of being distinctive and yet not being
> exclusive. For the sake of the Kingdom it needs both to
> be the Church and yet also to be for the world. (7)

So the rather dated twin aims of the nineteenth century still
remain, though in an updated fashion, as an integral element
in Church of England education - contributing to the
provision of general schooling in the neighbourhood, and yet
providing a specifically Christian form of education. It
follows naturally that the application of these twin aims will
result in more than one model of a Church of England
school.

The Bishop of London, Dr Graham Leonard, in a speech
in General Synod in 1985 emphasised the importance of
adopting these twin aims to Church of England school
governors who create admissions policies:

> Only so will schools be acting in accordance with the
> Biblical principle of which I spoke and fulfil the task of
> being a transforming witness to the world. To
> concentrate solely on denominational interests and
> purposes is to abandon that principle.
> These twin aims need to be applied both in
> relation to the curriculum and to the ethos of the
> School. The curriculum will need to reflect the insights
> of the Gospel both in its content and in the balance it
> achieves between different aspects of that content. The

ethos of the School will need to be developed through careful policy decisions regarding discipline in all its aspects, appointment of staff, admission of pupils, the pattern of worship and links with the wider community. But all these areas of concern need to reflect the Church's concern for the 'provision of general education in the neighbourhood' and must take into account the local community. (8)

Canon Regan's expression of the aim of the Roman Catholic school today would be acceptable to most Anglicans. It would not meet the community aim so easily, however, particularly if the local community was multi-faith for one would have to extend the aim of 'a vision of life based on Gospel values' to include something like 'in a school community with a significant number of non-Christians'. In the practical situation, however, as few Roman Catholic schools have over 10% non-Roman Catholic children in them, the Roman Catholic Church appears less concerned to meet the general needs of the local non-Roman Catholic community.

However, the 'Catholic child in a Catholic school with a Catholic teacher' is not a programme fully realised, especially in secondary schools. It is not fully realised and, for some Roman Catholics, it should not be, for they wish to relax what they consider to be the over-protective educational and religious environment of the Roman Catholic school. Equally, to hold twin aims in tension is a formidable task for many Anglican schools, their staff and governors. It can be too easy to accept the denominational image, particularly if a school is popular and over-subscribed. In some cases the Anglican school's role is interpreted as accepting only children of church-going families, a situation which draws it closer to the Roman Catholic model. Superficially, the aim of Roman Catholic school education and the twin aims of the Anglicans overlap to a considerable degree but it would be misleading to imagine there is a natural understanding between them, a sympathetic consonance; there are few joint schools established to make any such generalisations.

If one can understand the twin aims of the Anglican schools then there is no surprise in recognising the Anglican/Methodist link, for the Church of England is prepared to act ecumenically on occasions - some would say when the position suits it. However, it must be said that the

Anglicans have been able to provide an educational bridge between the Roman Catholics on the one hand and the Methodists on the other. There are, as yet, no Methodist/Roman Catholic schools and it may well be many years before any could be established, even if they were considered desirable.

More fundamental, however, is the question, Are joint schools ecumenical schools? The Education Act of 1944 does not, in effect, provide for ecumenical schools; it allows 'voluntary' schools to be established if certain criteria can be met. Are the principles of joint schools broad enough to be able to describe them as 'ecumenical'? It is to this question we must now turn. What is ecumenical education and can it only occur in a church school or a joint school? Recently, ecumenical education has been defined as: 'fostering understanding of, commitment to, and informed vision of the one, missionary church in the process of renewal'. (9)

Mary Hayward, in a recent paper prepared for an education conference in West Germany, drew attention to the notion of 'ecumenical learning' in the county school. Writing of an open approach to denominational distinctiveness and, in this, an encounter with commitment, she writes:

> Such learning (i.e. ecumenical learning) I prefer to express in terms of aim rather than content. Ecumenical learning might thus be described as a process of learning which enables students: to become aware of the different branches of the Christian church; to be aware of those elements in the Christian tradition which are held across the tradition (although perhaps with differing priorities), are fundamental to the tradition, are present within the tradition but also subject to different interpretation; to stand both aside from and alongside the churches they study; to understand what it would mean in personal terms to belong to and therefore to participate in the life of the churches studied. (10)

Ms Hayward's paper has an originality and inventiveness which in itself spotlights the lack-lustre approach characteristic of some ecumenical ventures. She recognises that learning about ecumenism may be a foundation for ecumenical activity but if it has any validity or credibility it has to be based upon sound educational objectives. There is a lesson too for those who choose to define 'ecumenism' in a narrow almost self-congratulatory sense:

> 'Oikumene' itself has an 'open' ring in religious education which, as it looks at one word, grapples first with its plurality of faiths and perhaps rarely with the multi-vocality of each. (11)

Perhaps of all one reads about ecumenism this last quotation is most unsettling. While it can be difficult to promote and engage in ecumenism between various Christian traditions, where are the initiatives to grapple with the notion of one world and its plurality of religions? It can be too easy and self-satisfying to speak of 'ecumenical schools' when what is meant is 'joint schools' and how concerned are Christian educators, Roman Catholic and Anglican, to struggle with the educational requirements of children from non-Christian religions, particularly if they attend the Church school?

In the voluntary school, Mary Hayward suggests there are three ways of providing opportunities for ecumenical learning. First, 'institutional ecumenism' (a phrase favoured by 'The Fourth R' (12) - a partnership of two or more churches in the provision of a voluntary school. Second, planned contact between voluntary schools in a particular place for particular purposes, for example for worship or charity work. Third, there are opportunities to plan the curriculum. It may be some schools will deliberately foster mutual understanding between Christians of different traditions. This may be approached through specific issues (e.g. birth control or celibacy) or through an historical or political situation (e.g. Northern Ireland) or, again, by a variety of other processes from breaking down stereotypes to meeting members of local churches, thus enabling students to develop new perspectives and new priorities by encountering a form of Christianity which contrasts with their own. Her paper concludes with an indictment: 'I sense impatience with "ecumenical learning", for these young people already share a perception of "ecumenical being" which the church does not fulfil.' (13)

Impatience is often associated with the young but they are not alone in being impatient with church hierarchies which continue to be suspicious of each other. One is aware of a willingness to utter ecumenical platitudes without apparently moving from a fixed position. The Anglican Roman Catholic International Commission (ARCIC) can examine theological and doctrinal issues but the ordinary worshipper has little interest with its esoteric concerns. Similarly a parish in which Roman Catholics and Anglicans share a church building may have a personal commitment to ecumenism but what effect does that have upon the church at large? A cynic may recognise in 'ecumenism' a similar approach to 'dialogue' of Christians with members of other faiths. Not all Christians are interested in dialogue; but some of those who are, regard it as a means of converting the non-Christian to their religion. Similarly, some religions are not interested in dialogue - for reasons that are not necessarily unacceptable - but individuals within those religions may join in dialogue either out of personal interest or some form of social concern. To be interested in ecumenism carries with it a similar length of shadow. Firstly, is it desirable that ecumenism should be a goal for Christians? Is ecumenism a move towards some form of domination by one church? Does it contain an expression of paternalism which treats other churches (and other religions) as if they were wayward children who will eventually return home? For those who join in ecumenical activity there can be little that is more rewarding or more frustrating. Impatience, yes, but let us also recognise that in reality to engage in any sort of ecumenical dialogue, be it practical or theoretical, will not make for an easy life.

To return to our earlier question: Are joint schools ecumenical schools? Well, as C.E.M. Joad would say, 'it all depends what you mean by "ecumenical"'. For example, it seems to be the case that in one Anglican/Roman Catholic secondary school there are no Baptists - the local pastor advises his congregation not to send their children to the school. Now whether he is justified in giving this advice or simply misguided and prejudiced, it is clear that the very existence of the school creates an open sore. Two churches may work together, but will that isolate others to create an even bigger divide? Ecumenical? Let us take a hypothetical case of an Anglican/Roman Catholic secondary school which admits 180 pupils each year. The admissions policy drawn up by the governors allows Anglicans and Roman Catholics 90 places each and the school is heavily over-subscribed. Should the 90 Roman Catholic places go only to the children of Roman Catholic parents? We cannot give an unequivocal answer, but given the defined aims of Roman Catholic education we have quoted it seems very likely that all 90 places would go to the children of practising Catholic parents. What of the 90 Anglican places given the twin aims referred to above? Are the 90 places to be given only to children of Anglican parents if by so doing the aim of service to the nation's children is denied? Perhaps some of these places, then, should go to children in the neighbourhood of the school be they Anglican, Methodist or nothing at all. So into the school entry would come 90 Roman Catholic children and 90 others, largely Anglican but with a liberal smattering of everything else. In this way a parallel admissions policy can be quite complex for, it could be argued, in such a joint school only one partner would be acting ecumenically through its admissions policy. In such a situation does the closely defined aim of one partner force the other either to be prescriptive in its policy or to assume the sole responsibility for ecumenism?

In a case such as we have hypothesised it would be possible for both partners in the joint school to claim a breadth of ecumenical interest even though the presence of a variety of Christian denominations would be the sole responsibility of one partner only. If this situation actually existed in a joint Anglican/Roman Catholic secondary school one suspects that it might be tempting for the Anglican admissions policy to match the directive Roman Catholic admissions policy. This would, in turn, create a denominational intake for children of Anglican parents and make the fulfilment of the traditional twin aims virtually impossible. Yet in A Future in Partnership, we read:

> the governing body of a Church of England Aided School which insists on operating admissions almost entirely by means of the simple criterion of the family's attendance at worship, is forgetting the general service to the nation's children that has always formed one of the twin aims of Church Schools. (14)

For joint schools to be ecumenical schools in any meaningful sense, then, it would be necessary for both partners to adopt the same aims regarding admissions otherwise the school would be likely to remain a joint school through the mismatch of its religious and educational aims.

On a visit to a joint school, one pupil commented that she had never imagined such wide differences could exist between various Christian groups - she was a Methodist. In the school, Religious Education was taught separately, because the then Roman Catholic Bishop of the Diocese felt that it would not be conducive for Roman Catholic children to share RE classes with non-Roman Catholics (shades of the 'heresy' of 1940 noted by Canon Regan). Sometimes worship took place together, but often Roman Catholics and Anglicans met in separate places. Now this report may be accurate, or it may not, but what is uncontrovertible was that a student registered impatience with diversity and difference in a startling way. She liked the school but found the protective cloak of denominationalism almost unbearable. It may not be totally unexpected that a joint school which appears to be a unity from the outside can create and support a divisive structure on the inside. To take the point a little further, the Headmaster of an Anglican Secondary School writes of the nature of his school's association with a Roman Catholic High School (not a joint school but two voluntary Church schools seeking a closer relationship) in the following way:

> The Associated VI Form provides the most overt example of ecumenical activity. This has now been in existence for twelve years. It would be easy to emphasise and perhaps exaggerate the nature of the liturgical and curricular features. The VI Form does, it is true, worship together: each month there is a joint assembly and in the week of Christian Unity we celebrate Communion together, an act of worship which causes more pain and questions than comfort because at the critical moment of the administration of the elements the Anglicans and Catholics go to separate altars in separate parts of the building. (15)

If these two impressions seem negative then perhaps one should remember that the frustration exists within a context of good will. As we have seen there is a basic and fundamental difference between Roman Catholic and Anglican aims making agreement extremely difficult, perhaps even unworkable. Yet if one is to be pragmatic one can argue that joint schools or separate schools with close liaison is a first decisive step on the long troubled road to ecumenism. The voluntary system does provide, however, through the governors of each school, a remarkable opportunity for experimentation in religious education. Joint schools allow an innovative approach to worship and RE which may not have reached its zenith but is at least underway. One needs to be looking well into the next century if one wishes to discover whether joint schools will push their respective Christian denominations towards a breakdown of barriers and removal of prejudice. Those people who are ready to criticise the thirty joint schools in existence do not have to look far within the United Kingdom to see how virulent antagonism and separation between the Church communities can even be expressed in violence and unrest.

Robert Waddington again:

> It must be recognised that in a situation of falling rolls some proposals for joint schools (providing some assurance of future pupil-places) may be based more on pragmatism than any sudden upsurge of ecumenical fervour. The truly ecumenical model would involve the collaboration of all the Christian Churches in the area round the school ... The ecumenical cause will not be served by attempting some pallid uniformity but by allowing the Christian community to face the nature of its own plurality; to face it positively in that it provides a rich mix in contemporary Christian experience and negatively in its contribution to division and disunity. (16)

The emphasis on pragmatism should not be taken as a disparaging comment. The Christian Church throughout its history has been nothing if not pragmatic and schools too have always been pragmatic by definition - they have to deal with the children regardless of political and financial pressures. They both have visions of the future, an ideal to be attained, but they respond to current issues as best they can. Behind Robert Waddington's comment lies the more profound regret that the Churches have not been creative enough to be truly ecumenical. This comes startlingly to the fore in the Education chapter of the publication of the Archbishop's Commission on Urban Priority Areas, Faith in the City (1986), (17) where one of the recommendations is that the Church of England, in partnership with other churches, should seek to establish an ecumenical secondary school in an urban priority area (Recommendation 13:91 (iii)). The suggestion is startling because the chapter ignores all ecumenical initiatives as such in its concentration upon the involvement of Church of England schools. It would have been more appropriate if the chapter had taken up Robert Waddington's final thoughts on this particular matter and considered practical issues, or forced upon the churches a strong act of will to bring the recommendation to the forefront of its thinking:

> Whilst there may already be joint schools, then, between the Church of England and the Roman Catholic Church or with the Free Churches, the ecumenical model is yet to be fully explored. The educational back-room boys raise questions of ownership, Trust Law, and difficulties of sharing places on governing bodies, but those who live with minutiae rarely wish to risk a moderately secure legality. Is it too much to ask that no new Church of England school should be established without the most serious consideration being given to the possibility of real ecumenical engagement? (18)

The frustration encapsulated in the question is in stark contrast to the bland recommendation of Faith in the City suggesting that the authors of that document were not fully au fait with the difficulties of creating ecumenical schools. For if there are to be ecumenical schools, truly ecumenical schools, then there has to be a strength of will that transcends pragmatism. Pragmatism may, under certain circumstances, enable a joint school to be created but an ecumenical school could only come into being as a firm act of commitment to the ecumenical ideal by the leaders of the churches. Is it likely? Are they ready? They may be but, even if they were, are the people ready? Will they take to the streets in protest in the battle for school places?

The vision of the Churches on mainland Europe too can exhibit depressing limitations. In 1986 it was mooted at a meeting of Christian educationalists in France that there should be a World Conference on Education. Only when the idea was probed a little was it realised that Roman Catholics were not to be invited - surprising when one remembers Roman Catholics represent half the world's population of Christians! If the Roman Catholics were invited, it was observed, there would be less room for the rest! If this is the ecumenical vision of the Christian Church then it is a barren walk across the desert to a dried up waterhole. However, the greatest contribution to ecumenical understanding in schools during the last forty years may not have come from the churches but from a reassessment and revaluation of the nature of Religious Education itself. The Education Act of 1944 created the machinery for an Agreed Syllabus of RE in every local authority; it also laid down that RE in the county school should be non-denominational. After all the denominations had been given the opportunity to create their own voluntary aided schools, therefore county schools should not contain the teaching of any particular denomination. In the years after 1944 the syllabuses reflected the common concern for the Bible. RE in the county school was dominated by the Bible and a quick glance at syllabuses of the '40s and '50s reveals page upon page of what were considered appropriate Bible texts. But RE changed and developed in the 1960s through the work (now much criticised) of Ronald Goldman, Harold Loukes and J.W.D. Smith. Syllabuses began to take on the form and content of the West Riding Agreed Syllabus of the mid-'60s. 'Relevance' became a key term - the Bible should be regarded as relevant to the lives of school students. In the 1970s the world religions explosion blew away much of that thinking though it still remained in the more sheltered areas of the country. The work of the now defunct Schools Council promoted a more objective look at religious phenomena and the phenomenological approach became fashionable. The 1980s witnessed a return to the study of Christianity but not now through Bible texts; the work of The Chichester Project, (19) in particular, encouraged teachers to look more objectively at the phenomena of Christianity. It was felt school students were not aware of the differences between Christian denominations, they were not aware of different approaches to Jesus, worship, ethical issues and the Bible. RE syllabuses began to reflect a new interest in Christianity which was very definitely both ecumenical and denominational - what do Methodists believe? How do the Orthodox worship? What happens at the Mass? The new GCSE syllabuses reflect this type of study, teachers (and students) write in great numbers to the churches asking them for details of what their church teaches and believes and they write for statements on various ethical issues.

The development of 'Christianity as a World Religion' has opened up major opportunities for learning about ecumenism. The students themselves may, of course, be members of no Christian denomination but through their studies they offer a challenge to the ecumenical vision of the churches. One hopes that the new syllabuses at 16+ will encourage Church schools to become more adventurous, not to look for a 'denominational option' which allows for that introversion so comforting for many church-aided schools. It is ironic that the major thrust towards ecumenism, by bringing it to the forefront of study, has had to come through the county system and has not been generated by the Church schools themselves. In fairness, this may be because the study of Christianity in a county school is divorced from any religious or emotional expectations of the pupil or the school itself. The greater freedom of the county school allows things to take place which would not happen (although they <u>should</u>) in many Church schools. The problem for the Churches is that this move in the county school has highlighted the narrowness and blinkered vision of many of those concerned with promoting their own Church schools. The divisions within Christianity can be quite bewildering to the pupil studying the Christian religion - they are also very difficult to explain.

We have then a range of opinions and views. There are those who feel the Church has done little in the educational field that will assist the cause of ecumenism. Others believe that the thirty joint schools do provide a threshold for future ecumenical activity. Whichever one of these views one takes, it has to have regard for the continuing debate about Church schools. Commentators inside and outside the Churches have been critical of the divisive nature of denominational schooling, and who can foretell what will happen in education over the next thirty years? In the context of the falling number of Church schools, perhaps the new initiatives do lie in the creation of genuine ecumenical models of schools; there must be more than one model, for an ecumenical school in the inner city would have to respond to different challenges from that of a rural ecumenical school. To the outsider it must seem that Anglican paternalism and Roman Catholic protectivism are the biggest obstacles to ecumenical schools. The Methodists also seem suspicious of the motives of the Roman Catholics and may well lack the financial resources to take new initiatives. However, these are massive generalisations which beg for contradiction and, more significantly, rejection by the Churches, but the time draws near for the latter to demonstrate their ecumenical concern rather than talk about it. Many of the qualities one looks for in denominational schools are shared by all schools; pursuit of excellence, establishment of good relationships, respect and concern for others. The following quotation from a recent publication sums up the dilemma of an ecumenical enterprise:

> Within a Catholic school the ultimate distinctive element is that its life is based on the vision of Christ in which all learning, growing, service, freedom and relationships are seen as part of a growth in the knowledge, love and experience of God. In other words there is a deliberate hope that the experience of belonging to the school will encourage personal commitment to Jesus Christ, will mark an important stage in the process of conversion and will lead to the discovery of the Christian vocation. It follows that a necessary part of the life of a Catholic school will be the guidance it gives to the articulation of their faith by its members. This will be achieved by its teaching of the principal truths of the Christian faith, by the way its life reflects the teaching of the gospel ... it must ensure that its teaching of the faith is done competently and professionally by believing and practising Catholics; it must endeavour to make its worship a true expression of the faith of the community. (20)

Many Christians would agree with parts of this statement - but it is a very Roman Catholic statement. Can all the churches display sufficient confidence in themselves, be prepared to be vulnerable enough to trust each other, in order to loosen the trenchant fears of denominationalism? It will take time, joint schools are a beginning not an end (perhaps a means to an end!), further discussions need to take place at all levels within the Churches and, who knows, perhaps the goodwill and unity now brought together in the Churches Joint Educational Policy Committee, currently under the Chairmanship of the Bishop of London, will bear fruit. One might, mischievously, suggest that an ecumenical school will only be of benefit to the Churches, it will contribute little to the state and be a deeper thorn in the flesh of those who oppose Church schools. Yet a keen observer of social behaviour might note that if the religions within a particular society are in harmony the society may well be more peaceful and productive.

Progress often happens under tension. Church schools are places where there is a genuine interface between politics, religion, the growing pupil, parents, governors, priests and laity. They create a maelstrom within which teachers and governors provide a fruitful environment for those in their charge. For the Churches not to be fully committed to education is unthinkable; for there to be ecumenical schools is a challenge that the Church must take up. The voluntary system is a partnership - a political, religious partnership shared by the community and parents; an ecumenical school is simply another form of partnership in which the balance, though delicate, could be even more fruitful.

Perhaps the Archbishop of Canterbury, Dr Robert Runcie, has uttered the final word:

> Education is never neutral. Everyone lives by his own convictions and attachments, however uncertain or ill-defined. We need to be able to acknowledge each other's beliefs and loyalties and focus attention on those areas of education where our own have important implications. For the Church to be able to exercise its important responsibility in education, we may have to disturb and invigorate the present ecclesiastical and educational structures and expectations. (21)

NOTES AND REFERENCES

1. Piers Paul Read, 'Catholic Class War', in The Spectator, 22 November, 1986.

2. Edwin Regan, 'The Catholic School - Past and Present' in RE News (Welsh National Centre for RE, Autumn 1986), no. 16.

3. Ibid., p. 4.

4. Richard Cunningham, 'The Vocation of Teaching', in Crosscurrent (The National Society (Church of England) for Promoting Religious Education, July 1986, No. 20), p. 5.

5. Robert Waddington, A Future in Partnership (The National Society for Promoting Religious Education, 1984), p. 12.

6. Positive Partnership (The National Society for Promoting Religious Education, 1985).

7. Ibid., pp. 24-25.

8. Ibid., p. 45.

9. J. Sutcliffe (ed.) A Dictionary of Religious Education (SCM, 1984).

10.   Mary Hayward, <u>Ecumenical Learning in School: Some Reflections on the English Situation</u>, an unpublished paper, 1985.

11.   Ibid.

12.   <u>The Fourth R</u>, (The National Society for Promoting Religious Education and SPCK, 1970).

13.   Mary Hayward, op. cit.

14.   Waddington, op. cit. p. 85.

15.   Mary Hayward, op. cit.

16.   Waddington, op. cit., p. 100.

17.   <u>Faith in the City</u> (Report of the Archbishop of Canterbury's Commission on Urban Priority Areas, 1986).

18.   Waddington, op. cit., p. 100.

19.   <u>The Chichester Project</u> (Lutterworth, 1982-86).

20.   <u>Signposts and Homecomings</u> (St. Paul's Publications, 1981), pp. 106, 107.

21.   Robert Runcie, A speech delivered at the General Synod of the Church of England, 3 July 1985.

Chapter Four

RELIGIOUS EDUCATION AND THE STATE SCHOOL

Derek H. Webster

Rabbi Yitzhak used to tell this story about his grandfather, the holy Rabbi Nahum. Once, at the conclusion of a sabbath, his grandfather's disciples were seated together examining their souls. Pious and good men, they were overwhelmed by the awe of God. In their humility, they felt that they were totally without hope. Their only consolation was that they were utterly devoted to their teacher, the great Rabbi Nahum. Only he, they decided, could uplift and redeem them. So immediately they set out for his house.

At the end of the same sabbath, Rabbi Nahum examined his soul. In his fear of God, it seemed to him that he had sinned very greatly. He felt that his only hope lay in the comfort and guidance that his disciples, good men who were earnest in prayer, might offer him. So he went to his door to go to them. Opening it, he saw them coming to him. And at that instant, commented Rabbi Yitzhak ending his story, two arcs fused into a ring. (1)

The hasidic tale is a reminder that the axis of education is the relationship forged between teachers and their students. It is this which truly educates. The teacher teaches not as a conveyor of information nor as one who leans down from above to the uninitiated below. He educates standing as one human being before another human being in a creative interaction. It is the person more than the content, the being present more than the intention, which educate; for these confer dignity upon and confirm the value of others.

This foundation, this relationship out of which education is bodied forth, is profoundly dynamic for it meets the needs of the present at a radical level. None of this is to deny value in scientific approaches to education. Recent years have witnessed an explosion of curricular thinking which has offered to teachers a richness of resources, a novelty of ideas and an imaginative means of development which are impressive. Education has become a marvellously polychrome affair and curricular vigour seems to be undiminished. Yet accelerating fashions and the avalanche of new thinking accompanying them should not obscure the fact that behind all education stands, directly or indirectly, a meeting of persons. To forfeit this is to forfeit awe. To diminish the strangeness of education is to disregard that mystery which lies behind the ways of being. In the last analysis, teachers and taught stand together as irresolvable questions themselves. (2)

A programme for religious education emerges as teachers reflect upon their relationships in school and set them firstly, within those concerns pressing upon young people today and, secondly, against the best understanding of their own academic disciplines which they can achieve. Such a programme rests upon philosophical foundations. The 'how' of method and the 'what' of content are determined ultimately by the 'why' of theory. At the theoretical level, questions which ask for a response from teachers concern:

1. the justification of religious education in the school curriculum,
2. the distinctive nature it can be argued to have,
3. its aims.

A   THEORETICAL CONSIDERATIONS

1.   The warrant for religious education in the curriculum

There is a logically prior question to that of justification which is, of course: Is religious education possible? Only if it is possible does the question of its curricular worth arise. It is assumed here that it is possible. The epistemological grounds for this assumption will become evident indirectly in the course of this chapter.

Any subject area expecting to hold its place in the curriculum faces sharp questions of justification. For religious education these questions are at present crucial. The very fact of legislation guaranteeing its place in schools raises rather than settles questions of warrant. For some, the very notion of an education which can be qualified by the word 'religious' is incoherent. For others, earlier justifications fail because they lack the multi-faith understanding of religious education. It is then surprising to find so few recent attempts to justify the place of this subject in the curriculum. Very occasionally in the academic literature arguments are offered. (3) Yet the majority of teachers, particularly non-specialists concerned with teaching young children, find little time to pursue these arguments. All teachers do, however, have access to the agreed syllabus in religious education for their own particular area. It might then be expected that guidance would be given within it. Yet this is far from the case. The syllabuses rarely raise the question of justification. In those that do offer thoughts on it there is a lack of sustained argument. This is probably only to be expected, for syllabuses tend to be very concise documents. It is all the more important then that what is said concerning the warrant for this subject, albeit by way of conclusions from arguments not given, should be satisfactory. Unfortunately, for the most part it is not.

A legal justification?

It is commonplace at the beginning of all syllabuses to draw attention to the legislation which requires religious education to be taught in schools. The ILEA Chief Inspector (Schools) reminds his teachers that 'religious education is in the curriculum by law. The Agreed Syllabus is the method by which the law is implemented.' (4)

Although the fact of the legislation is not used in an explicit way as a justification, its position and prominence immediately raise that very question. Informal conversations with many teachers show that the position 'I teach religious education because the law requires it' is widespread. This argument should not be taken lightly, for in a democratic society there is a strong presumption that

(i) the law should be obeyed and
(ii) the law represents a widespread and usually majority opinion.

Yet despite (i) above, there is also a recognition that this need not imply a total obligation, for laws are sometimes seen to be inadequate and are subject to change. There is a clear contradiction in a position which, at one and the same time, could offer a justification prescribing the teaching of religion in schools (as in England) and proscribing this teaching (as in the USA). What this argument fails to do, and yet what it is required to do if it is to be a proper justification, is to state precisely why religious education is being authorised. The question: What is it about this subject which makes it worth legislating for? needs to be answered.

Despite (ii) above, which really becomes an appeal to public opinion, it is necessary to make a distinction between professional opinion based on specialised knowledge and general opinion. This distinction does not deny a role for public opinion in educational practice; it does, however, suggest that in matters of a technical nature it is a very limited role. Questions relating to the authorisation of subjects in the curriculum are generally taken to be of a technical nature.

A cultural justification?
This argument is clearly put in the Warwickshire Agreed Syllabus.

> There are many good reasons why the study of religion should be part of the curriculum of all schools. Such a study helps pupils to understand better their own cultural heritage ... (5)

Certainly educationalists would attach importance to the transmission of the cultural heritage of their society to each new generation in schools. Some would think that this was one of the key social functions of education. Yet this is not an argument offering a justification. It does not show that a particular tradition displays a worth or a value such that it is deserving of preservation into the future. To set this argument in the context of the present situation in Northern Ireland, where Protestant and Catholic traditions and historical perspectives are so sharply dichotomised, is to see its weakness. To invoke the cultural heritage argument as a justification for religious education would require the presentation of criteria for discriminating among the elements to be imparted. These the argument does not give.

A moral justification?

The Berkshire Agreed Syllabus suggests that 'there are four main reasons why religious education is important'. (6) The third of these states

> Religious education contributes to moral development: along with other aspects of the school curriculum, it develops consideration for other people, respect for moral legal obligations, and concern for fairness and justice in society at large. (7)

Religion and morality can be linked very closely indeed. Some religious people will view their God as a moral being and feel that this influences the quality of relationship which is possible with him. They may evolve patterns for living - like 'discipleship' or the 'imitatio Christi' - which display clear moral obligations like charitable giving or caring for those in need. Nevertheless, a perceived intimacy of relationship between religion and morality in certain contexts cannot count as a curricular justification. There is simply no evidence to demonstrate conclusively that to engage in religious education is to improve moral behaviour. A great deal of material, empirical evidence of a largely statistical kind, would be needed to establish this, and it is not forthcoming. Further, there is little agreement among philosophers and theologians that any final conceptual patterning which sets out the logical relationship between religion and morality in a generally acceptable way has been arrived at. By simple observation it is clear that religion is not essential for the discovery of the difference between right and wrong. Moral obligations can be perceived by reason alone. Indeed, to suggest, as some parents and teachers do, that religious education should be included in the curriculum because it checks disagreeable behaviour, seems to damage the integrity of both religion and morality. Thus, as neither moral action nor moral understanding is dependent on religious education, this justification crumbles.

A justification in terms of usefulness to other subject areas

A final argument, often popular among teachers, is that religious education can be justified in so far as it is of value to other disciplines, areas of knowledge or curricular subjects. It 'provides insights into the role of religion in international affairs'; (8) it stimulates 'art, architecture, music and literature'; (9) and it contributes 'to community relations within Britain'. (10) There is, of course, a role for religious education in co-operation with other disciplines. Integration can offer striking perspectives; but this role, which is purely secondary or subsidiary to the main purpose of religious education, cannot offer a justification. A justification can only arise from an argument about the distinctive nature of religious education, and not from a view about its merit as an instrument for the furtherance of the aims of other subjects in the curriculum. This is a view which needs to be strongly made, particularly in those places where the totality of religious education has been absorbed into schemes of personal and social education.

Laudable, then, though many of the sentiments expressed in the agreed syllabuses are, they tend to be confusing and inadequate when analysed as justifications. Perhaps one of the clearest positions is that adopted by the Humberside Agreed Syllabus. (11)

> The warrant for religious education in the curriculum rests on its educational significance. Religious education is about a distinctive way in which men and women express their experience of life. This means that it is valuable as an area of knowledge. Ultimately its justification does not arise from the legislation which prescribes it, nor from its possible moral consequences, nor from the strength of public opinion. Rather it is worthwhile for what it is in itself.

2.   The distinctive features of religious education

Religious education has a place in schools because it displays four features which are quite distinctive. These features, if omitted from the curriculum, would not be covered by other subjects or areas of study. They concern concepts, beliefs, language and experience.

The first distinctive feature of religious education is its understanding of concepts which are formally religious and which interrelate with each other. The various religions have theologies which offer believers means of reflection and a language to convey faith. Central to theologies are concepts, e.g. holiness, sin, righteousness. Concepts link with each other to elaborate positions or teachings which become doctrines. Doctrines relate to each other, often in very complex ways so that faith may be systematised. It is then part of the teacher's task to explain terminology and to delineate doctrines. This amounts to clarifying the patterning of ideas in religious faiths.

The second distinctive feature of religious education concerns an understanding of the reasons supporting or disproving religious beliefs. The criteria by which evidence is weighed are analysed and the procedures used in reaching conclusions are judged. There is an investigation of the methods used in distinguishing between both beliefs and faith systems. A teacher then is involved in the assessment and evaluation of argumentation in religion.

A third feature is the apprehension of the ambiguity of religious language. Within religions there is a rich tradition of myth and a many-layered understanding of symbol; there is poetry, paradox, riddle and mystery. All are used to prompt insight. Achieving this often involves language being used in special ways. Statements are not always descriptive in accustomed ways nor are predicates applicable in literal senses. So teachers illuminate the logical peculiarities, the parabolic nature and the irreducibly paradoxical status of religious language.

The final distinctive feature is an understanding of religious experience. Those who espouse religions claim particular experiences. Often these are shared and bind believers into communities. Some would say that the experiential side is so fundamental that it integrates and legitimises the other three features. Teachers need to foster an awareness of the religious dimension of experience so that their pupils can perceive this dynamic in the lives of believers.

These features offer a warrant for the place of religious education in the curriculum which is educationally acceptable. The balance between them in any particular phase of education, the emphasis each may receive and the timing and means of their introduction within classrooms are all methodological matters requiring professional judgements from teachers. The four features do not presuppose any particular curricular arrangement. In fact, as religions raise so many key questions fundamental to being human, there will be myriad ways in which teachers may seek to deal with such questions. This is not, however, a licence to abuse the nature of religious education. Where one or more of the distinctive features is not recognisably present then the subject is probably not being taught. There is really only one exception to this. Teachers in the early phase of education have agreed that the exploration by children of themselves and their environment is acceptable as religious education:

> The early years of schooling develop those skills and that understanding which are necessary foundations for religious education. Thus what is called religious education can, at this level, be a preparation or pre-religious education. (12)

3. The aims of religious education

There is firm agreement among religious educators of young people in county schools in England and Wales that their subject is focused primarily on understanding. The Cambridgeshire Agreed Syllabus speaks for nearly all when it says 'the aim of religious education is to enable pupils to understand the nature of religion, its beliefs and practices'. (13) This concurrence should not disguise the fact that understanding is used in several ways in the syllabuses and that religious education actually has a prior aim to this one of understanding.

To take the question of understanding first, it is obvious that it is currently used in a variety of ways. Examples could be: 'I understand what telfillin are'; (i.e. I can point them out and name them correctly); 'We understand what Elizabeth and Zechariah felt at the birth of John for we too had a child in later years' (i.e. We have, at first hand, shared a common experience); 'I understand how Peter felt after the betrayal.' (i.e. Imaginatively I am able to attune myself, both emotionally and spiritually, to this experience); 'I understand how to blow the shofar' (i.e. I have mastered the sensori-motor patterns which enable me so to co-ordinate movements that my blowing produces the right sound. Or, I've now got the knack); 'I understand why David refused to kill Saul' (i.e. I appreciate the motives which regulate his behaviour).

This list is not exhaustive and does not imply a particular typology of understanding. However, it does suggest certain modes of understanding. (14) There is, first of all, a sensori-motor mode from which many of the 'how to do it' understandings are derived. Secondly, there is an empathetic mode of understanding which comes from a person being able to put himself into the position of another. Thirdly, there is an analytic mode which stems from the ability to separate, discriminate and label correctly. Finally, there is a synthetic mode which seeks, at both the cognitive and affective levels, to detect or create more holistic perceptions, often through the use of symbol and metaphor. Each of the modes ranges over a continuum of forms from simple to very complex. They may interrelate and in some cases presuppose each other.

While the agreed syllabuses refrain from any conceptual analysis of understanding, they show through usage that they hold a broad view about its range of meaning:

> ... if pupils were to understand the nature of religion they would need a knowledge of religions ... an exploration of those aspects of human experience which raise questions about the meaning of life; skills of interpretation to help understand the significance of religious beliefs and practices; a sensitive attitude towards other people's deep convictions and towards their own maturing ability to think about questions of belief and value. (15)

It is usually left to teachers to ensure that they stimulate all four modes of understanding and, in doing so, 'continue a movement which is intrinsic to a learner's growth process'. (16)

The success of this stimulation depends on the extent to which there is an awareness of the dynamics of understanding, a theme not even raised in agreed syllabuses. The importance, complexity and richness of these dynamics have been exhaustively demonstrated by Bernard Lonergan. (17) Most teachers will probably be interested in that particular process which lies at the centre of creative understanding, for it is here that they interact with their young people in very significant ways. (18) It is a process which occurs within the context of a desire to know or of an intellectual curiosity such that 'before we look for answers we want them'. (19) The process has five phases and a sequence which is unchangeable, though as it is circular it can commence at any point. (20) Deeper understandings of importance to self growth seem to begin as a conflict arises which ruptures a person's equilibrium. Such tension often appears when the meanings a person has do not correspond with the reality he experiences. This can be the first phase in the process towards creative understanding. Its second phase arises as intentional thinking fails to find a resolution. When this occurs the mind allows a pause or a cessation of activity. This suspension can be momentary or it may be prolonged. Quite serendipitously within this relaxation an image, symbol or insight may surface which integrates the conflictual elements and constitutes a third phase. The fourth and fifth ones relate to the restoration of equilibrium which is now achieved and its interpretation through some means of communication. This understanding then is 'shot through with penetrative insight whereby the agent sees and grasps the inner character and hidden nature of things'. (21)

This understanding brings joy and has been called an 'ecstatic intuitition of relations'. (22) A clear biblical example of this process of conflict, pause, integrating image, restoration and interpretation occurs in the story of Peter and Cornelius in Acts 10. Peter, after an experience which made him reflect on his understanding of what was clean and unclean, says:

> God has shown me that I should not call any man impure or unclean ... I now realise how true it is that God does not show favouritism but accepts men from every nation ... Can anyone keep these people from being baptised with water? (23)

There are many other examples in the standard literature of creativity studies. (24)

To return to the second question, that of the prior aim of religious education, not only does the subject have distinctive features, it shares with other areas of knowledge a unifying focus. This focus lies behind the formal aims of all elements in the curriculum. Fundamentally, religious education seeks the development of the human. It strives to achieve this by encouraging an openness to those disciplines within the sciences and the arts which speak of the humanity of men and women. It fosters a consideration of the fears and failures as well as the hopes and aspirations of the human spirit. It asks about a mystery within persons which continually through history has evoked wonder and reflection, action and concern:

> Perhaps when creation overwhelms; when fantasy, imagination and intuition are loosed; and when the inner

vision of each human being is valued, then an understanding of that horizon of existence, explored within and central to religion becomes possible. (25)

The heart of religious education is a relationship with young people such that they are enabled to respond at depth to what is ultimate for them. It is a relationship which encourages them to ponder the thousand contingencies of human life and its irrevocable dependencies; which helps them correlate contemporary symbols and images, dreams and visions with what is everlastingly mysterious. It is a relationship which prompts them to reflect on that service which accepts duty and obligation; on the freedom that lies within responsibility and involvement; and on the love which discerns self-fulfilment in self-emptying. It is a relationship which engages young people in the fresh 'old quest for truth'. (26)

It is necessary to say two things about this prior aim. Firstly, the humanity it seeks is both an actuality and a possibility. Not simply a natural endowment, it has to be realised in living and dying; or it may be betrayed. It was Gerhard Ebeling who pointed out that only a human being can be inhuman. Secondly, to locate humanity properly involves moving beyond what is empirical - though without diminishing the value and importance of materialism for an understanding of men and women. To refuse to journey outside strictly empirical boundaries in the hope of remaining scientific and value-free is to restrict understanding. It is to subscribe to a view which itself arises from a seriously defective value system.

To perceive the height and depth of what it is to be human implies a concept of knowledge which embraces the widest possible understanding of reality. Such a concept cannot be limited to the view that all knowledge starts with observation or is propositional in form or can receive perfect expression. It does not imply that the empirical sciences offer a mode to which all knowledge should correspond. Nor does it accept that the role of the disinterested observer is paramount in acquiring knowledge. Rather it accepts the value of imaginative, intuitive hypotheses. And it affirms that a person who is genuinely committed to relationships will, in the encounter with others and in a participation in the life of the world, receive a knowledge not otherwise available. Knowledge requires art and skill as well as objective thought. Further it requires

60

participation. It was St Thomas Aquinas who observed: 'A thing is known by being present in the knower: how it is present is determined by the way of being of the knower.' (27)

Clearly, the argument about the prior aim of religious education is an argument about the philosophical framework on which not only this subject but the venture of education rests. To consider this aim is to detect norms and assumptions. It is to perceive a pattern of presuppositions and values. This pattern presents a view of reality which the curriculum expresses. There is a sense then in which the school curriculum becomes a window through which students and teachers perceive themselves and their worlds.

B PRACTICAL CONSIDERATIONS

When Rabbi Zalman was in prison he was visited by the chief of police. They spoke of the Scriptures and the visitor asked the holy man a question which was puzzling him. He said, 'If God is all-knowing, how may his question to Adam, "Where are thou?" be understood?' The rabbi asked: 'Do you believe that the Scriptures are eternal and that every era, every generation and every man is included in them?' 'I believe this,' said the other. 'Then know,' said the rabbi, 'that God is asking where you are.' (28)

The hasidic tale is a reminder that the process of education is an awakening to truth which removes the mesh of self-deception. To this extent, teachers and their students are on the same path. The operations of teaching and learning are a mutual introduction, exploration and interpretation of living which witness to the involvement of those who teach in the lives of those who learn. Practical problems are raised here for teachers. It is essential to perceive that they do not need to control all learning to be effective. Their competence is demonstrated in so far as they understand just what can be achieved in the teaching situation and know what is worth achieving. They may advise on the ways in which their students should face the ladder that is before them; they may structure a suitable environment for its climbing; they may organise the means of ascent. However, they cannot actually go up the ladder for their pupils. All teachers face this difficulty though the metaphors and images in which it is understood in the various subject areas are legion. The problem created by the freedom of the individual and his move towards greater autonomy is resolved as teachers deepen their understanding of the teaching relationship which lies within their own subject areas and evolve a curricular content which expresses this. It is worth looking at both of these in a little more detail.

1. The teaching relationship

Embedded within the teaching relationship are problems relating to human development and an understanding of persons. It is obvious that there is change and development in each person's understanding of his being. The nature of reality to which he commits himself and the overarching vision of his place within it are never wholly static. Those who work within the field of religious education are familiar with the earlier theoretical formulation of growth patterns by Piaget, Erikson and Goldman as well as the more recent ones of Peatling, Moran, Kohlberg and Fowler. (29) All of the patterns have contributed rich insights which now form part of teachers' understandings. Through them curricula have been changed, allowing a better congruence of content with learning operations. Even so, all of the growth patterns offered by the theorists suffer inadequacies. Developmentalism is concerned with commonality and leaves little room for diversity. Indirectly, it raises conceptual barriers between people and diminishes genuine encounter by prompting 'set pattern' relationships. All of the theories claim a comprehensiveness which is very vulnerable to charges of over-simplification. They explain too much, threatening to dominate the moral life with juridical ethics and shielding reason from acknowledging its roots in subjectivity and passion. Increasingly, the criticism is made that these theories 'attempt to raise white, middle-class North American male values to the level of human universals'. (30)

The most popular of current theories of development is that delineated by Fowler. It offers a depth and range unequalled elsewhere and is impressive in the seriousness with which it approaches formidable problems of faith development. Committed to responsible scholarship and the clarification of difficult ideas, it rather deflects criticism by claiming to be a report of ongoing work as yet provisional in character. Nevertheless, to the extent that this is experimental work in human psychology, criteria relevant to the assessment of such work apply. At present, questions relating to the sample, the nature of the statistical support available for conclusions and the use of the theories of Piaget, Kohlberg and Selman need to be resolved before the theory can be accepted as properly scientific. (31)

To reflect on teaching as a relationship offers a corrective. Instead of concentrating on what students must become and how this might be achieved, teachers can limit their power and narrow their range. They cannot really control the experience of their young people in the way some unreflective bureaucrats and myopic technocrats claim. Their central role is to engage in a genuine dialogue of interpretation over selected contents and experiences.

Two elements ensure the genuineness of this dialogue. The first is a teacher's honesty in an understanding of his own being. His life, like that of his students, is a 'wonder voyage into the unknown'. (32) If his life is the act of weaving his own story, then it must be worth both pondering and sharing. Iris Murdoch's view is that 'we live in a world whose mystery transcends us ... morality is the exploration of that mystery in so far as it concerns each individual.' (33) It is an insight which prompts men and women to perceive that, inescapably, they are related to and react to what is mysterious. There are many ways of dealing with this and many responses to make. Curiously, mystery remains whether it is accepted or rejected. It is as much affirmed in the disbelief of atheism and the dubiety of scepticism as in the belief of religion. This is so since the transcendental nature of a person stands within all of his thinking and feeling as its prior grounding and the 'enabling condition of his freedom'. (34) This mystery is the source of all of those experiences and questions which give rise to structures of meaning whether they are expressed in science, philosophy and religion or more informally in story, myth and allegory. The Baal Shem Tov sets this within the dimension of a particular religious tradition with his suggestion that all people think of God but that 'what varies is their way'. (35) So there is no particular stage setting for mystery. This is not to be expected since it is not the seen but the basis of seeing, not the known but the basis of knowing, not a value but the ground of values and not the particulars but their source. 'There is no vantage point from which to spy on mystery.' (36) Where then is it to be found? Obviously this can only be from within. The witness of many is that where the foil of life is tautly stretched it may resonate with that rhythm which surrounds it. Traditionally, mystery is perceived when people move to those boundaries which question their understanding of the everyday world and its common routine: the coming of new life, terror at the suffering of those who are loved most, the strangeness of new places or the grief that can overwhelm at the coming of death. Mystery can be present when people are driven to behave in ways which spring from inner conviction. Convictions when they have the force of conscience and lie deeper than argument can compel an allegiance, a fulfilment of duty, a meeting of obligation and an acceptance of responsibility, which persist when there is and can be no success. Mystery can appear at those points when life is recast: when retirement is faced or unemployment, when children leave home, when it is clear that life is ending or when there is an alienation stemming from total isolation. Mystery can arise

> as people tap the roots of that ultimacy which can only be spoken of haltingly: they discern in the fleeting loveliness of life a promise that such beauty will remain forever, they find that that hope which bears them through the bitter and deceiving world has an unknown strength, they see that their freedom is such that no earthly compulsions can wrest it from them, they find that the silent and dark emphasis of the universe is the sound and cloak for that mystery which dwells above all harmony and is the dazzling radiance of an unapproachable light. (37)

So it is that teachers, if they are to convey the mysterious nature of life to others, will need to reflect on the paradox which lies within themselves.

Beside this honesty, there is a second element which ensures the genuineness of the teacher-student dialogue. It is a pondering on method, on the means of communicating with others. So far as teachers of religious education are concerned, the problem of language is fundamental. How is a person to say what cannot be said? At one level, of course, there is no problem. Artefacts can be described, ceremonies pictured, history presented, biography drawn and liturgy enacted. Stories can be told, buildings visited, speakers attended to, maps coloured and projects organised. But how is all of this to be done in a way which facilitates the apprehension of meanings which believers perceive? Within county schools this needs to be done in ways which preserve the integrity of young people with no particular faith stance.

Many teachers find that it is within the context of a story that the significant experiences of life, both in contemporary living and from the traditions of the world's great religions, can best be imaged forth. Others find that a poetry can be created whose precision is richly suggestive. Still more use a thinking which is properly analogical or deeply symbolic to guide beyond the bars of sense perception. Sound, gesture, movement and form as well as parable, icon and allegory offer what is oblique and indirect as means of touching what could not otherwise be apprehended. None of this dethrones reason. The canons of openness, rationality and critical assessment so popular with educationalists remain. (38) This approach, however, makes two things clear with respect to reason. Firstly, it is not the only goal for either teachers or students. In the venture of religious education there is a need for those outside of faith, if they are to understand those within, to grasp that point when for the religious person the brokenness of understanding is revealed. It is a matter of using understanding to perceive the limits of understanding. Secondly, in the living of life in relationship reason can be pressed to those levels which many would see as negative. Openness may become that crippling indecision which elevates inaction. Rationality may pull itself to that point of total scepticism which refuses to take life seriously. The critical spirit can degenerate into cheap iconoclasm and become parasitic on constructive thinking. (39)

2. Curricular content

In <u>Curriculum 11-16</u>, Her Majesty's Inspectorate provides a check list of areas of experience which should be offered by the curriculum. (40) Among them is the spiritual area. This is not new. As early as 1947 the West Riding Agreed Syllabus spoke of the development of 'the spiritual nature of the pupil'. (41) What is novel is the emphasis this area has received in recent years. There have been interesting attempts by Holley, King and Priestley to locate this area in education in general and in religious education in particular. (42) It is held that 'Rightly understood all education is a

65

spiritual activity' (43) and that 'successful religious education is primarily the provocation of spiritual insight.' (44) It is true, however, that teachers often first come into contact with these ideas in their agreed syllabuses. Typical of the present trend are the statements of the Hertfordshire Syllabus:

> Religious education is concerned with the spiritual growth of the individual, with those feelings and beliefs which arise out of experience and that influence the search for meaning and purpose to life (45)

and the Bradford Syllabus:

> Religious and spiritual experiences are seen as an essential element in the growth and development of children and young people. These experiences are partners in the search for truth alongside the scientific and historic. (46)

The current emphasis on the spiritual in education is curious. There are two reasons for thinking that the heart has moved in advance of the head in asking teachers how they might enhance the spiritual in the lives of their children. Firstly, there is no sequence of maturation in spiritual matters which secular educationalists would find acceptable. What work has been done relates to growth within faith communities and inevitably uses concepts, is informed by categories and makes assumptions, which those outside cannot share. Despite this, the work of Loder, Dykstra and Batson presents a means of understanding the pattern of spiritual growth which might be transposed to the secular order. (47) They emphasise the role of creative imagination in human development in ways which bring new insights into how educationalists might deal with spiritual development. It is arguable that 'the five-fold process of creative imagining is central to all of the indicators of psychological development and is the only means by which they can occur'. (48)

Secondly, there are no clear definitions available which indicate what the notion of the spiritual may mean when used in educational thinking. The concept can be so broad that it says nothing and becomes a bit like the Bellman's map in The Hunting of the Snark, 'a perfect and absolute blank'. (49) It may be so narrow when used within a faith context that it is interpreted to fit as a thread within particular theological positions. Clearly, if it is to have value for education, it needs to have relevance within and without religions. It requires rooting within the human person and needs to function within a network of concepts whose relative importance is established. A helpful direction is offered by the Inspectorate:

> The spiritual area is concerned with the awareness a person has of those elements in existence and experience which may be defined in terms of inner feelings and beliefs; they affect the way people see themselves and throw light for them on the purpose and meaning of life itself. Often these feelings and beliefs lead people to claim to know God and to glimpse the transcendent; sometimes they represent that longing and striving for perfection which characterises human beings but always they are concerned with matters at the heart and root of existence. (50)

Another view is that

> ... the spiritual is a category of being whose form is the personal, the co-ordinates of which are thought, freedom and creativity and the expression of which is in commitment, aspiration and valuation ... (51)

The spiritual area is a dimension which suffuses all education. In particular its force is felt in the quality of a school's teaching relationships and in the manner in which it infuses the areas of knowledge of the curriculum. In facing the question: What religious education will occur in the classroom if the spiritual area is enhanced? two things may be considered. The first concerns the way in which teachers and young people relate and the second how content is perceived.

If those teaching in schools establish relationships of any depth, then such relationships can be understood from three perspectives. These perspectives affirm the transcendence of the persons in relationship; demonstrate a creativity in the breadth that such a relationship achieves; and display a means of communication within the relationship which is characterised by dialogue.

A relationship of transcendence is affirmed where what enhances or enriches life develops. Transcendence negates the view that life is fixed and human nature unchanging by continually pressing for what most truly humanises existence. The horizons of the self are nudged back, the boundaries of what circumscribes are crossed. The means of doing this are ever changing and never ending for, as Schleiermacher observed, humans have 'a sense and a taste for the infinite'. (52) Within education, the giving of self in a relationship results in greater self-realisation.

Where a relationship demonstrates creativity, the potentiality of freedom has been seized and given a direction. Where it is positive, that direction leads towards a deepening of humanity. For the adventure of human life is to mould with and for others from what is as yet unknown, to shape a nature from fictile possibility. Curiously, as David Jones says, '... one is trying to make a shape out of the very things of which one is oneself made.' (53) The facticity of life, all of the obvious limitations imposed by genes, history and culture do not remove or annihilate creative freedom; they do, however, condition it.

Where the form of communication in relationship is through dialogue, there is a mutual affirmation in the lives of the people involved. This affirmation both precedes and is the prior condition of what is generally known as successful teaching. In dialogue, persons are present for each other, discovering how realities and truths may be further expanded or integrated. This implies a relationship of sincerity, responsibility and trust which does not seek to insulate from risk or controversy. In it each one is available to the other, which enables each to know the other in a special way and to know themselves more deeply. The dialogue is both a gift for the present and a promise for the future, for human beings are secrets which are everlastingly disclosed.

Implicit in this argument is the assumption that teachers bring to their relationships an expertise in relevant areas which makes possible a creative interaction with their pupils. Sadly, religious education is very vulnerable here. In a league table of all subjects, religious education

> ... has the lowest place with regard to teachers qualified to teach it. It is estimated indeed that in maintained secondary schools only forty per cent of tuition in religious education is given by teachers properly qualified for teaching it and that twenty-nine per cent is in the hands of people with no qualification

whatever in religious education. (54)

When this is coupled with the reduced number of places available for training religious education teachers in colleges, polytechnics and university departments of education during the last decade, clearly there is little hope of major improvement in the near future. The effects of this on schools are parlous. Senior management teams accord religious education a low status within the curriculum and among their staffing priorities. The option system in most schools tends to push it out of sight for examination purposes. Consequently, numbers taking it at CSE, O level and A level continue to decline. This, of course, has its effects on those wishing to teach it. In the short term, there are problems here regarding retraining, in-service provision and the widening of opportunity in training institutions which are of such financial magnitude that they are inevitably political. In the longer term, educationalists and parents in particular, and perhaps the community more generally, must reflect on the extent to which they are prepared to take seriously the claims of religious education to a place in the curriculum.

Moving to the second consideration, if all that has been said so far about the cruciality of relationships is correct, then there can be no set of absolutely fixed rubrics or series of closed pedagogical prescriptions ensuring the presence of the spiritual dimension in a person's teaching. To think that these are possible is to misunderstand the nature of teaching, ignore the importance of creative freedom and diminish the natures of both students and teachers. What can be said about the religious education programme in the classroom is that if teaching is informed by certain broad approaches, which take account of the variety of individual skills, circumstance and opportunity, then this dimension is more fully present. These approaches could move in several directions.

Firstly, attempts may be made to cultivate to continually deeper levels that amazement which human beings have as they find themselves cast into existence. It arises from what might more formally be termed ontologic experience. At one level there is an astonishment at creation which is grasped from within and can be articulated but falteringly. St. Augustine is speaking for all when he comments:

> For we both are, and know that we are, and delight in
> our being, and our knowledge of it. Moreover, in these
> three things no true-seeming illusion disturbs us ... And
> truly the very fact of existing is by some natural spell
> so pleasant, that even the wretched are, for no other
> reason, unwilling to perish ... (55)

This is as much a matter for the scientific disciplines as for
the artistic ones. (56) Not simply quantitative, although the
immensity of the space displayed by telescope and
microscope may be the question that prompts it, it is
qualitative, posing ultimate issues of meaning, truth and
being. For the poet amazement may be part of a 'sense
sublime', for the artist an intuition of the ineffable; for the
ordinary person it may be the perception that within the
commonplace (a piece of bread, a posy, a shell and an act of
friendship) as well as the extraordinary (the symphonies of
Mahler, the architecture of Chartres, the lives of martyrs)
lies what is common to both. At another level, astonishment
has its darker side as the brutal aspects of life within nature
and human societies are understood and the feelings of pain,
helplessness and sadness are experienced. The agreed
syllabuses give opportunities for the exploration of
amazement when the suggestion is made that each child
needs to 'widen his interest in the world around him' and
explore human 'experience of and response to beauty and
harshness in nature'. (57)

Secondly, efforts can be made to urge children and
young people to consider what lies beyond the boundaries of
their present understanding in the intellectual, moral and
aesthetic realms. Widening frames of reference provide
more accurate and inclusive patterns of understanding.
There are many possibilities here. As the range of the sense
organs is explored, together with their limitations, two
questions are fundamental. They are: Is the world really as
we perceive it to be? and What lies outside the senses? As
the notion of time is investigated, young people may puzzle
over what the identity of the self is. Changes of physique
and abilities over time induce the questions: Am I the same
person now as I was then? and What will I become? As the
meanings of words are learned and work with a dictionary
begins, there can be a problem with language. If the
meanings of words are all given by other words, what do any
words really mean by themselves? As the human body and
developing skills are appreciated and as it is understood that

one may lose hair, teeth, nails and possibly - through accident - an arm, the question: What or Who is really me? presses. As children share interests in activities like stamp- or coin-collecting, the processes of classification give rise to questions which push beyond taxonomy to epistemology. Reflection on relationships, on expectations of parents or peers, leads to a probing of moral areas and questions of responsibility, duty and freedom. Moving to new boundaries not only gives more unifying structures, it can change persons, sometimes in a subtle way, occasionally more radically. For example, sixth-formers who have mused on the night meeting of Priam and Achilles in the Iliad, on what drives Alyosha Karamazov to kneel to the stars or on the battlefield conversation of Arjuna and Krishna in the Bhagavad Gita may find their lives changed as their boundaries of emotional understanding are stretched. As frames of reference are restructured and limit situations approached, there is a need for great sensitivity in the teaching relationship. There are situations where teachers need to intensify conflicts within their students' understandings and refocus questions to make them even more demanding. Good teaching can make children dissatisfied with themselves and uncomfortable in their thinking. Security, important though it is, is not always overriding. There is often emotional pain and insecurity, anxiety and stress as ideas grow. Teachers need to exercise their knowledge of their children here. Well-timed challenges can produce rich growth; ill-timed ones can threaten and upset:

> To reflect upon these boundaries seriously is to raise the ultimate questions of our existence. The way we face them reveals the kind of being we are, for the way a finite being holds itself with respect to its ultimate limits is the very core of that being ... to become evasive or confused about these limits is to confuse our existence at its very core. (58)

The agreed syllabuses give opportunities for this approach, encouraging their teachers to have an aim for their work which will help their pupils 'to think for themselves about ultimate questions of meaning and value (e.g. Who am I? What is life for? Who is my neighbour?)'. (59)

Thirdly, an alertness to the fact that the meaning of life is not completely given from without, but is also

71

constructed from within, can be promoted. The agreed syllabuses locate a fundamental aim for religious education in the personal search for meaning. This subject

> helps young people to identify and foster those personal values, allegiances and commitments that are beginning to take shape in their hearts and mind. (60)

Pupils are engaged 'in their own personal quest for values and beliefs by which to live'. (61) There is much that can nourish this voyage among all of the branches of knowledge in the curriculum. Certainly, the teachings of the major traditions in the great world religions raise for those who study them profound questions about the meaning of their lives. To read the key scriptures of these religions is to be interrogated about personhood and have the search for final values intensified. Reflection on their myths, symbols and revelations, on their parables, icons and rituals offers a sharpening of experience and an enrichment of humanity. Religions pose for each new generation the enduring problems of men and women: Why must I suffer? Why do the wicked prosper? Where is justice to be found? Is there immortal life after death? How can I find the truth? Often the answers that religions give need to be lived out in committed lives. Thus questions of commitment: What do I value most? What am I prepared to die for? arise. Yet because the stories which religions tell are many-layered, they can lead to further development and further questioning even when there is no commitment. Tackling the issues embedded within the world's religions can shift young people towards more authentic, more honest living, whatever their life stance. Above all, however, the world religions bring young people to face the host of questions which surround belief in God. What counts in religious education is not the particular views that are held but that a journey is begun, that the innate yearning after what is inconceivable and unsayable is attended to. What matters is that, through a sincere wrestling, an honest searching and a trenchant questioning, an approach is made to the frontiers of the spirit.

Fourthly, an attempt to reflect on those aspects of personal experience which seem significant to young people can be made. It focuses on their personal and inward response to life. The Bedfordshire Agreed Syllabus suggests that teachers should draw on 'pupils' experiences' (62) and develop

> an awareness of a dimension beyond the purely physical
> ... a sense of mystery about what it is to be human ... a
> feeling of dependence upon (the natural world). (63)

The unspoken assumption behind this is that experiences of
relativism, contingency and temporality will pose questions
of ultimacy. The joy as well as the anxiety of living raise
the problem of the unconditioned within which is found
either a presence or an absence. The research of Robinson
and Hay has shown the importance of transcendental
experiences in people's lives. (64) Such experience is
common enough within a given population, though it is not
of great frequency within an individual life. What religious
education can do is to help young people probe not only the
special experiences but also the meaning and worth of a
wider range of feeling and knowing. The Nottinghamshire
Religious Experience Research Project has had interesting
success in doing just this and has established its worth. (65)
The sharpest test of the value of this approach is seen
in the topics teachers are often very wary of using in their
classes. Death and dying, terror and loss as well as grief and
pain lie more within the experience of children than is often
realised. Their lives are seldom pastoral idylls and fear is
felt by all. If the school is a place where the shadows and
darkness of living can be faced, then children have an
opportunity for growth. The effect of looking properly at
death can be to determine to live properly, rejecting the
stereotypes and expectations which do not foster personal
integrity.

> It is through accepting the finiteness of our individual
> existences ... that we are able to find the strength and
> courage ... to devote each day of our lives ... to growing
> as fully as we are able. (66)

There are rules for dying as well as for the celebration of
living, for grief as well as for laughter. (67) Here, both
teachers and students can find themselves involved in the
same problems and perhaps track through them in like ways.

CONCLUSION

If religious education is to flourish in state schools in the twenty-first century, it will need to offer a programme which takes full account of the diversity and richness of the great religious traditions of the world as well as the particular historical and cultural situation in which it is set. Its programme will be quite separate from the nurture given to the young by faith communities where this implies commitment and assent. It will have two features. The first of these is an openness and flexibility to an unknown future, the second is the promotion of what is unique and distinctive to religious education. This latter is found in the understanding of the patterns of religious belief, the language in which these are expressed, the means of evaluation of argument in religion and the experience of believers.

However, the programme itself will need that basis which is given when the teaching relationship is seen as dialogic and when the whole teacher-student interaction is drawn within the spiritual dimension. To achieve this many practical problems of supply, training and time-tabling need to be faced, as well as more theoretical issues relating to the nature of religious education. The Report of the Working Party of the National Association of Head Teachers is the best current guide to these and makes informed and very realistic recommendations. At a time when, having survived the problem of absorption into integrated humanities schemes, religious education finds itself threatened by assimilation into programmes of personal, social and moral education, it is helpful to have this support. (68)

In a sense, there can be no conclusion. The comment of Rabbi Levi-Yitzhak of Berditchev is a reminder to those who write about holy things of the degree of their own ignorance. On being asked the question: 'Why do all Talmudic tractates begin on page two,' he said: 'To remind us that even if we know them from one end to the other, we have not even begun.' (69) Just so.

NOTES AND REFERENCES

1.   M. Buber, Tales of the Hasidim: the Early Masters, (Schoken Books, 1961), p. 172.

2.   St. Augustine, Confessions (Penguin Classics,

1961), p. 76. (Factus eram ipse mihi magna questio.)

3. e.g. D. Meakin 'The Justification of Religious Education', British Journal of Religious Education (1979, vol. 12, no. 2); M. Phillips-Bell, 'Justification and Multifaith Religious Education', British Journal of Religious Education (1983, vol. 5, no. 2); W.G.M. Elliott 'An Examination of Religious Statements and Implications of this Analysis for Religious Education', unpublished PhD thesis, (University of London, 1965). (I am happy to acknowledge my debt to the above in this section.)

4. Religious Education for our Children (the Agreed Syllabus of the Inner London Education Authority, 1984), p. 4.

5. Religious Education in Warwickshire Schools and Colleges, (the Agreed Syllabus of Warwickshire Local Education Authority, 1985), p 1.

6. Religious Heritage and Personal Quest, (the Agreed Syllabus of Berkshire Education Authority, 1982), p. 2.

7. Ibid.

8. Religious Education in Warwickshire Schools and Colleges, (the Agreed Syllabus of Warwickshire Local Education Authority, 1985), p. 1.

9. Religious Education for Living in Today's World, (the Agreed Syllabus of Bradford Metropolitan District Council, 1983), p. 3.

10. Religious Heritage and Personal Quest, (the Agreed Syllabus of Berkshire Education Authority, 1982), p. 2.

11. Agreed Syllabus of Religious Education (Humberside Education Authority, 1981), p. 5.

12. Ibid., p. 6.

13. A Framework for Religious Education in Cambridgeshire, (the Agreed Syllabus of Cambridgeshire County Council), 1982, p. 1.

14. C.F. Melchert, "Understanding" as a Purpose of Religious Education' (Religious Education, 1981, vol. 76, no. 2) p.181.

15. A Framework for Religious Education in Cambridgeshire, (the Agreed Syllabus for Cambridgeshire County Council, 1982), p. 1.

16. C. Melchert, loc. cit., p. 185.

17. B.J.F. Lonergan, Insight (Darton, Longman and Todd, 1958).

18. Vide C.D. Batson, 'Creativity and Religious

Development' (unpublished ThD, Princeton Theological Seminary, 1971); C.R. Dykstra, 'Christian Education and the Moral Life' (unpublished PhD, Princeton Theological Seminary, 1978); J.E. Loder, The Transforming Moment (Harper and Row, 1981).

19.   B.J.F. Lonergan, op. cit., p. 9.

20.   J.E. Loder, 'Transformation in Christian Education', (Religious Education, 1981).

21.   R. Holley, Religious Education and Religious Understanding, (Routledge and Kegan Paul, 1978), p. 75.

22.   Ibid.

23.   Acts 10:28, 34, 47, New International Version of the Bible, (1979).

24.   Vide S. Arieti, Creativity (Basic Books, 1976); B. Ghiselin (ed.), The Creative Process, (University of California Press, 1952); R. May, The Courage to Create, (Collins, 1976); R.W. Weisenberg, Creativity: Genius and Other Myths, (W.H. Freeman & Co., 1986).

25.   D.H. Webster, Playing Hide and Seek with God (Christian Education Movement, 1981) p. 15.

26.   R.S Thomas, Later Poems 1972-1983, (Macmillan, 1984), p. 60.

27.   Thomas Aquinas, Summa Theologiae, 1. 12. 4.

28.   M. Buber, Hasidism and Modern Man, (Haper and Row, 1958), p. 130.

29.   J. Piaget, The Moral Judgement of the Child (Routledge and Kegan Paul, 1932); E. Erikson, Childhood and Society, (Norton, 1963); R. Goldman, Religious Thinking from Childhood to Adolescence, (Routledge and Kegan Paul, 1964); J. Peatling, Religious Education in a Psychological Key (Religious Education Press, 1981); G. Moran, Religious Education Development, (Winston Press, 1983); L. Kohlberg, The Philosophy of Moral Development, (Harper and Row, 1981); J. Fowler, Stages of Faith, (Harper and Row, 1981).

30.   S. Thistlethwaite, 'From Theory to Practice', (Religious Education, 1982, vol. 77, no. 4), p. 426; C. Gilligan, In a Different Voice, Harvard University Press, 1982.

31.   D.H. Webster, 'James Fowler's Theory of Faith Development' (British Journal of Religious Education, 1984, vol. 7, no. 1). (A reply to some of the questions raised concerning Fowler's theory in the above is offered in M. Smith, 'Answers to Some Questions about Faith Development', (British Journal of Religious Education, 1986, vol. 8, no. 2).

32.   P. Pacey, <u>David Jones and Other Wonder Voyagers</u> (Poetry Wales Press, 1982), p. 9.

33.   I. Murdoch, 'Vision and Choice in Morality', (I. Ramsey (ed.), <u>Christian Ethics and Contemporary Philosophy</u>, Macmillan, 1966), p. 208.

34.   K. Rahner, <u>Theological Investigations</u>, (Darton, Longman and Todd, 1975, vol. 13), p. 123.

35.   E. Weisel, <u>Souls on Fire</u>, (Penguin, 1984), p. 25.

36.   J. Shea, <u>Stories of God</u>, (The Thomas More Press, 1978), p. 19.

37.   D.H. Webster, 'Religious Education and a Rediscovery of the Spiritual: a Pathless Path', (<u>News and Events</u>, The York Religious Education Centre, 1984), pp. 25-6.

38.   P.H. Hirst, 'Education and Diversity of Belief', (M.C. Felderhof, (ed.), <u>Religious Education in a Pluralistic Society</u>, Hodder and Stoughton, 1985).

39.   M.C. Felderhof, 'Introduction', (M.C. Felderhof (ed.), op. cit.,) p. 2.

40.   H.M. Inspectorate, <u>Curriculum 11-16</u>, (DHS, 1977), p. 6.

41.   <u>Syllabus of Religious Instruction</u>, (the Agreed Syllabus of the County Council of the West Riding of Yorkshire, 1947), p. 46.

42.   R. Holley, <u>Religious Education and Religious Understanding</u>, (Routledge and Kegan Paul, 1978); U. King, 'Religious Education: Transcendence and Liberation', (<u>Celebration and Challenge</u>, 1984, Report on a Conference held at King's College, University of London); J. Priestley, 'Teaching Transcendence', (M.F. Tickner and D.H. Webster (eds.), <u>Religious Education and the Imagination</u>, Aspects of Education, 28, the University of Hull, 1982).

43.   U. King, op. cit., p. 16.

44.   R. Holley, op. cit., p. 145.

45.   <u>Hertfordshire Agreed Syllabus of Religious Education</u>, (the Agreed Syllabus of Hertfordshire County Council, 1981), p. 5.

46.   <u>Religious Education for Living in Today's World</u>, (the Agreed Syllabus of Bradford Metropolitan District Council, 1983), p. 3.

47.   Vide note 18 above.

48.   D.H. Webster, 'The Spiritual Development of Children', (<u>The Clergy Review</u>, 1985, vol. 70, no. 1).

49.   L. Carroll, <u>The Hunting of the Snark</u>, (Penguin, 1973), p. 56.

50.   H.M. Inspectorate, Supplementary Note: What the Spiritual Area is Concerned With, (DES, 1978).

51.   D.H. Webster, 'Spiritual Growth in Religious Education', (M.F. Tickner and D.H. Webster (eds.), Religious Education and the Imagination, Aspects of Education, 28, the University of Hull, 1982).

52.   F.D.E. Schleiermacher, On Religion, (Harper and Row, 1958), p. 39.

53.   D. Jones, The Anathemata, (Faber and Faber, 1972), p. 10.

54.   B. Watson, 'Theology in the Classroom within the Present Educational Setting: Problems and Prescriptions', (J. Barnett (ed.), Theology at 16+, Epworth Press, 1984), p. 92.

55.   St. Augustine, The City of God, Book 11, Chapters 26 and 27, (W.J. Oates (ed.), Basic Writings of St. Augustine, Random House, 1948, pp. 168-9).

56.   Vide A. Peacocke, God and the New Biology, (Dent, 1986).

57.   Agreed Syllabus of Religious Education, (Lincolnshire County Council, 1980), pp. 10-11.

58.   J. Wild, Existence and the World of Freedom, (Prentice-Hall, 1963), p. 28.

59.   Agreed Syllabus of Religious Education (County of Avon, 1976), p. 6.

60.   Religious Education in Warwickshire Schools and Colleges, (the Agreed Syllabus of Warwickshire Local Education Authority, 1985), p. 1.

61.   Religious Heritage and Personal Quest, (the Agreed Syllabus of Berkshire Education Authority, 1982), p. 34.

62.   Bedfordshire Agreed Syllabus of Religious Education: Planning Secondary RE, (Bedfordshire Teaching Media Resource Service, 1980), p. 13.

63.   Ibid., p. 11.

64.   E. Robinson, The Original Vision, (Religious Experience Research Unit, 1977); E. Robinson, This Time-Bound Ladder, (Religious Experience Research Unit, 1977); D. Hay, Exploring Inner Space, (Penguin, 1982).

65.   D. Hay et al., Inside Information, 1984-6. (Newsletters of the Religious Experience Research Project, the University of Nottingham.)

66.   E. Kubler-Ross, Death: the Final Stage of Growth, (Prentice-Hall, 1975), p. 164.

67.   Vide R. Ricketts (ed.), Bid the World Good-Night, (Search Press, 1981); E. Schneiderman, Voices of Death,

(Bantam Books, 1982); C. Saunders, <u>Beyond All Pain</u>, (SPCK, 1983); I. Ainsworth-Smith and P. Speck, <u>Letting Go</u>, (SPCK, 1982); E. Collick, <u>Through Grief</u>, (Mirfield Publications, 1982).

68.   <u>Religious Education in Schools</u>, 1985, the Report of the Working Party of the National Association of Head Teachers. (Support is given to the view that 'for all 11-16 year olds, there should be a minimum provision of two (35 minute) periods per week per class on Religious Education and Moral Education. This should be complementary to any additional work done on personal and social education elsewhere in the curriculum ...', p. 32.)

69.   E. Wiesel, <u>Souls on Fire</u>, (Penguin, 1984), p. 80.

Chapter Five

CHRISTIAN EDUCATION IN A MULTI-CULTURAL SOCIETY

Edward Hulmes

A PRELIMINARY QUESTION

At first sight there is something re-assuringly practical about the title of this chapter. Here at last (it might be said) there is a thoroughly down-to-earth issue that it would be pointless to complicate with theoretical considerations. The facts speak for themselves. In recent years the composition of society in Britain has substantially changed. And this change (it might be claimed) calls for a ready response, especially from teachers, to meet new social circumstances and the needs of a changed student constituency. In purely descriptive terms Britain is both a multi-racial and a multi-faith society, to a degree that was unknown only a few decades ago. Precise figures for different ethnic and cultural groups may not be available yet, but the demographic trends are apparent even to the casual observer.

It is one thing to describe Britain as a multi-racial or a multi-faith society. It does not follow from this that Britain is, or indeed ever can be, a multi-cultural society, in anything other than a superficial sense. It is arguable that when it comes to questions of educational theory and practice, for example, Britain is still a fundamentally monocultural society. This raises an important educational question, with theoretical as well as practical implications. The question suggests that the present crisis in education is primarily philosophical rather than economic. How realistic is it to speak of Christian education in a multi-cultural society, when it is difficult (even for Christians) to reach agreement about the meaning of the former, and questionable that any existing society (including Britain) can reasonably be described as the latter? The question raises issues that it might be useful for anyone interested in education, as well as those professionally involved as teachers or administrators, to reconsider.

There are several points to be clarified. What is meant by the phrase Christian education? What meaning is to be attached to the phrase multi-cultural society, a phrase which at first sight looks like a contradiction in terms? What is distinctive about Christian education, and about a multi-cultural society, and how does the one relate to the other? (I) Do both phrases conceal ideological aspirations that it would be useful to uncover? The issue here is one of definition, rather than of usage. In this chapter I would like to comment on some of these questions by considering what, for me, is an intriguing paradox. The paradox is implicit in the juxtaposition of the two discrete phrases contained in the title. My intention is to make the paradox explicit, and thus to make a contribution to the discussion of the central theme of the book. I approach the exercise in the light of my interest in the theology of education, or more strictly, the comparative theology of education.

CULTURAL DIVERSITY AND THE NOTION OF A MULTI-CULTURAL SOCIETY

The words Christian education in a multi-cultural society suggest several things to the reader. To the crusading spirit they might suggest both an opportunity and a challenge. More defensively, perhaps, the reader might reflect on the real, but restricted, role for Christian education within the overall framework of an educational system which is not based upon Christian principles. Will Christian education survive within such a system as a form of Christian presence in a secular society? Or does the preservation of Christian education require Christians to withdraw from the state (that is, the secular) system of education? It might well be concluded that the answer to the last question must be yes, if it turns out that the aims and objectives of Christian education are incompatible with the goals of a multi-cultural society. And what may be true of one cultural tradition in Britain may be true of others.

Among the responsibilities to be discharged by the members of a developed society is that of making adequate

provision for education. Decisions have to be made about
aims and objectives, about the content of the curriculum
and the preferred methods of teaching, about the initial and
subsequent training given to teachers, and about the
deployment of available human and material resources to
meet special needs. In education, no less than in other areas
of social interaction, there is a tension between the old and
the new. In education this tension is not always creative. In
an increasingly litigious age it would not be surprising to
find that teachers, like their medical and legal colleagues,
prefer to take as few risks as possible with their clients'
future prospects and with their own careers. So teachers,
with notable (or notorious) exceptions, tend to practise their
profession <u>defensively</u>. The qualities attributed to P.K.
Theodore's celebrated captive creature are still found useful
by many who are supposed to kindle sparks of interest in
unreceptive minds. 'Cet animal est très méchant; quand on
l'attaque il se défend.' But today there is an additional
factor which has changed the situation in a qualitative way.

The tension today between older and newer approaches
to education is maintained, as before, by the criticisms that
the younger generation has usually reserved for the methods
of its elders. But it is not just a matter of choosing
innovations which, in their turn, will serve long-established
aims and objectives which remain intact. That element
remains, but there is an additional factor which is now
beginning to be recognised for the serious challenge it
presents to the dominant philosophy of education in the
western world. For good or ill the nature of British society
has changed. The change is qualitative as well as
quantitative. It is a change that presents society as a whole
with problems as well as opportunities. In the early phases
of adjustment to these changes two rather unhelpful
responses are heard. One exaggerates the incidence, and the
disruptive effects, of the acts of violence which are said to
be caused by racial and cultural tension in a comparatively
few parts of the country. The other response to social
change effectively <u>limits</u> the contribution that cultural
diversity might otherwise make to the enrichment of
society, by concentrating attention on its more trivial
aspects. This raises an important question. Is Britain a
multi-cultural society?

Statements are often made to the effect that Britain <u>is</u>
<u>a multi-cultural society</u> (or is in the process of becoming
one), and that education should, in consequence, reflect the

levels of cultural diversity now to be found in this country. A society which consists of individuals and groups from different cultural backgrounds is clearly multi-cultural in one sense, but this does not take us very far. The presence of so many small or large ethnic minority groups which have arrived here comparatively recently, or of the larger and more established communities which have been domiciled here for a long time, is insufficient in itself to make society multi-cultural. It would be inaccurate to use this description of society as if it were objective and demonstrable. And it would be naive to object to criticism of its use on the grounds that social action designed to help the underprivileged and to remove injustice - in schools or anywhere else - should be supported by whatever name it is known. If subjective opinions are to be allowed it might be preferable to take account of the views of those who might be expected to benefit most from the elimination of injustice. But there is increasing evidence to show that the members of ethnic, and other, minority groups would not agree that society in this country is multi-cultural in a significant sense. Ethnic minorities in Britain and elsewhere in the world have a different perception of reality. They are isolated from each other, and from the dominant majority, by cultural difference. They experience segregation and economic deprivation, not least because they lack the political power to bring about a fairer distribution of resources.

The word 'society', like the word 'community', implies a high degree of affinity among the members of a homogeneous, rather than a heterogeneous, group. It refers to a group in which certain values are inherited (or otherwise chosen), shared, preserved, and transmitted. This degree of affinity is founded upon an identity of interests and concerns. Personal relationships between individual members of such a group may range from the distant to the intimate, but there are always limits to what is acceptable. From time to time disagreements may give rise to hostility and violence, in which case a particular act may be censured in the common interest, and defined as anti-social. But all these relationships within the group are grounded in an organic unity of shared values and tradition. The acceptance of some quite specific values and social objectives is essential for the health of any society.

There is a kind of tolerance which expresses mutual acceptance and understanding. There is another kind of tolerance, of <u>toleration</u> perhaps, which masks indifference. Both varieties have been characteristic of the cultural life of this country for a long time. For centuries the rights of individuals and of minorities have been defended in pursuit of democratic ideals in Britain. The cultural map of Britain has been changing since the end of the second world war. During that same period the challenges to tolerance of both kinds have been mounting. Immigrants from many parts of the former Empire, and from elsewhere, have come to live in this country, bringing with them their own distinctive patterns of culture, their own religious and moral beliefs, and their own understanding of the relationship between education and the community. Within the population at large minorities have established and preserved distinctive ways of life. New elements have been added to the cultural mix, and these new elements seek to retain their identity within the wider community. Some have sought assimilation and integration. Others have not been able to resist either. The problem, by no means a new one, is that the values which distinguish the cultural life of a particular group frequently do not coincide with the values of the larger community. Does an increase in the number of distinctive cultural elements mean that society is more pluralist in fact? Of all the questions which present themselves in an avowedly pluralist and democratic society few are more difficult to answer than this.

Changes in social attitudes, in religious beliefs and practices, and in moral values, reflect the growing secularisation of society since the end of the second world war - and not only in Britain. These changes have introduced a new level of cultural diversity into this country. It is still an open question as to whether or not the extent of cultural diversity will ever be recognised as fully as it might be, even when the notion of pluralism is entertained in principle. When a <u>notional</u> assent is given to pluralism in education, it is only given in terms which exclude at the outset the possibility of any serious challenge to the dominant theory of knowledge. The introduction of teaching about world religions in courses of religious education may be taken as an index of the will to recognise the fact of religious pluralism. The study of world religions, now well established, undoubtedly provides some of the most imaginative innovations in curriculum development. The decision to extend the boundaries of religious education to include non-theistic life-stances such as Humanism provides additional evidence of the willingness of many teachers to acknowledge the fullest possible range of pluralism in Britain.

Other observers, outside as well as inside schools, are less convinced of the value of such a wide-ranging curriculum. They take the view that despite the existence of religious and cultural difference in this country it is <u>Christian</u> education (or more vaguely, education in the Judaeo-Christian tradition) which must regain the dominant position it once held. In the hands of such critics this appears, in effect, to require that education become explicitly instrumental in order to induct students into Christian values and beliefs. Assuming for a moment that the more appropriate approach to education in this country today is that which reflects the pluralism of society, however incompletely in practice, it is still necessary to insist that the inclusion of teaching <u>about</u> different religions and life-stances may, paradoxically, preserve a <u>monocultural</u> approach to religious pluralism. It is not easy to see how students from <u>different</u> cultural backgrounds can be protected from the potentially indoctrinatory effects of this western cultural domination, which tends to focus attention on the study of religion in descriptive, or experiential, terms - but which ignores the epistemological differences of cultural diversity.

These differences are fundamental, and so far as education is concerned, they are not just methodological. It is not merely that in <u>this</u> culture the importance of rote-learning is stressed, whilst in <u>that</u> culture little attention is given to that method of memory training. The differences have more to do with what is to count as knowledge, and what is to count as evidence. It follows from this that different cultures may have very different ideas about how knowledge is to be acquired. One way of making students more aware of the approach to knowledge so widely adopted in western systems of education would be to encourage them to extend their study of world religions to include a consideration of the <u>educational</u> implications of cultural diversity as an important aspect of pluralism. (2)

In other words, there are at least two questions, not one, to be considered here. The first reflects curiosity about a wide variety of unfamiliar customs and beliefs. If it serves to emphasise differences, it can also prepare the way for understanding and empathy. 'What difficulties are faced by Christians (or Jews, or Muslims, or Humanists, for example) in practising their faith in Britain today?' The second question draws attention to differences of another order, differences which have to do with the function of education itself in society. 'What would it be like to be educated as a Christian (or a Jew, or a Muslim, or a Humanist, for example)?' This second question suggests that there might be an altogether new dimension for cultural enrichment in a pluralist society, and that education itself might one day feel the gale-force effects of cultural diversity. To be in a position to answer this second question requires some knowledge of the principles of Christian, Jewish, Islamic, and Humanist education.

A good example of the partial nature of the concessions made to the demands of pluralism in a democratic society is thus provided by education itself. It is not yet clear at what point the appreciation, or the tolerance, of cultural diversity ceases in society as a whole. In education the picture is clearer. The assumption that each element in society can contribute to what is described as multi-cultural education, designed for a multi-cultural society, already shows to some extent what is expected. Ideas and principles which may be valuable, even essential, in preserving the distinctive cultural life of a minority may also be useful to the majority. Education could provide a forum for the exchange of this information. The principles upon which the theory and practice of education are built in the different cultural traditions now represented in Britain are not easily reconciled to serve a common interest. On the other hand the concept of pluralism is simply ignored in practice if the approach to knowledge, and to the acquisition of knowledge - in short, to education - is effectively monocultural. In spite of the considerable advances that have already been made in schools in recognising the existence, and the special needs, of minority groups in this country there is little evidence to show that the principles and praxis of education have responded to cultural enrichment.

The description of Britain as a multi-cultural society is probably premature. At the point where most help for minority interests is required there is often a lack of awareness of one of the most immediate causes for concern. This cause for concern focuses on educational aspirations among minority groups, and is based upon their understanding of the relationship between education and society. Help is provided, but it is not always the right kind of help. In recent years a great deal of effort has been devoted to the development of multi-cultural education. In several parts of the country specialist teachers and advisers have been appointed to plan, co-ordinate, and monitor activities in this field. A society, whether multi-cultural or not, cannot be constructed overnight out of disparate multi-racial or multi-faith elements, either by social engineering or by educational fiat. It is true that there are still large numbers of Christians in Britain, but society is no longer (or not yet) Christian. There are even larger numbers of British citizens who belong to other communities of faith, or who profess no religious beliefs. Yet society cannot be described as Jewish, or Islamic, or Humanist, with any greater measure of accuracy. It would be simpler, and more accurate, to describe Britain as a secular society, with relativist tendencies.

Is there any other way in which it might reasonably be maintained that Britain is a multi-cultural society in anything other than a narrowly demographic sense? That is to say, is the description of this society as multi-cultural merely a recognition of the existence of discrete religious and ethnic types? There is undoubtedly a genuine admiration for the interesting and colourful differences in dress, social customs, beliefs, values, music and food, which are typical of ethnic, and other, minorities. That such differences are noted and appreciated means little. Anything out of the ordinary may be temporarily diverting. The danger is that cultural enrichment should be defined in such limited terms, and even restricted to this rather superficial level. It is important to recognise, to appreciate, and to enjoy, these comparatively trivial and non-threatening differences. The real test for a society which claims to be multi-cultural lies elsewhere. Education provides a touchstone. Would it not be the mark of a multi-cultural society that it actively promotes an understanding of cultural diversity by allowing in the theory and practice of education the fullest possible exploration of pluralism?

CULTURAL DIVERSITY AND THE NOTION OF CHRISTIAN EDUCATION

The notion of Christian education has been discussed and analysed in several places recently. (3) Other chapters in this book deal in various ways with points of detail. It is appropriate here to mention some of the characteristic presuppositions of Christian education, without which the use of qualifying adjective is misleading. Christian education is predicated on the contingency of the world, the creative and re-creative work of God, the salvific and redemptive mission of Jesus, the beginnings and subsequent history of a community of believers, and the freedom of individuals to explore the implications of Christian faith. This freedom is made unconditional by the love which permits it, so that it opens up the possibility that human beings may actually choose to take leave of God. That God can be known is not unique to Christianity. That God can be known <u>uniquely</u>, both through the historic ministry of Jesus, and through the exercise of human reason confronted by the evidences of the created natural order, is the distinctive <u>Christian</u> claim. The communication of this knowledge, of these beliefs, of this faith, is the business of Christian education, by whatever means are considered suitable.

For the believer <u>education</u> is not a preparation for life, but a continuing journey through life. Its 'Christian' quality is assumed. Every experience is potentially an opportunity for acquiring knowlege of what God has revealed in Christ, for developing the critical faculty, for enlightening the intellect, for strengthening the will, and for directing the individual towards his creator. In a more restricted sense Christian education relates to what is consciously planned in school, or church, to initiate the Christian quest, and to provide for the harmonious development of all the powers of the human being - physical, social, intellectual, moral, aesthetic, and spiritual. Ideally, this formal education complements the educational influence of the home.

Christian education has three essential features. First, it <u>establishes</u> faith in Christ as the foundation and guide for correct thinking and right action. Second, it is <u>integrative</u>, serving to bring together elements in individuals or in society that tend towards fragmentation. It is thus concerned with human beings, 'whole and entire', catering for their moral, as well as for their intellectual, needs at each succeeding stage of life. Third, it <u>enables</u> individuals to decide for themselves whether they will believe or not, by exercising their capacity for reason as well as for faith. From an educational point of view there is one aspect of Christian education which is of special interest in a situation where the unity of any society threatens to crack along the fault-lines of cultural diversity. It may be that the most significant task for Christian education at the present time is to provide bridges, not cement. Ideally, if not always in practice, Christian education promotes more than an understanding of one particular kind of religious faith. From the theology of dereliction which is at the heart of Christian faith and experience, Christian education proposes an understanding of human vulnerability, and difference. It encourages the exploration of pluralism, with regard to doubt as well as to faith. The image of the suffering God is more than an icon. Christian education begins where it ends, with the enigmatic figure of Jesus. In every generation it focuses attention on a startling claim which might otherwise remain unknown.

Simply stated, the claim is to the effect that in Jesus the whole of creation is provided with a unique vision of the Creator's will and purposes. This is the matrix of Christian education, and its continuing dynamic. A knowledge of this divine initiative is 'necessary for salvation', however variously the word salvation is interpreted. The difficulty is that Christians have never been able to agree about the content of Christian education, or about its methods. Because of this it is sometimes easier to think of it more in terms of what Christians happen to do when they are involved in education. In this respect Christian education differs from Islamic education, for instance, where the function of education is an Islamic society is explicitly instrumental in preparing Muslim citizens for life in the community (ummah).

> Education which is designed to produce 'men of knowledge' should regard the cultivation of the knowledge of Islam as the primary goal. (4)

In Christian terms the organic society, or community, is (or should be) the Church. We are not speaking here of one or other of the branches of an ecclesiastical organisation, still less of buildings. The Church is the believing community of Christians. Local differences of liturgical practice and theological emphasis cannot obscure the underlying unity of belief among Christians. This is not the place to enter into a discussion of the theological basis of Christian belief, nor to give an account of the divisions (often bitter and lasting) which have arisen among Christians in various parts of the world as a result of different interpretations of the Christian story. But it is worth noting that one of the distinctive features of the

Christian community is that membership is extended beyond the grave. The Christian creeds include references to the communion of saints. For many Christians, if not for all, these allusions refer to a relationship which unites the living with those who have gone before them in faith.

This adds an important dimension to the concept of Christian education. Christian education is not just this-worldly, nor other-worldly. It is simultaneously both. In consequence the story of a brief exchange between the famous headmaster Alington and the parents of one of his pupils is less morbid to Christian ears than it might be to others. Asked by the mother of the boy what he was educating her son for, Alington replied, 'In a word, madam - for death'. Christian education has some distinctive long-term objectives, but is not so preoccupied with the next world that it loses touch with the reality of the present. Even so this dual concern makes it impossible that Christian education, despite its imperfections in practice, should remain parochial. It has universal, if not cosmic, aspirations. No more than Islamic education can it be reduced to the level of a constituent element in secular education.

There is already a world-wide community of Christian believers, yet the Christian gospel is to be preached 'to the end of the earth'. (5) This imposes a dual responsibility on Christian educators. First, they have the responsibility for transmitting the faith they hold inside the Christian community. This amounts to what has often been described as Christian nurture, by means of which new members (especially the young) are inducted into the tradition and confirmed in the faith. Christian education of this type may be catechetical and heuristic within certain prescribed limits. On the other hand there is another broad type of Christian education that has arisen in response to what Christians believe to be a dominical command.

> Go therefore and make disciples of all nations, baptising them in the name of the Father and of the Son and of the Holy Spirit, teaching them to observe all that I have commanded you; and lo, I am with you always, to the close of the age. (6)

These words, attributed to Jesus since the time of the earliest Christian communities, have been quoted down the centuries by Christians in support of missionary activity, and in support of Christian education as an instrument of mission.

The degree of homogeneity that is to be found today in British society exists in spite of, and not because of, cultural diversity. It is assumed that individuals have a common interest in improving their standards of living despite real or suspected cultural differences which divide them. This was illustrated in the consultative document, Education in Schools, published almost ten years ago. (7) It contained the government's response to some of the issues raised by the Great Debate on education. Anyone reading this document today will be struck by what is omitted, and by the scarcely concealed appeal to self-interest. No principles appear to be invoked, other than those which relate to the pursuit of natural excellence and competition. There is no reference to an overall vision of the purpose of education, such that Christians, Jews, Muslims, Humanists, and others, despite their differences of approach, would immediately recognise as an acknowledgement of the spiritual dimension of human existence. Commenting on this deficiency Richard Wilkins wrote:

> For lack of anything more definite, the aim of education appears to be this: to prepare the individual child for life in a society dependent on productive industry and international trade; a society of producers and consumers which happens to have a cultural, political, and ethical past from which useful lessons might be learned, and which now happens to be multi-racial; a society which only aspires to remain a going concern, and which expects the same of its education system. (8)

During the decade that has passed it has become obvious that the stability of manufacturing industry and international trade cannot be guaranteed. Educational systems directed towards preparing children to be consumers and producers according to the norms of either the west- or the east-European form of capitalism are likely to be overtaken by events. Touched (or untouched) by compassion, they prepare children for a society which does not exist. What does exist is a complex society in which the incidence of failure, or comparative failure, is inescapably much higher than the incidence of success. Education (and this at least must be true of Christian education) cannot be primarily concerned with the attainment of what the

91

secularised western world, with its predominantly material values, identifies as success. As an instrument for correcting the prevailing tendency for society to define success, and then to honour the successful, Christian education may still have a vital role to play in bearing witness to an alternative approach. This alternative approach does not seek to belittle success, but it recognises the reality of failure. Christian teachers do not believe that:

> Education alone can re-route the future. But they reject the idea that their job is merely to provide the skills, information, and experience, which will serve the ends of a smooth-running community of happy materialists. That is not their controlling aspiration, nor is it that of the large Christian public to which they belong. They believe that there is a style of life more self-reliant and less acquisitive than that encouraged in our society, and that children should be made aware of it. Above all, their belief in mankind's divine origin and destiny underlies their formulation of individual and national goals, and so radically affects their attitude to the school curriculum. (9)

Is there still a place for Christian education in such a society? An affirmative answer might be expected, or assumed, in a country like Britain where the influence of Christianity on the development of our institutions and services, including education, is undisputed. Many Christians (and this includes those who were not born in Britain) are involved in education at various levels out of a sense of Christian vocation. Few would deny that Christians have made significant contributions to education. Despite differences of opinion between them over matters of educational as well as theological detail, their service to education is acknowledged even when it is criticised. It is assumed that Christians will continue their tradition of helping to provide for present and future educational needs. Yes, it would appear that there is a place for Christian education in Britain, and not only in separate Christian schools. Or rather, that there is a place in education for Christians who are prepared to accept that their professional obligations are to further the interests of a secular society.

This is an important qualification. At this point we are not necessarily concerned with Christian education, even though Christians may be very much involved. Christians may be ready, if not actually required, to distinguish between private beliefs on the one hand and professional responsibilities on the other, in the interests of education built upon secular principles. But the assumption that Christian education can be accommodated as a distinctive element of the needs of a multi-cultural society needs to be examined if misunderstandings are to be avoided. Individual Christians (or for that matter, individual Muslims, Jews, Hindus, Humanists, Sikhs and others) may be useful, under certain conditions, in an educational system devoted to the creation of what is described as a multi-cultural society. It may not be so straightforward for <u>Christian</u> education to be accommodated as one of several elements within a wide range of educational possibilities.

This prospective difficulty can be illustrated by changing the terms of an earlier question to allow for the range of cultural diversity which may be presumed to prevail in a pluralist society. Is there a place for <u>Islamic</u> education, or for <u>Jewish</u> education, in a multi-cultural society? The point at issue is not whether there should be adequate private provision within a pluralist society for Christians, Jews, Muslims, and others, to educate their own children in their respective religious, ethical and social traditions. Nor is it about the inclusion of teaching <u>about</u> world religions in education. Neither of these special provisions is being disputed here. The point is that special arrangements for minorities may actually militate against the best interests of society as a whole. Wherever there are conflicting, or potentially conflicting, cultural interests <u>society</u> is under threat. It is essential to the health of any society that its members share common goals. If they do not, and if they are permitted to follow their own separate social goals to the point of creating separate schools with widely differing educational methods, they cannot expect to belong to the same society in any profound sense.

What begins to take place in such a situation is the gradual change from a coherent society to a kind of wary federation at best. The phrase <u>multi-cultural society</u> can mask a paradox, or a contradiction in terms. The <u>imposition</u> of multi-cultural aims on society, with a view to eliminating existing differences in the course of time once again invests the educational system with an instrumental function. This time the aim is to train the future citizenry to take their places in a society which is tolerant of cultural difference only to the point at which such difference presents no serious threat to the new secular consensus. In this case one set of educational principles, considered to be logically prior to any other set of principles derived from any of the constituent cultural traditions, retains its dominating influence on the direction of education. Cultural diversity may be sustained for a time by nostalgia, but it is steadily eroded by neglect, assimilation, and integration. If this happens then violence is done to minority rights, intentionally or unintentionally, and pluralism is revealed as a euphemism for secularism. The word minority can be misleading. In the cases of some minority groups - Muslims and Christians, for example - the numbers are substantial, and quite probably increasing.

In practice little serious regard is given to the development of new approaches to education (not merely to religious education) which reflect this cultural diversity. How far will the influence of alternative approaches to education ever be permitted to transform what happens in British schools? The absence of a consensus about educational aims and objectives creates a gap at the centre of education, but it should not be assumed that Christian education can help to fill this gap. Christian education, for example, may have no role to play in an educational system which is founded on principles which, if not actually inimical to Christians, may be incompatible with Christian educational principles. It may be that if Christian education is to survive, it will only do so in separation from the state system of education, rather than by integration within it. Such an arrangement would depend upon the degree of freedom permitted to minority groups in a pluralist society. But the reluctance to consider alternative approaches to educational activity which are integral parts of the various cultural traditions that comprise British society, still less to allow such approaches to influence the dominant theory of knowledge, shows that there are in practice limits to pluralism, as there are limits to tolerance. Minorities might well discover that their freedom to protect their cultural traditions may be severely curtailed in what is taken to be the majority interest.

CONFLICTS AND CONTRADICTIONS WITHIN CULTURAL DIVERSITY

The lack of precision - one might almost say the reluctance to be precise - in the use of the phrases Christian education and multi-cultural society is not really surprising at a time of uncertainty and change. No doubt this owes something to the widespread indifference to the subjects to which these phrases refer. The steady secularisation of society has already been mentioned. The convictions of agnosticism have become at least as widely respectable as the certainties of religious faith, and often as inaccessible to scrutiny. In consequence neither phrase counts among the most frequently used in ordinary conversation, so the imprecision which attaches to their occasional use is seldom thought to be a matter for general regret. And when these phrases are used it is often with a decidedly partisan intent, in campaigns for changes in society which suit the particular interests of the spokesmen in question. In cases where the sloganising of special pleading takes the place of reasonable advocacy, precision in the use of language is rarely a high priority.

The problem for those engaged in education is to know how to deal with cultural diversity at a time when the majority of students, not to speak of their teachers, have become alienated from the religious beliefs which underlie the cultural differences. Part of an essay on 'Education and Tradition' by the Jewish scholar Martin Buber highlights some of the issues which confront teachers in a country like Israel, which has first to achieve independence, and then to preserve it without compromising the ideals of freedom, tolerance, and pluralism upon which its institutions are built. His comments apply equally well to teachers who have to face the challenge of cultural diversity in re-defining the aims and objectives of education in Britain:

> We must provide them (i.e. the present generation of students) with a truly national education, and this means that we must convey the primordial utterances of their people to their ears and their hearts. We must surmount the prejudice of this era which claims that those utterances can have interest for us only as literary history, as cultural history, religious history, etc., and that instruction should treat them only as the chief literary creation of the nation, as the source for

the study of its ancient culture and the oldest document of its religious beginnings. We must surmount the superstition of the era which seems to hold that the world of faith to which those utterances bear witness is the subject of our knowledge only, and not a reality which makes life worth living. We must keep the younger generation free from the bias that says: 'We know all about ourselves and the world, and in any event these utterances can no longer exert an authoritative influence on our lives.' (10)

Buber remained sceptical of Zionism, and even when he returned to live in Israel he continued to try to build bridges between people of different cultures who found themselves caught up in conflict in the Land which is holy to Jews, Christians, and Muslims, alike. He did not find it easy. Criticism came from fellow-Jews, who suspected his motives. Similar suspicion fell upon a Jew of a later generation, Meron Benvenisti, himself a native born Israeli (sabra). Benvenisti has recently described the conflicts and contradictions which he experiences daily in Israel. Here is a country which members of at least three different cultural groups call their homeland, but which has not yet been able to create a community from the elements of diversity.

Jews, Palestinian Arab Muslims, and Palestinian Arab Christians, are in open conflict about possession of the same homeland. For some years Benvenisti devoted himself to the task of improving the relationship between Jews and Palestinian Arabs in the city of Jerusalem. Humanly speaking he failed, because as a politician in a city divided by cultural differences and political aspirations he was unable to convince the dominant Jewish majority that pluralism means very little if it does not also mean the sharing of political power. Benvenisti's understanding of the concept of moledet, 'homeland', 'the land of one's kindred and the place of one's birth' (in his case Israel), is comprehensive and inclusive. And in their own terms the attachment of his Palestinian Arab friends to the same land is no less complete. The Hebrew word moledet is not easy to translate. In this respect it is rather like the Latin word patria, which carries similar nuances. It is a comprehensive and inclusive concept. In some ways the situation he discusses in the state of Israel is not unlike the situation which faces the people in this country. More specifically, he compares the situation in Jerusalem to that in Belfast, with

96

its conflict of cultural minorities and the end of any pretence about organic unity. He quotes a short poem which will be familiar to many Israeli children, from their lessons in school:

'Grandpa, grandpa!'
'Come here grandchildren.'
'Tell us, grandpa - we heard on the radio that we have gone to defend our moledet ... What is moledet?'
And they fixed me with the inquisitive gaze of children, waiting for my answer.
'Moledet?' I whispered with awestruck soul, 'It's every person and all the people. It's grandfather, grandmother, mother and father. And the grandchildren. And the neighbours. And the children. Young and old. All the people and every person. Moledet is everything. It's made up of mountains and valleys, sights and sounds ...
All this is moledet. It's the quivering of the leaves on the tree and the shining azure sea,
The red roof-tops, the silver of olive groves,
The first dawn light touching the mountain-tops and the sparkling droplets of dew;
The joyous sound of bird-song, the dancing rays of sunlight,
And the laughter of infants, lightsome and strong.
All that, all that is moledet.' (11)

The mistake, however, is to insist that moledet is everything, when it is far from being everything. By neglecting its unique religious origins and history it may lose much of its power as a unifying symbol, even for Jews. The conflicts and contradictions in society begin to re-appear. The generation of Jewish pioneers, for example, who went to Palestine to build a new homeland on the basis of Zionism and socialism, established legendary working communities (kibbutzim) in the process. Long before Israel achieved independence in 1948, these pioneers attempted to construct a pluralist society in which the practice of religion was safeguarded, but not required. For those who needed it religion provided a solace. Such, at any rate, is the view of a native-born Israeli like Benvenisti, who suggests that the polarisation of Israeli society today is, at least partly, the consequence of attempts to separate the tradition from the religion which gave it birth, in the interests of secularism.

This point of view is of some importance for the

97

present discussion. From what has been noted above it is clear that an education that is genuinely Christian cannot be contained in a parochial way, or consigned to a reservation marked 'Christian'. In the nature of the case it will have a universal outreach. It cannot merely be a constituent element. On the other hand the phrase multi-cultural society, despite its obvious weaknesses as a description of an empirical reality, expresses an aspiration for a harmonious society in which freedom and diversity are respected in a way which is not inconsistent with Christian ideals. There is a long way to go before these ideals are realised. For Christians who are involved in education today there is a two-fold task. The first is to bear witness to the coherence of the Christian analysis of the human predicament, no matter which subject is being taught in the curriculum. The implication of this last remark is that Christian education is not just something that Christians can leave to other Christians who work in religious education. Religious education enjoys a special position in British state schools that may be lost in time. It is an important subject but it suffers from the unique statutory protection it enjoys, and from the fact that the statute is increasingly disregarded. What effect the ending of compulsory religious education in state schools would have is difficult to predict. But Christian education is not dependent upon statutory provision for religious education, any more than it is dependent on the continuing existence of educational institutions as we have come to know them. Christian teachers have a joint responsibility in the second task as well. This is to enable students to see that behind the apparently contradictory beliefs which they hold there may lie similar, if not identical, interests and aspirations. From the Christian point of view this exposes the central paradox in the exploration of cultural diversity, which is that cultural differences provide the raw material for common affirmations.

NOTES AND REFERENCES

1.   I have tried to deal with this subject at greater length in a book to be published in November 1988 by Longman, with the title, Education and Cultural Diversity. The book is primarily concerned with the different approaches to education which are characteristic of the

distinct cultural traditions in Britain today.

2.   In his book <u>Orientalism</u> (New York, 1979) Edward Said considers some of the ways in which western scholars have approached a culture and a religion such as Islam. Their critical and descriptive methods, he complains, have resulted in a false picture of Islam in the west. What they have presented to western students is, in Said's view, a western construct which does not, and cannot, adequately interpret Islamic culture. This is a criticism that Muslims often make of western attempts to study Islam. From the Islamic point of view, the tools of western critical scholarship are incapable of revealing the glory of Islam.

3.   See, for example, <u>The Fourth R: the Durham Report on Religious Education</u>, the National Society, SPCK, 1970; various papers have been written for the Christian education seminar organised by NIECE (North of England Institute for Christian Education). Further information is obtainable from the Director of NIECE at the School of Education, University of Durham.

4.   Khurshid Ahmad, <u>Principles of Islamic Education</u>, (Lahore, 1968) p. 16.

5.   Acts 1.8.

6.   Matthew 28: 19-20.

7.   HMSO, July 1977.

8.   <u>Education in Schools: a Christian Rejoinder</u> (Association of Christian Teachers, London, undated), p. 1.

9.   Ibid., pp. 1-2.

10.   Martin Buber, 'Education and Tradition' (re-published in <u>Contemporary Jewish Thought</u>, edited by Simon Noveck, B'nai B'rith Books, Washington D.C., 1985), p. 274.

11.   This modern Hebrew poem, translated by Marcia Kretzmer, is quoted at the beginning of Chapter 2, 'An Image of Homeland', in Meron Benvenisti's <u>Conflicts and Contradictions</u>, (Villard Books, New York, 1986), p. 17. The poem is apparently used in the second grade of schools in Israel. Benvenisti notes, 'In the school curriculum and in the army the subject (<u>moledet</u>) is known also as <u>yedi'at haaretz</u> - "knowledge of the land". Those who coined that phrase were undoubtedly aware of the biblical meaning of <u>yedi'a</u>, an act of sexual possession: "And Adam knew Eve, his wife." <u>Yedi'at haaretz</u> features in the school curriculum and in army courses as a subject in its own right, incorporating geography, geology, history, ethnology, botany - and all this is directed not simply to increasing knowledge but to nurturing a deep attachment to the country: "instilling youth

with love of country".' ibid, pp. 19-20. Elsewhere he adds, however, that although the Jewish Bible is often used as a handbook by Israeli students in their explorations of the Land, its traditional religious message is rarely heeded.

Chapter Six

CONFLICT OR COMPROMISE? RELIGIOUS AND MORAL EDUCATION IN A PLURAL CONTEXT

Brenda Almond

'I can understand how someone who has lived in circumstances contrary to my own may also have contrary ideas.' Stendhal, who made this remark, went on to say that he could see the reasons lying behind all opinions, while still holding his own as strongly as anyone else. The problem of achieving a resolution of Stendhal's potential dilemma is, and always has been, central to the issue of toleration. Particularly where religion and morality are concerned, it is the problem of avoiding the pitfall of indifferentism, whilst still leaving room for others to maintain their deeply felt differences.

Traditionally and historically, toleration has presented itself first as a political problem, and then subsequently, when toleration has been politically and legally established, as a social problem. Today migration and mobility, with consequent intermingling of cultures, have been facilitated by speed and ease of travel, as well as by the way in which laws concerning citizenship and nationality are complex and technical, based on arbitrary specifiable requirements rather than on instinctive recognition of a natural identity. Contemporary liberal societies, confronted by the problems posed by suddenly and dramatically increased cultural and ethnic diversity, have in general responded with strong anti-discrimination laws. Sometimes these laws extend into the less formal area of social relationships and here again, the principles to which a liberal society is committed are those of toleration and mutual understanding. But political, legal and social resolutions of ancient problems, inevitably imperfectly achieved as these may be, serve only to bring into focus a further problem - one that is likely to be in the long run the most difficult to solve. This is the problem of how, in a plural society, to approach the task of religious and moral education.

Particularly for the religious, the terms in which the dilemma is posed in the title of this chapter are likely to be unsatisfactory. How could anyone opt for conflict when the question is one of educating a generation of children - children destined to form in common the society of the future? But how, too, on the other hand, can anyone opt for compromise where the nearest, most sensitive and most important aspects of life - particularly those encompassed by the religious and the moral - are concerned? To be, for example, a compromising Christian is hardly to be Christian at all; while to be a Moslem or a Jew who compromises with regard to the rituals and practices deemed most important for a Moslem or a Jew is to be, at least, neglectful in terms of those religions.

So the question is, where <u>differences</u> are inevitable, can <u>conflict</u> be avoided in some lesser or limited sense that will produce harmony in the classroom and lead to a similar harmony in the wider society? And is there a compromise available which would provide a blueprint for a unified programme of religious and moral education, offensive to few, but not so watered-down as to be incompatible with a positive commitment to children's moral and spiritual development? The answers to these questions must depend to a considerable extent on what is taken to be the purpose of religious education, the deepest division being between those who believe its aim is to induct into a faith and those who see it as a matter of informing <u>about</u> faiths. Since the first of these alternatives can itself be taken in two ways, three possible positions on religious education can be identified:

1.   There is the view that religious education is a unique area of the curriculum because its task is to inculcate belief or faith; that its purpose is to give students an 'inside' understanding of the concept of God, of prayer and of worship. On this view a degree of commitment is necessary for a full understanding of religion. If a person is able, for example, to win prizes or pass examinations in religious knowledge, but is lacking this kind of 'inside' understanding, then his or her position, defenders of this view will claim, is similar to that of a blind art expert. No matter how one respects that person's acquired knowledge, it cannot amount

to an understanding of art of the kind available to a sighted person.

2.   There is the view that the kind of insight described by defenders of the first view is indeed the goal of religious education, but that this consideration does not make the case of religious instruction significantly different from that of education in any other curriculum area: generating a scientific attitude, for example, is part of the purpose of science education; drawing out an aesthetic response an essential aspect of art education or the teaching of literature.

3.   The third view differs from both of these in holding that as far as religious education is concerned, its purpose is only to inform students about the psychological, sociological and historical facts relating to religion, and to familiarise them with its literature. On this view, acceptance of a religion is a personal private commitment that cannot be the business of education, since education is the province of reason, not of feeling.

These are questions, then, about the purpose of religious education. They are questions with both factual and evaluative aspects. There is the factual issue of what actually is intended, as well as debate about what ought to be intended. As far as the factual question is concerned, what the 1944 Education Act established as a compulsory requirement was 'religious instruction not distinctive of any religious denomination'. There has been some argument over what was intended here, but the use of the term 'denomination' suggests that what was envisaged was Christian education of a non-denominational kind, supported by the notion of an Agreed Syllabus. It is unlikely, too, that any distinction was recognised between the 'inductive' and information-giving goals. In today's multi-faith rather than multi-denominational society, this has been reinterpreted so as to mean religious education which is not distinctive of any particular religion, i.e. not Christian, nor Hindu, nor Muslim, and this new conception may be supported by an Agreed Syllabus (for example, like that of Birmingham) in which other faiths than Christianity play a role. This goal is difficult to reconcile, however, with either the first or the second views about the purpose of religious education. Thus there is a tendency for this conception of the content of religious education to be necessarily tied to the third approach, i.e. the one that associates religious education with a primarily information-giving function. This is the position represented by the Swann Report with its demand for an end to mainly Christian compulsory religious education, and its recommendation of courses based on respect for other faiths in predominantly secular schools.

To some extent, the debate is a replay in contemporary terms of a problem familiar in various countries of Europe and America in the nineteenth century. For today's differences between Christians, Muslims, Jews, Hindus and others reproduce in terms of feelings roused and sensitivities offended, the differences and disagreements between different types of Christians - in Holland, France and Germany between Protestants and Catholics, in Britain between Anglicans, Protestants and nonconformists - that marked the introduction of compulsory education. Different countries solved the problem eventually in different ways. In Britain there was, after painful debate and delay, the Agreed Syllabus. In France, parents were expected to arrange their children's religious education on a specific afternoon of the week when normal lessons would be suspended. In the United States, the principle accepted was that state education would not discriminate against any pupils, and while this was for many years considered compatible with Christian prayers to start the day, and with the celebration and recognition of Christian festivals such as Christmas and Easter, this position has in the last two decades been challenged, so that these observances have been repudiated in some schools, creating in some cases a wholly secular education which would not be out of place in an Eastern European society officially committed to atheism.

Britain's position is distinctive in two ways: hence the problem implicitly posed in the title of this book. Unlike the United States, Britain does recognise Christianity in the Anglican form as its established religion. And secondly, no doubt for this very reason, Britain does include religious education as a compulsory, indeed the only compulsory, subject in the school curriculum. It also makes the daily act of worship at school assembly a compulsory element, but since this requirement is subject to physical possibility - it was recognised that a school might simply be too large for everyone to gather in one place at one time - the requirement has been more respected in the breach than in the observance. The process of neglect started, then, less as a response to the multi-cultural society than as a consequence of major school reorganisation - in particular the large split-site comprehensive schools of the sixties and seventies. Of course, not all head-teachers felt able, or disposed, to take a quasi-clerical role, and physical difficulties may have reinforced in some cases personal reluctance and a lack of sympathy for the objective. After all, it was no doubt unwise of the Victorians to lay down the manner of religious observance, attempting to perpetuate in schools the daily communal prayers that have long ago died out as a household practice. No-one today is expected to follow the instructions of Mrs Beeton's cookery book, although many people still take seriously the art of cookery!

Behind the practical difficulties, however, lie important theoretical and philosophical issues. If any light is to be cast on the practical difficulties it will be necessary to look more closely at these underlying problems, which fall into two main categories, the epistemological and the ethical. The epistemological difficulties are concerned with the question of truth. Is there, where religious and moral beliefs and assertions are concerned, a fact of the matter? Is anybody's opinion as good as anyone else's? Or are some people right and others wrong? What is it to be right or wrong about religion or about morality? What kind of evidence would settle disputes in these matters? empirical evidence? logical reasoning? intuition? Or is there perhaps a special kind of religious or moral truth which fits into none of these categories but nevertheless has its own validity?

Difficulties of the second sort are essentially ethical in character. What sort of respect do we owe to other people? Have they a right to their own opinions, no matter how misguided or irrational these may be? And if their opinions involve actions and practices which impinge on other people, where should the limits be set to legal and social toleration of these practices? How far are we responsible for each other and how far independent? These are issues of rights and autonomy which are first and foremost moral questions, but they rapidly become issues for society with legal and political implications.

Within the school, they are questions about the presentation of alternative ways of life and alternative conceptions of living, as well as about the weighting and respect to be given to these alternative conceptions. In this case, a liberal society finds itself caught in the classic dilemma of liberalism: on the one hand, it is committed to pluralism in a permissive sense; on the other, it is first and foremost a <u>society</u>, and if it is to perpetuate itself and retain its distinctive character, then its own cultural traditions, which include the moral and ideal elements of liberalism, must play a role in the education of the young.

Liberalism is often thought to be committed to an atomistic and individualistic view of society; the notion of community may be placed in opposition, as it is, for example, in Alasdair MacIntyre's <u>After Virtue</u> (1) as well as in a recent thoughtful article by John Haldane on 'Religious Education in a Plural Society'. (2) But liberal values are not empty, although their content is often taken for granted, and the sharing of these values within a society can provide a sense of community in a deeper cultural sense than is acknowledged by liberalism's critics.

However, these ethical and social considerations are best approached in the light of a clearer understanding of the epistemological issues involved. It would therefore be appropriate to consider these first, before attempting to define some of the moral requirements and ethical principles that are relevant to the practical problems of religious and moral education in a multi-faith and multi-cultural society.

TRUTH AND KNOWLEDGE IN RELIGION AND MORALS

Most religious believers are willing to acknowledge the role of faith in their religious commitment. To some, faith is essentially opposed to reason. Its basic characteristic is that of <u>un</u>reason, or irrationality. What could be more irrational than the prayer 'Lord, I believe; help thou my unbelief'? And indeed historically, at times of extreme religious persecution, the case for toleration has sometimes been made out on the basis of, and by appeal to, this fundamental assumption of irrationality. For it was perceived that the mysterious basis of religious conviction is not amenable to normal physical modes of coercion. As Luther put it, 'You cannot strike it with iron or burn it by fire'. And this inaccessibility to ordinary or extraordinary modes of inducement of belief appeared to make intolerance and persecution themselves irrational, as Locke argued in his <u>Letter on Toleration</u> (1689).

However, as the history of the period demonstrated, not everyone accepted this position. Indeed, a parable in the New Testament was sometimes taken as justifying physical

106

coercion of recalcitrant unbelievers because of the injunction it contains that those who refuse to come to the feast should be 'compelled to come in'. (3) It would seem, however, that in the case of adults, this kind of coercion, along with crude processes of brainwashing, while it might produce lip-service or compliance, cannot produce religious belief in any real or important sense.

The same may not be true of children, however, for they are conspicuously amenable to coercion, and prone to propaganda. This is a consideration to which it will be necessary to return later, when discussing the ethical issues of autonomy and rights. For the moment, however, while this caveat must be borne in mind, it would be reasonable to proceed on the assumption that religious belief is at least distinctive - distinctive, that is to say, in the sense that it is a matter of deep rather than shallow or surface conviction, the product of commitment rather than of cold deliberation.

This feature of religious belief is, no doubt, both its strength and its weakness. As Anthony O'Hear puts it:

> ... for the religious believer religious belief is a personal commitment, something nearer to a love for one's family or loyalty to one's country, than to that calm and provisional acceptance of some abstract theory which is sometimes taken to characterize the attitude of the ideal scientist towards his currently favoured scientific propositions. (4)

So is the concept of religious truth inherently mistaken? Is there no such thing as religious knowledge? - a term incidentally mostly long obsolete as the name of that slot on the school timetable devoted to religious education. There are two ways in which religious belief could be assimilated to established categories and ways of knowing, and one way in which, whilst hardly a matter of assimilation to an established or an acknowledged category, a case might still be made out for describing religious awareness in cognitive terms. The two familiar ways involve assimilating religious knowledge to either ordinary empirical knowledge, or to deductive reasoning, while the less common strategy involves accepting the possibility of an intuitive or mystical gateway to truth. All of these positions have their adherents, though the deductive strategy has been most prominent historically.

The assimilation of religious truth to empirical truth

involves interpreting characteristic religious claims regarding, for example, God's existence, or the efficacy of prayer, as factual or scientific claims - claims which may be refuted by the evidence of the senses, this being an essential feature of empirical truth. But this is an implausible position to maintain, since there is seldom only one way to interpret events in the physical world, or the sequence of events which follow on prayer. These sequences of events are public features of our common human experience which can be and are variously interpreted by different individuals. What one person sees as evidence of creative design, another sees as the product of blind evolution. What one person sees as evidence of the love of God - a good harvest, for example - another will set against the drought in the Sahara as no such evidence, or evidence to the contrary. And either a positive or a negative result may be interpreted as an answer to prayer. A prayed-for recovery from illness, for example, will be received with gratitude, while death will be seen as a 'merciful release'. But what is susceptible of conflicting explanations in this way can hardly be taken to share the normal or accepted standards of scientific proof.

Where deductive certainty is claimed, the problem is rather different. Arguments familiar from ancient times that establish the being of a God by analysis of, for example, the concept of perfection (perfection would not be perfection if it lacked the attribute of existence) have been found unsatisfactory in their own terms, but are subject to a more telling general objection. This is that conceptual, logical or deductive truths are essentially empty. They do not contain new or substantive information. But for the religious believer, it is important to insist that the truths of religion are substantial truths; that they are meaningful in the most full and important sense of the term; they make a difference to life.

Neither of these ways, then, offers a satisfactory interpretation of religious claims. There is, however, a third way in which religion may be presented as a form of knowledge, albeit of a unique sort. This is the way of intuition or mystical insight. Here, where the first two strategies make religion a familiar form of knowledge, the mystical answer divorces it from all other practical modes of knowledge and implicitly divorces it, too, from the experience of most ordinary people - and, pertinent in this case, particularly from the experience of children.

Conflict or Compromise?

It is impossible, or at least unreasonable, to deny mystical insight. The problem is that it is confined to the person who experiences it - it has, one might say, only one-person validity. Passed on, it becomes secondhand and worthless, as is the testimony of one who claims to have seen a ghost, when this unsupported testimony is presented as evidence for the occurrence of psychic phenomena. So it is not even possible to give the name 'knowledge' to what the mystic believes or claims to see, for it is a peculiar feature of the term 'know' that the person who uses it endorses the claim that is embedded in the knowledge statement. No other individual can endorse the mystic's unique and deeply personal insight, and so, no matter how impressive in itself, it must remain irrelevant as a characterisation of religious knowledge to others who are not themselves initiates.

Some, impressed by these considerations, will reject altogether the attempt to establish the rationality of religious belief in terms of familiar and accepted categories of knowledge. For, they may say, such criticisms and calculations are based on a misunderstanding of the nature of religious claims and, in particular, of the language in which those claims are couched. Different types of statement, they suggest, follow different rules: scientific statements, for example, are not rejected as meaningless because they do not fit the mould of deductive logic, just as the syllogisms and arguments of deductive logic are not rejected because they are not subject to confirmation or refutation by empirical means. As the philosopher Ludwig Wittgenstein noted, there are many language-games that people play. (5) The 'language-games' of science and logic, then, are not the only ones available. In particular, the way in which aesthetic, moral, or religious statements are validated may be as distinctive and characteristic as are the concepts they employ. In another terminology, these are all 'forms of thought'. (6)

But while some will be satisfied with the brief answer that both religion and morality are sui generis, that their validity is internal to them rather than independently established, others will see in this answer a concession to the enemy. For these critics, it will seem that religion must have something in common with our other modes of thinking and judging if it is to be taken seriously by any intelligent person.

There is some justification for this second reaction.

109

For this 'brief answer' may amount to no more than a facile relativism. As such, it will be seen as damaging to both religious and moral belief. For it appears to accept a contrast in these cases between belief and knowledge which, it may be implied, does not exist in the case of 'harder' forms of knowledge, such as science and logic. A little reflection reveals, however, that even in those cases, the contrast between what is true and what we <u>believe</u> to be true is problematic.

This can be interpreted either sceptically or reassuringly. The sceptical interpretation is associated with such scientific irrationalists as Thomas Khun and Paul Feyerabend, who have explained the 'hard truths' of science in terms of beliefs of those culturally defined as 'scientists'. For them, science is what scientists believe, and Kuhn's theory of paradigm change seems to interpret shifts of received opinion in science as subjective fashion-preferences rather than as rational reappraisals of objective external features in the environment that compel a change of opinion. (7) If religious belief and moral belief are subjectively explained in a similar way, then for these, too, no contrast exists between what is the case and what is believed; science, religion and morals fall victim alike to a common scepticism.

But a reassuring interpretation is also possible. For science has not been shown to be uncertain in any way that casts doubt on our everyday practices and assumptions. On the contrary it is, along with logical reasoning, the model that we, as human beings, take of certainty. There is nothing, then, in the argument that contrasts belief and knowledge to prevent religion and morality being seen as sharing a common reliability with other modes of thought rather than a common uncertainty.

Neither the sceptical nor the reassuring interpretation, then, justifies a contrast between 'harder' forms of knowledge on the one hand, and the case of religious or moral claims on the other that would have implications for school curriculum or organisation. It is worth, however, looking a little more closely at the distinction between belief and knowledge on which this contrast is based.

First, it is clear that only an outside observer may make a distinction between what, for example I believe, and what is the case - I cannot sort my own beliefs out into these two categories. (Admittedly, I could sort my beliefs out into those I am <u>more</u> sure about and those I am <u>less</u> sure about, but this contrast relates to my state of mind rather than to the world outside.) Unlike the hypothetical observer, then, I cannot make a distinction like this myself. The posited observer in this case would, however, having made his pronouncement, no longer be an outsider, but another participant in the dialogue about whatever it is that is in dispute - this time coming down on one side or another by his or her pronouncement as to the validity of my belief. Moreover, if I talk in more general terms about what we as human beings believe - as opposed to what I believe - then the hypothesis of an outside observer becomes even less meaningful. In summary, then, if a distinction between what is true and what I believe to be true is impossible for me to make, then a distinction between what human beings believe to be true and what really is true is impossible for human beings to make. It is not necessary, then, to view religion from a purely irrationalist standpoint. Its subjectivity, such as it is, is definable only as something it can arguably be maintained to have in common with other widely respected areas of cognition.

As far as moral, as opposed to religious claims are concerned, the application of a strict 'either empirical or logical' criterion seems to place the moral objectivist, like the religious believer, in a difficult position. But in this case, too, irrationalism and a sceptical or impartial relativism are not the only alternatives to the choice posed by the strict empiricist or positivist.

In the case of morals, the point is probably best made by demonstrating that this kind of relativism is itself irrational. Once again, this follows from the necessity it generates to postulate an outside observer, from whose point of view all moral standpoints are judged equal. Even more than is the case with religion, in morals no external standpoint is available, for all are obliged to adopt a moral position in the ordinary process of living and interacting with other human beings. There is no genuine amoralist position, for the possibility of morality follows from the necessity of choice.

What kind of objectivity, then, is involved here? It is the objectivity that arises from the possibility - it cannot be more than that - of shared values and a common recognition of universal rights and moral norms. Some will see a similar possibility in the case of religion, because they will see behind some at least of the world's religions the possibility of a common conception of God, and common consequences of this conception for the relationship of humans with each other (in ancient terminology, the brotherhood of man - the notion that we are all brothers and sisters under God). This kind of moral objectivity might be described, in a phrase used by the American philosopher Hilary Putnam, as 'objectivity for us'. (8) This is not the 'God's-eye' view so appealing to the unabashed objectivist, but neither does it involve the intellectual and moral void of relativism.

These kinds of considerations, then, suggest the possibility of a positive conception of the goals of religious and moral education that is compatible with the first or second views set out earlier. This conception does not in itself confine religious and moral education to a limited information-giving function. If the question of epistemological constraints, however, can be set aside, there are still constraints of a different nature, in particular those involving ethical principles, to consider.

PLURALISM: THE ETHICAL CONSTRAINTS

Whatever the possibilities of religious and moral consensus, then, the fact remains that these are areas where people and groups will continue to disagree. What, in the interim, while like-minded people work for consensus, are the ethical constraints that should guide policy in the area of religious and moral education? Since a full relativist position has been rejected here, these constraints need not start from the perspective that all views are equally valid or merit equal respect. Indeed, views may in some cases be wrong, misguided, immoral or irrational; but it is a feature of a liberal society that these are not thought to be grounds for suppressing them. There is, however, where education is concerned, a gap between not suppressing a point of view and actively promoting it by education and information, which could be significant.

The first consideration for a liberal society must be that freedom of religion is one of the pillars on which it is built. However, since a religion that is not transmitted to the next generation is a religion chopped off at its roots, a complete conception of freedom of religion must carry with it a right to bring up one's children in the religion in question. (9) This is a principle that would no doubt be accepted in contemporary British society by Christians, Jews, Muslims and Hindus. Religion, however, is embedded

112

in wider cultural practices, and an education that stops with one's own children is only a partial fulfilment of a religious believer's aspirations. Nevertheless, if a society is itself politically and institutionally committed to no one religion, then this partial solution may well be the best available. And the history of, for example, the Jewish religion has shown that it is possible for a religion to survive on the basis of private family transmission in the absence of wider social endorsement.

But if a society is, historically and currently, committed to a particular religion, why should it not institutionalise the process of intra-generational transmission of that religion? Why not see that children, unless their parents dissent, are initiated into that religion, and the culture and values associated with it? The paradox involved in pressing for an end to specifically Christian teaching on the grounds of sympathy for other religions is underlined in these remarks by Haldane:

> How could it satisfy the Muslim wish for their own religious schools, to be required to send their children to secular institutions? And what view should they form of a society that would respond to their expression of deep attachment to tradition by casting off its own inheritance? Of course the latter gesture is a demonstration of tolerance and acceptance of pluralism but, if the host society has so little respect for its own culture as no longer to require transmission of its religious tradition and the associated system of values, might one not doubt the seriousness of its regard for Muslim and other essentially religious, immigrant cultures? (10)

Haldane accuses this, which he calls the 'reformist' argument, of being based on a superficial notion of cultural pluralism, trivialising of culture and religion. It focuses, he argues on such issues as sexual mores, diet and dress as distinguishing culture, and ignores the fact that these details reflect different and deep religious and ethical commitments - as he puts it, they are 'not mere ornaments which can be detached from the structure of religious doctrines and moral virtues in which they occur'.

Contrary to this, it is often assumed that neutrality on such matters as culture, religion and morals is a necessary stance on the part of a liberal state. But this assumption

113

probably flows from a misunderstanding of the functions of a state. While an individual can only hold to one view, it is the function of the state, and particularly a liberal state, to preside over contradictory viewpoints so that they do not become a source of danger or conflict for its citizens. Politically and legally, then, there must be religious toleration, but that does not preclude a liberal state's commitment to the values implicit in its nature. And liberalism, as it happens, has a special connection with the Christian religion, at least in its Protestant forms - one which is missing in the case of some other religions - in the doctrine of the equality of all believers. It is peculiarly committed, then, to leaving open the greatest number of possibilities to its citizens, and a maximum of freedom for the exercise of choice.

So long as some want religious education, then, this must be permitted by a liberal state. Freedom of religion goes hand in hand with freedom of religious schooling. True, this principle requires some qualification. The principle cannot apply where a religion is itself repressive and intolerant, or where it represents a threat to individuals. But subject to this proviso, there cannot be a case for outlawing even a committed form of religious education. Only the method and source of its provision is at issue. Is it to be provided, for example, in separate religious schools, or through religious education in state schools? If the former, should those schools be publicly or privately financed?

The general reasons just given for permitting religious education would also, it seems proscribe any legal ban on the existence of separate religiously-based schools. But this does not mean that the public purse must provide such schools or even subsidise them. Even the claim that people who provide their own schools for their own children are entitled to some refund of their expenditure is questionable. For it is a general principle of taxation that no allowance is made for a publicly provided service which a taxpayer chooses not to use, whether this is a nuclear umbrella or a local swimming-pool. And in the case of religious schools, there is also another principle involved: that the general taxpayer should not be asked to support a religious training which contradicts his or her deeply felt convictions. Morally and politically, then, while separate religious schools must be permitted by a liberal society, they need not be financed by it.

As far as publicly-funded schools are concerned, it has

been argued here that these should have regard for continuity of culture and tradition, and meet parents' reasonable requirements in this respect. Clearly, too, parents must continue to be able to withdraw their children from religious education that offends their own convictions. It may be necessary to add, at this point, that as children grow older, their own rights in this respect should begin to take over from this parental right, so that from twelve years on, students' own objections or preference must begin to be allowed to weigh.

Briefly, then, the basic principle involved is this: the state should respect the autonomy or later mature independent judgement of individuals, and, moreover, it is implicit in the very nature of a liberal state that it should do this. What this implies in practice is a combination of independently supported religious schools and a non-indoctrinatory, though not necessarily non-committed, approach to religion in state schools. In these schools, where the great majority of the nation's children will be educated, the principle applied is simply a more direct form of the principle of respect for autonomy. What this means in terms of teaching-programmes is a practical task for negotiation by those most directly involved. It would be a mistake to expect consensus where religion is concerned, but nevertheless the essentials of religious feeling and awareness are a common factor between religions, and communicating these as well as bare information about literature and rituals is part of a complete conception of religious education.

The rewards for reaching the right conclusions on these matters, difficult and complex though they are, are great, if T.S. Eliot was right when he said that 'the dominant force in creating a common culture between peoples each of which has its distinct culture, is religion'. (11) However, it is worth remembering that Eliot believed that it was one particular religion that possessed this binding power: the Christian religion. If in Britain, we are moving towards a view that a wider religious perspective can be found to unite rather than divide the various people living within the same borders - if we are trying to compose a coat of many colours - we should perhaps heed his warning and move only cautiously towards that wider conception, for, as Eliot put it:

> ... You cannot put on a new culture ready made. You must wait for the grass to grow to feed the sheep to

give the wool out of which your new coat will be made.
(12)

NOTES AND REFERENCES

1.   A. MacIntyre, <u>After Virtue</u> (London: Duckworth, 1981).

2.   J. Haldane, 'Religious Education in a Plural Society', (<u>British Journal of Educational Studies</u>, Vol. XXXIV No. 2, June 1986).

3.   For an account of the history of the debate about toleration, see Kamen, H., <u>The Rise of Toleration</u> (London: Weidenfield and Nicholson, 1967).

4.   A. O'Hear <u>Experience, Explanation and Faith</u> (London: Routledge and Kegan Paul, 1984), p. 1.

5.   Wittgenstein's remarks on this subject are to be found in his <u>Philosophical Investigations</u>, para 2 (3rd ed., trans G.E.M. Anscombe, Oxford, Blackwell, 1968).

6.   For a discussion on the 'forms of thought' as characterised by a distinctive set of concepts and distinctive methods of validation see P. Hirst, <u>Knowledge and the Curriculum</u> (London: Routledge and Kegan Paul, 1975).

7.   See Feyerabend, P., <u>Against Method</u> (New Left Books, 1975) and Kuhn, T.S., <u>The Structure of Scientific Revolutions</u>, (2nd ed., Chicago: University of Chicago Press, 1970).

8.   Putnam, H., <u>Reason, Truth and History</u>, (Cambridge University Press, 1981), p. 55.

9.   For a further discussion of this point by the present author, see Cohen, Brenda, <u>Education and the Individual</u>, ch. 5, 'Religious Freedom'.

10.   J. Haldane, op. cit.

11.   T.S. Eliot, <u>Notes towards the Definition of Culture</u>, (London: Faber, 1962, first pub. 1948), p. 122.

12.   Ibid.

Chapter Seven

THE DILEMMA OF POLITICAL AND RELIGIOUS TEACHING: THE CASE OF PEACE STUDIES AND RELIGIOUS KNOWLEDGE IN SCHOOLS

James O'Connell

INTRODUCTION: A STUDY IN CONTRASTING SUBJECTS AND SOCIETIES

In this chapter I intend to contrast approaches to two school subjects, one apparently uncontroversial, the other highly controversial. One subject, religious knowledge (here considered in its Christian form) is as old as the school system; the other, peace studies, is new as a subject, though its content and focus are as old as religion. There is an initial slightly odd contrast between these subjects in that religious knowledge is in relative decline in schools, while peace studies is slowly - but only very slowly - growing as a teaching subject.

While some proponents of concern for education on peace issues have been arguing strongly for the inclusion of peace studies in school curricula, others, more critically-minded, have drawn on experience with religious knowledge; and they have concluded, from the perceived failure of religious knowledge teaching to influence pupils in the subsequent practice of religion, that formal teaching about peace is not necessarily a good way of turning out peaceful persons. The decline in religious practice, which teaching about religion in schools has manifestly failed to reverse or halt, reflects influences as diverse as the lack of foresight and planning of the churches in dealing with rapid urbanisation during the nineteenth century, the failure of theologians to confront new historical methodologies, and challenges from science to the Christian faith. Moreover, the religious decline itself undermined in schools the will to teach effectively about religion.

The conclusion to be drawn from widespread religious teaching and concomitant religious decline is that schools alone cannot reverse or counter dominant trends in society. This conclusion must have dismaying implications for subjects such as religious knowledge or peace studies, if it is now true that the dominant values of society are secularising and that they are militaristic (in the sense that national security is seen as mainly dependent on the possession of, and will to use, military force). Yet the situation is rather more complex than such simple correlation and it merits being looked at in the light of the experience of another subject, viz., language teaching and its differing results in three contrasting countries: Israel, Belgium and Ireland. Language teaching in these states offers a way of observing and verifying the roles of families and of the state in the success of a teaching effort.

In Israel, from its founding, Hebrew has been taught with conviction and pertinacity as a symbol of national identity and a means of integrating groups of Jews from diverse linguistic origins. The State and families have combined to make the mission successful. In Belgium where the teaching of Flemish to Walloon children languished - in spite of directives from the education authorities - until the mid-'60s, French-speaking parents gradually became aware that job prospects, especially in the public services and in Brussels, depended on being able to speak Flemish. The Flemish had by this time used their superior numbers and control of State structures to make clear that in political and economic terms Flemish as a language was no longer optional for Belgians. Generational change was also taking place: Dutch, which is essentially the same language, had gained prestige from its use within the Common Market institutions and taken away from Flemish a peasant and uncultured appearance. Sensitive French-speaking Belgians had come to realise that bi-lingualism was becoming crucial to the unity of their country. In consequence, Flemish became the subject of serious study for Walloon children and they made strides in mastering the language that would have been unthinkable for previous Walloon generations. These two cases form a contrast with the Irish case. In Ireland, the State between 1922 and 1960 made enormous efforts to promote the revival of the Irish language: the government insisted on compulsory Irish language teaching in all schools, primary and secondary, and made a knowledge of Irish a pre-condition for university entrance and public service jobs.

Yet the revival efforts broke on the rock of parental resistance and apathy. The Irish population generally refused to take the revival effort seriously: they offered little home support to the government and school initiatives; they feared the economic consequences of not retaining English as a spoken language and considered bi-lingualism impractical; they compared unfavourably the cultural content of Gaelic literature with that of English literature; and they were satisfied with a distinctive use of English that had produced Yeats, O'Casey and Joyce and saw no compelling reason for abandoning it. By the 1970s the Gaelic revival had petered out in its official nationwide thrust. It is worth adding that this linguistic failure in education took place in spite of the best efforts of two generations of dedicated school teachers.

Does this set of language teaching experiences, and the decay of religious knowledge teaching, suggest that schools reflect society only and cannot innovate against the values of families and generally prevailing values in society? The answer is broadly in the affirmative. But broad answers - like broad generalisations - need to be qualified. First, family values are often not reflected upon and remain open to modification. Indeed, in the case of religious instruction, parents favoured the teaching of a religious faith that they did not themselves practise because, on the one hand, they accepted uncritically what was prevailing practice in schools, and, on the other hand, with a vague religiosity that characterises British attitudes, believed that a modicum of Christian and religious teaching was good for children. Second, social values and trends tend not to be homogeneous or coherent. Third, certain approaches to teaching may anticipate future trends in society and already draw on social factors moving in directions away from prevailing ones. Fourth, in certain instances where a teaching has a rational and compelling case built into it, it may pierce the lethargy of received opinions and reach pupils in a convincing way. Were this last possibility not there, schools would mostly face towards the past rather than cope with the present or prepare for the future.

TRADITION, CHANGE AND THE SHAPE OF THE FUTURE

Against the background of these considerations, peace studies in primary or secondary schools appears to struggle against (a) a generation of parents whose views are traditional in the sense that they see British security based on strong military defence, including nuclear weapons, and (b) a state apparatus that, at government level, has been hostile, and at other levels mostly hostile. Moreover, parents, especially middle class parents, have come increasingly to monitor the content, style and values of teaching in schools where their children are and to protest where these factors are not to their liking. This general situation suggests why, in spite of support from certain local authorities, few peace studies courses have been established in British schools. In particular, since formal peace studies courses are usually thought to be linked to the issue of nuclear weapons which divides the Conservative and Labour parties, head teachers and others seek to avoid charges of political partisanship and few offer encouragement to teachers anxious to introduce such courses.

Yet things are not quite what they seem to be. Some school surveys reveal that while peace studies courses are rare, teaching with a peace focus and with a content that could readily form part of a peace studies module is reasonably widespread in British schools at the present time. (1) What has happened is that those teachers who are concerned about peace issues have introduced a peace focus and content into other courses. These latter courses tend to be development studies, global studies, multi-cultural studies, race relations, studies in international understanding, integrated social studies, geography and, not least, but especially, religious studies. Many also have introduced a peace focus into traditional subjects such as history and English. This approach has enabled teachers to avoid an excessive preoccupation with the nuclear issue and to take up issues of understanding, justice and co-operation among groups, issues that taken together add up to teaching about peace. Apart from avoiding the reproach of being obsessed with the nuclear issue, this approach has three other advantages. First, it enables peace teaching to be carried on without having to bid for extra time and place in already over-crowded time-tables. Second, it enables a peace focus and content to be introduced naturally into subjects ranging from history and English to physics and biology. Third, it reaches in this way many more pupils than could be reached through formal peace studies courses.

Cynically one might have noted a fourth reason for a peace focus rather than a peace course by noting that, in this way, it is possible to evade the fate of unloved and mostly languishing religious knowledge courses. Yet there are formal peace studies courses; and there is a case for teaching them. Where they exist, they have also often been successful in attracting pupils freely - the peace studies course in the international baccalaureate at Atlantic College in Glamorgan is a good example - and they have been taught by teachers with more than usual dedication. They have also been based on good syllabuses that concentrate on issues directly relevant to our times. Yet one must have reservations over the possibility of similar courses being taught by conscript and less enthusiastic teachers. In other words, there is a case for peace studies courses where teachers are able and willing to teach them. There is not a good case for such courses to become more widespread until the general social ethos has changed and until such time as teachers have been trained to deal with them.

Peace studies courses - whether taught as such or as elements in other courses - possess one crucial advantage over the common run of religious knowledge courses: they are much more directly geared to contemporary concerns. Peace itself is an issue that is not going to go away while the threat of nuclear destruction hangs over our world, and while technology makes the world go on growing smaller - with increased awareness of comparative living conditions, functional interdependence, and growing competition for scarce resources. The agreed religious syllabus is, in contrast, constructed around biblical stories that are seldom properly related to their historical context and almost never reflected on for doctrinal teaching and exposition of a theological-metaphysical relationship with God. At best these biblical stories are given a moralising interpretation. So they have historically kept alive a vague sense of religiosity and have convinced British children that religion is chiefly concerned with relatively superficial moralising about good and not-so-good ways of acting. In short, peace studies courses are able powerfully to confront the present and to face towards the future, while religious teaching in its commonest forms draws feebly on the past and too often copes without insight or pungency with the present.

THE THEMES OF PEACE STUDIES

At this stage it seems reasonable to ask what the focus and content of a peace studies course might look like. The broad focus is the maintenance and repair of peace. Peace itself has two dimensions: a positive dimension that seeks co-operation among persons and groups for security, justice and freedom; a negative dimension that seeks to avoid or to eliminate violence, especially the organised violence of war. Peace taken in this two-fold sense is extremely wide. For that reason, it needs to be organised for teaching purposes into manageable categories. Obviously these categories and their content will vary according to age and attainment but the following six themes suggest possible practical approaches:

1. Philosophy of non-violence: The broad nature of peace; practical approaches to non-violence; the theory of just war; the role of pacifism; case studies of non-violent action, including Gandhi and Martin Luther King.
2. Individual, family and school peace: Psychology of personal peace; conditions of peace in families, school organisation and peace; roles of various groups in school, including teachers and pupils.
3. Nuclear issue: Politics, strategy and ethics of nuclear weapons; East-West political relations; security, freedom and justice in relation to peace in a nuclear age.
4. Peace and development: Development and justice; development and compassion; the uneven allocation of world resources; the process of development and its costs in developing societies; development, changing international relations and the threat to peace.
5. Problems of industrialised societies: Race and multi-cultural relations; industrial firms, management and worker participation; the issue of social class and national community.
6. Case studies: Northern Ireland, Central America, the Middle East.

Two further comments are appropriate. First, the contents sketched here can be covered over several years and can be approached according to the ages and needs of school classes. Second, abstract categories and values are best dealt with by being incorporated into case studies that put flesh and blood on them for young persons.

THE PEACE OF GOD: FAITH AND RELEVANCE

Earlier it was said that religious knowledge was one of the subjects made use of most frequently by teachers to include a peace focus and content. I have also suggested that those teachers who are presently concerned about peace issues are among the most lively and enthusiastic teachers. It may well be that there is a moral here, namely, that just as I have argued that peace studies teaching has a future because it is relevant to our time, so religious teaching may find renewal in taking directions closely aligned with peace and justice. In that way it may bring a new vision into religious teaching as well as relating it to the most generous instincts of our young contemporaries. In consequence, I wish to argue that those themes that touch pupils in peace studies courses are such as to prompt reflections on great religious themes and combine the search for peace in our time with the option for the poor that liberation theology, one of the most vibrant contemporary forms of theology, puts forward. Christ began His own ministry by citing the words of Isaiah: 'The Spirit of the Lord is upon me, because he has anointed me to preach good news to the poor' (Luke 4:18).

Before starting on this venture it is worth considering an immediate objection to it, namely, constructing religious knowledge courses around peace themes is equivalent to hijacking religious teaching and manipulating it into the service of peace teaching. Were this subservience to be the case, there might be merit in the objection - though it is important to remember that peace lies at the heart of Christianity: Christ is the peace of God and is our peace. This approach is not however meant to suggest that religion does not have a doctrinal content, forms of worship and community linkages that transcend teaching about peace or working for peace. What is being argued is not that religious teaching should be an instrument of peace teaching but that the concerns of peace teaching should stimulate religious themes. Throughout the centuries religious teaching has been conditioned and enlivened by the social and intellectual background of its time. The development of doctrine has been intimately linked to such factors: Augustine and Aquinas were influenced respectively by Neo-Platonism and Aristotelianism; Luther owed much to new European nationalisms and to the invention of printing; and recent biblical scholarship has relied heavily on a modern historical methodology that was evolved in the wake of the romantic movement. Hence, it is not only relevant but necessary to the elucidation of religion, to consider what happens when our world, suddenly grown small, is faced with, on the one hand, a technological capacity to provide a reasonable subsistence for all its inhabitants, and, on the other hand, a capacity to destroy all living things.

What then have those who seek to improve religious teaching within the Christian tradition and who argue that its vibrancy depends on opening it up to central issues of contemporary living, not least issues of security, justice and peace, to say about the focus and content in such teaching? It seems best, as in the case of peace studies, to suggest broad themes: a sense of God, brotherhood, community, and reconciliation:

1. A sense of God: At the heart of religion is a relationship with God, the ground of reality, the Alpha and Omega, who can never be captured fully in human concepts but who can be glimpsed through His creation, especially through those creatures possessing knowledge and love who are persons; and not least among the latter is Christ who is the image of the invisible God. A.N. Whitehead perceptively argued some generations ago that too much religion consisted of ministers seeking to persuade people to come to God, whereas religion consisted rather in the adventure of a common search for God. God, the foundation of reality, 'in whom we live and move and have our being', is the ground of the belonging to one another of all things that exist. Moreover, in sharing an eternal love He offers the hope of surviving the demise of time, not least for human love. (2) In a world that is worked on by the creativity of science and technology there is a place for understanding human co-operation in creativity as well as for sharing the ultimate Creator's benign concern for all that exists. In a negative way the same co-operation is needed not only to avoid nuclear destruction but also ecological and other damage that may follow from warped human exploitation of science and technology. In the Christian tradition and its scriptures there is a certain sureness of touch in reflecting on the nature of God and in overcoming human sinfulness in approaching Him. But underneath approaches in faith there also has to be the constant work of reason - not only to seek the evidence for God in the world but also to ensure that within a religious tradition there is constant reference to the test of reason. Young persons will not in the longer run

thank teachers whose appeal is less to the scrutiny of reason than to the authority of established interests.

2.   Brotherhood/Sisterhood: Central in religious approaches is a belief that the relations of men and women to God are one side of a coin of which the other side is their relation to one another. Where a concept of creation is accepted, the fundamental unity of all persons - Jew and Greek, bond and free, male and female, Russian and American, European, Asian and African - is accepted. In other words, there is a common humanity which can be respected only in an ethic of justice and love. This common humanity is harmed by division; and it is warped by stereotypes. Theologians are under no obligation to pretend that historically religions, not least Christianity, have lived up to their ideals. But the ideals can be suggested and their doctrinal foundations uncovered. At the same time, students may be invited to discuss why Churches, for example, at different times have not lived up to their ideals. In this context the social class of churchmen and nationalism of their congregations may be looked at. Students can be asked to match the weight of class and nation against the strength of religious belonging and to make their judgements on where their own allegiances lie. Similarly if a religion accepts that all peoples are brothers and neighbours, students may be asked to discuss why problems of just sharing within nations and between nations still remain outstanding. Finally, it can be suggested that where peoples are brothers, sisters and neighbours, demonisation of leaders or of peoples is inconsistent with an acceptance that they are the children of God and open to the Spirit of God.

3.   Community: The belonging that is generated by a recognition of brotherhood and sisterhood brings with it the notion of community. Community is a sense of belonging to persons, sharing objectives with them, and willing a common good. The idealised picture of the early Church in Jerusalem that Luke paints remains a cogent inspiration: 'Now the company of those who believed were of one heart and soul, and no one said that any of the things that he possessed were his own, but they had everything in common ... There was not a needy person among them, for as many as were possessors of land or houses, sold them and brought the proceeds of what was sold and laid them at the feet of the apostles; and distribution was made to each as any had need' (Acts: 4-32, 34-37). Christian living has sought community at many levels, ranging from families and local communities

through ethnic groups and nations to reach out to the whole world. Where there is community there is bound to be the co-operation and the absence of violence that make up peace. Community in itself threatened where there are divisions among persons and groups. But, historically, it was often difficult to extend a sense of community from one group to other groups and persons both because physical distance was a serious obstacle and because, in a context of scarce resource, groups preferred to restrict a sense of community rather than be under pressure to share resources. Only in our times as the scientific renaissance has become operative through the industrial revolution have problems of distance and scarcity begun to be resolved. In the process it becomes easier to translate a Christian understanding of humanity and its relation to Christ into a sense of global community, based on a struggle for justice and measured by the worth of peace. As the writer of Ephesians with remarkable vision put it: God

> has let us know the mystery of his purpose, the hidden plans he so kindly made in Christ from the beginning to act upon when the times had run their course to the end: that he would bring everything together under Christ, as head, everything in the heavens and everything on earth (Ephesians: 1:9-10).

Again, elsewhere, the Pauline tradition links the themes of creation and reconciliation in Christ:

> Before anything was created, He existed, and He holds all things in unity ... God wanted all perfection to be found in Him and all things to be reconciled through Him and for Him, everything in heaven and everything on earth, when He made peace by His death on the cross (Colossians 1:17, 19-20).

The world is as small now as Britain was in the young Disraeli's time. The latter reckoned that there could not justly or sensibly be two nations, one rich and one poor, in his country. In our world, there is no gainsaying a Christian logic that accepts a sense of community that seeks for peace and that is committed to building global justice into a stable peace. It is a task that many others as well as Christians need to take part in. And in working with others, Christians play a proper human role, as well as carrying out

126

their own mission of unity.

4. <u>Reconciliation</u>: In a world where peoples have inherited historical divisions, and where goods are unevenly shared, injustices and grievances are not going to be easily coped with. In this situation, a Christian doctrine of reconciliation that recognises sin and hard-heartedness has much to offer. Beyond basic forms of justice and love, Christian theology reflects on teachings that propound how enemies have to be loved and injuries forgiven; how the face that has been struck on one cheek turns the other cheek; and how with one who forces a man to go a distance the man goes voluntarily a greater distance. Christianity acknowledges the fact of division; it offers powerful motivation for overcoming divisions; and it suggests that the strength of God is available to those who undertake the task. Here we also come back to understanding that peace, which is the fruit of reconciliation, is also the means of reconciliation. Paul, who calls Christ 'the peace of God', sketches in vivid language the work of reconciliation: 'It was God who reconciled us to Himself through Christ and gave us the work of handing on this reconciliation ... God in Christ was reconciling the world to Himself, not holding men's faults against them, and He has entrusted to us the news that they are reconciled' (2 Corinthians 5:18-19).

Reconciliation, like peace, is part of process. G.M. Hopkins has expressed this insight in powerful lines:

> ... And when peace here does house,
> He comes with work to do, he does not come to coo,
>   He comes to brood and sit.

To learn to turn the other cheek, to recognise in our times American, Chinese and Russians without distortion, and to recognise at home Bengalis, Punjabis and West Indians, as well as the Jews and the Greeks in the scriptures, is to live with and work with process. In reconciling there are no easy solutions. Christ went to the cross to overcome human divisions. In our times similar challenges exist to which there are no solutions but only relentless efforts to deal with them. The crucifixion of Christ, its suffering and its victory, remains the path and the strength of those seeking human unity. In a profound sense, history is process. And so its future belongs to those who use vision, determination, and patience, to handle process.

To sum up what I have been arguing in this section:

religious teaching for contemporary pupils comes best to
life when it draws on the generosity of young persons and
shows that it is related to the great problems of the world
around them. In particular, in being related to issues of
justice and peace, religious teaching may be constructed
around four central Christian themes: creation, brotherhood
and sisterhood, community, and reconciliation. These
simple, if profound, themes also avoid presenting
Christianity in a complicated way. They enable other great
themes, Eucharist, Baptism, Ministry to be integrated into a
whole that is meaningful for our contemporaries; and they
take up the central religious and secular challenges of our
time.

OBJECTIONS TO PEACE STUDIES

I want to shift the focus of this chapter back now to peace
studies and to look at objections that have been put to it as
a subject. One recurring objection is that it is not a <u>true</u>
academic subject. This particular objection is one that other
subjects - not only sociology, but electrical engineering -
have met before. Perhaps the objection is partly countered
by noting briefly how the subject emerged. In the years
after the First World War, and in response to the breakdown
of the pre-1914 order, the discipline of international
relations emerged and took its place alongside the science
of politics. In the wake of the Second World War, new needs
were perceived. It was then that the subject of peace
studies began to emerge. The founder of peace research in
Holland, Bert Röling, called it 'the science of survival'.
Survival became a global issue in the years after 1945. Out
of such beginnings came peace studies - which in academic
language is an area study, that is, a subject in which
differing disciplines focus on a common theme or objective.
In the case of peace studies, political science and sociology
for the most part - but also history, economics and
psychology - converge in an interdisciplinary way on the
theme and problematic of peace. In the context of an
objection that calls into question the legitimacy of the
academic study of peace, it is worth drawing attention to
two longer established area studies that have much in
common with the methodology of peace studies: human
geography and medicine. In the case of human geography,
economics and sociology are focused by a concern for the

uses of the earth; and in medicine a whole range of disciplines from chemistry to psychology are joined by a concern to maintain and restore health.

A second objection is that supporters of peace studies do not weigh sufficiently the claims of security, justice and freedom against those of peace. Two replies may be made. A first reply is simply to say that unless we resolve the issue of nuclear peace there will be no other issue to resolve. Also, even in the most unlikely event of being forced to a choice between being dead and being red, it seems worth saying that the former choice would be permanent and the latter not more than highly temporary. In other words, in terms of that condition of just war which is the principle of proportion it seems difficult to offset the choice of nuclear war and its mutual or all-round destruction against ends that might conceivably be attainable through contemporary war. A second reply is more important. In the first place, those concerned about peace take up its cause in spheres much wider than the nuclear (a range of peace themes has already been outlined). Moreover, those who are not pacifists - which in practice means most of those involved in teaching about peace - accept a theory of just war. In this connection too, it seems worth adding that much positive research has been carried out by peace theorists on the means of defending Western European by the use of conventional weapons. (3)

A third objection, which is related to the second, is that teachers of peace studies are 'partisan'. In Britain this contention tends to stem from the policy differences between the Conservative and Labour parties on the possession of nuclear weapons. In reply, it is worth stating that peace studies deals with issues much wider than the nuclear issue. Moreover, even if many teachers of peace studies in this country tend to oppose the British possession of nuclear weapons, few among them fail to realise that they owe it to their pupils to be fair and not partisan; and they realise that fairness is the only long-run guarantee of teaching influence. Moreover again, they know that parents, especially middle class parents, monitor teaching carefully and quickly pick up orientations in school to which they are opposed. It seems clear enough that efficiency, integrity and prudence work together to prevent the stereotypical partisanship that certain conservative theorists are over-ready to suspect. Partisan indoctrination is not a quick, easy or acceptable option for teachers concerned about peace.

In a roundabout way, this third objection against peace teaching brings us back to the same issue in religious studies. Some writers who argue the charge of 'political indoctrination' against peace studies argue that:

> ... there is a serious case for exempting religion ... from our strictures against indoctrination. Religious instruction in school can certainly be harmful, debilitating, and dogmatic. But it can also be a warm sustaining part of that moral education without which no child can survive in the world. Religion shores up the certainties of morality with vague but deep foundations. The exposure to alternatives may defeat the purpose of religious education as much as it defeats the purpose of morality: it offers to place idle curiosity where there should be certainty and trust. The crucial feature of religious belief is that, unlike political belief, it is essentially addressed to the individual, his conscience, and his salvation ... If political indoctrination is harmful it is partly because it closes the mind in respect of questions that are genuinely open, and which must remain open if we are to agree to live on terms. Religious indoctrination closes the mind about a question that is incapable of a rational answer. (4)

The double thrust of these views, namely, their opposition to the social dimension of Christian living and their anti-intellectual stance in relation to reasoned questioning and deepening of faith, situates them a long way from positions argued in this paper. For one thing, hardly a contemporary theologian of worth would defend this kind of individualistic approach to Christian faith; and it removes Christian moralists from seeking to influence public or political morality, whether on the nature of apartheid or the incidence of inner city poverty. For another thing, it is historically far removed from an intellectual tradition that moves from Augustine through Aquinas to Hooker and Temple: intellectus quaerens fidem, fides quaerens intellectum. A faith that is not rationally grounded is in danger of running counter to reason; and a faith that does not reflect on its reasonableness neglects to work with intellectual creativity and will quickly stagnate in a barren fideism. It will not stand up to anything except ghetto living. It is going to go on being badly eroded in a secular and multi-cultural society. It stands no chance of resisting the influences that pour in from the communications era that has latterly come upon us. With individualist and anti-intellectual protectors, religion scarcely needs enemies. Peace studies teachers, since they are not teaching a widely accepted subject, are at least spared the temptation to avoid reflection and argument and know quite well that all they put forward will be scrutinised in a tradition that has historically revered military defence and that tends to envisage a future as having to be wrested from an adversary rather than worked out with one who even in defeat has the power to destroy utterly. In short, religious studies and peace studies at their best respect the social dimension of human living and accept the test of an intellectual approach to truth.

CONCLUSION: THE INELUCTABILITY OF THE STUDY OF RELIGION AND PEACE

In our time there is no escaping concern for religion or peace. To let science replace religious explanation is to permit description and transformation of what already exists to obscure ultimate questions of origin and destiny. In turn, to ignore a concern for peace is to ignore how the technical development of weapons and the growth of co-operative relations between states remain as yet out of equilibrium. There would be an extraordinary failure of academic teachers at any level - an ultimate trahison des clercs - were they not to seek to undertake a systematic study of the foundations of contemporary peace. Together with the nuclear issue, however, must go all the other issues of peace. In one form or another, while humans live, peace will remain a human ideal and a human problem. Those who know the hope and strength of God, who share the springs of a common humanity in fellowship and reconciliation, and who accept the slow and patient task of conserving existence and participating in the task of creation, will work together in those intellectual and practical areas where religion and peace meet and mingle.

NOTES

1.   Surveys have been carried out by two full-time

researchers, David Lawson and Kevin Green, attached to the School of Peace Studies at the University of Bradford.

2.   I am following the traditional reference to God in male terms. Being beyond sex, God is no more male than female. I have much sympathy with those who refer to God as 'Father-Mother'.

3.   See, for example, the studies by the Alternative Defence Commission on defending Europe with conventional weapons: Defence Without the Bomb (Taylor and Francis, London, 1983) and The Politics of Alternative Defence (Paladin, London, 1987).

4.   Roger Scruton, Angela Ellis-Jones and Dennis O'Keeffe, Education and Indoctrination, (Education Research Centre, London 1985), p. 46.

PART II

Chapter Eight

THE CHURCHES AND EDUCATIONAL PROVISION IN NORTHERN IRELAND

John E. Greer

Strange as it may seem, religion was not a major issue in the hedge schools which were set up throughout Ireland in the late 18th and early 19th century, perhaps because there was no system, with regulations, but only individual schoolmasters who depended for their livelihood on the fees of individual pupils. (1) But religion became an issue when educational societies were established whose aim was to convert Roman Catholics from the errors of their ways to Protestantism, though these societies in the main followed the policy that the scriptures should be read in schools without note or comment. The board of Commissioners, established in 1831, was concerned that in the new system of national schools there should be no interference with the religious beliefs of the children. The Commissioners wished to ensure that 'while the interests of religion were not overlooked, the most scrupulous care should be taken not to interfere with the peculiar tenets of any description of Christian pupils'. (2) Children were to be given moral and literary education in class together and separate religious teaching by clergy who had access to children of their own persuasion in the schools. But this seemingly fair system broke down because it prevented the bible being read during 'secular' instruction. It also failed because the Protestant Churches had a strong inbuilt tendency to use their schools to recruit members for their own denominations and could not accept the obligation to allow children of other traditions to leave while denominational religious teaching was being given. (3) The effective denominationalisation of the national school system was in fact a matter of satisfaction to Protestant and Roman Catholic Church leaders alike. (4)

In the early twentieth century, primary schools in Northern Ireland were small, mostly one teacher, and denominational in management, being vested in and managed by the clergy.

> The unchecked growth of denominational schools had resulted in much overlapping and duplication in the field of primary education. The relative poverty of the country meant that many schools were provided as cheaply as possible and were badly designed and poorly equipped. The system often produced a hybrid type of building which had to serve as both school and church hall and was not well adapted to the purposes of either. (5)

There was an urgent need for the reconstruction of the whole educational system, and this task was undertaken by the new government of Northern Ireland which came into existence in 1921.

The story of the reconstruction of education in Northern Ireland from 1921 has been told by Corkey (6), Fulton (7, 8), Sutherland (9, 10), Darby (11) and Akenson (12), among others. The most recent and the best accounts of the period up to 1930 have been written by Farren (13, 14). Briefly, the government planned to bring into existence a system of schools similar to the national schools of the 19th century which all children would attend. These schools would provide denominational teaching outside compulsory school hours, given by clergy, or other suitable persons, including teachers. But this proposal pleased no one, and was seen as an attempt to secularise the schools by Protestant and Catholic alike, though the Minister of Education, Lord Londonderry, was not a secularist and wanted to establish a system of non-sectarian but not secular schools. (15) The Roman Catholic authorities would settle for nothing less than Church schools managed by the clergy, employing Catholic teachers to teach Catholic children, and they held out for and finally achieved their own voluntary schools, largely paid for by the state. Unwilling to pay capital or maintenance costs to voluntary schools in 1923, in 1930 the government decided to pay voluntary schools 50% of capital expenditure and 50% of costs of maintenance, and these payments were increased to 65% in 1947. In 1968 a generous offer was made to voluntary schools which agreed to accept 'maintained' status, whereby public representatives (2 out of 6) were accepted on school management committees. This offer proposed capital grants of 80% and maintenance grants of 100% for maintained schools, and subsequently in 1975 capital grants were raised to 85%.

The leaders of the three main Protestant Churches, the Church of Ireland, the Methodist Church and the Presbyterian Church, settled in 1930 for controlled schools owned by the local authority, in the management of which Protestant clergy had a guaranteed role as the representatives of those who had transferred their schools, in the curriculum of which bible teaching had an assured place in school hours, and in which Protestant teachers were employed to teach Protestant children. (16)

In 1968, when maintained status was offered to voluntary schools, a small concession was made to the Protestant Churches which had transferred their schools in that provision was made 'for the appointment of transferors' representatives to the management committees of county primary schools in areas of new housing'. (17) This provision explains why today Protestant clergy but not Roman Catholic clergy are invited to serve on the management committees of new controlled schools. Murray has argued that this demonstrates an acceptance by statutory bodies that 'state' schools are de facto Protestant schools. (18) Controlled schools are largely Protestant by custom because they are attended by all who do not attend Roman Catholic schools, but they are also de jure schools with Protestant transferor representation on their management. We may end this account of the development of the dual school system with a brief reference to the 1978 (Northern Ireland) Act which made possible the education of Protestant and Roman Catholic children together by creating a new category of 'controlled integrated' school, 'an Act to facilitate the establishment in Northern Ireland of schools likely to be attended by pupils of different religious affiliations or cultural traditions'. (19)

How this establishment of a system of Catholic voluntary schools and a parallel system of Protestant controlled schools accords with the Government of Ireland Act 1920 is still a puzzle to many constitutional lawyers. Section 5 of the Act provided that:

In the exercise of their power to make laws under this Act neither the Parliament of Southern Ireland nor the

Parliament of Northern Ireland shall make a law so as either directly or indirectly to establish or endow any religion, or prohibit or restrict the free exercise thereof, or give a preference, privilege, or advantage, or impose any disability or disadvantage, on account of religious belief ... (20).

If this kind of prohibition were to be applied strictly, as may happen in the United States, the whole of the present system could be in violation of the Act, for 'the state pays the bulk of the cost of the Church schools, and church representatives take part in the management of state schools'. (21) In his detailed discussion of this issue, Graham points out that 'Northern Ireland remains an essentially Christian community and 'establishment' could be said to have retained its original meaning of prohibiting any preference being given to one denomination over others'. (22) Moreover it may be argued that as part of the free exercise of religion, children should be brought up in a religious community in which religious teaching is provided and that children should not be disadvantaged by attendance at secular schools. The inclusion of a conscience clause for teachers in controlled schools in the 1947 Act, against the strong wishes of the Protestant Churches, appears to have overcome some at least of the legal problems. Teachers in controlled schools may be excused from teaching religion or from attending or conducting worship if they make their request 'solely on grounds of religious belief' according to the 1947 Act (23), a ground for excusal which was widened to 'solely on ground of conscience', in the Education and Libraries (NI) Order 1972. (24) Unlike the 1944 Butler Act, the 1947 Act and the 1972 Order did not pass the task of inspecting Religious Education to the inspectorate. Instead it gave this task, along with the opportunity to give denominational instruction, 'to ministers of religion and other suitable persons (including teachers of the school) to whom the parents do not object'. (25) It may be noted that Church control of the Religious Education curriculum is exercised through the work of clerical inspectors. (26)

So far, attention has been focused on primary or elementary education which catered for children up to age 14. In the post war period of the Butler Act of 1944, and the 1947 Act in Northern Ireland, an attempt was made to provide a secondary education for all children, and the school leaving age was raised to 15 in 1957 and to 16 in

1972. One peculiar feature of secondary education in Northern Ireland has been the existence of a large number of grammar schools. In 1986 this amounted to 56 grammar schools under voluntary management and 21 managed by Education and Library Boards. The raising of the school leaving age meant the rapid expansion of a new type of school called intermediate, or secondary intermediate, or more commonly today called high schools, for pupils who were judged to be unsuitable for an academic course of study. In 1948 there were 8 newly created local authority intermediate schools in old buildings and two voluntary intermediate schools. By 1986 there were 88 maintained intermediate schools and 89 controlled schools of this type.

Thus there developed from 1923 until the present day in Northern Ireland two parallel systems of schools, one largely Catholic and the other largely Protestant and the numbers of pupils and schools in these systems in 1986 may be seen in Table 8.1. (27) This table does not include nursery schools, preparatory departments of grammar schools or special schools, nor does it include independent schools of which there are now 11, some primary and others all age from 5-16 years. (28)

From this table it may be seen that at present there are approximately equal numbers of pupils at controlled and maintained primary schools (circa 90,000 each) and approximately equal numbers at controlled and maintained secondary (intermediate) schools (circa 50,000 each). The large number of pupils at voluntary grammar schools may be contrasted with the much smaller numbers of pupils at controlled grammar schools. At present, no precise analysis of school type by religious denomination has been carried out which would indicate the affiliation of pupils attending Church related and controlled schools. But one report, which appears to use the term 'state schools' in a loose way to include both controlled and Protestant voluntary schools, 'shows approximately 99.5 per cent of Protestant children in state schools and 98 per cent of Catholic children in Catholic schools'. (29) In another recent province-wide survey of schools by Darby et al. called Schools Apart? the degree of 'exclusivity' was examined. None of the 67 Roman Catholic schools which responded had less than 95% Roman Catholic school population while 86.6% of these schools were attended exclusively by Roman Catholic pupils. Of the 84 Protestant/controlled schools which responded, only 5.9% had a Roman Catholic population of more than 5% and

Table 8.1: Number of Schools and Pupils in Northern Ireland by Management Type in 1986

Type of School	Primary		Secondary Intermediate		Secondary Grammar		Totals	
	No. of schools	No. of pupils	No. of schools	No. of pupils	No. of schools	No. of pupils	No. of schools	No. of pupils
Controlled	516	90,014 mainly Protestant	89	50,362 mainly Protestant	21	13,280 mainly Protestant	626	153,656
Maintained	481	90,762 mainly Catholic	88	48,883 mainly Catholic	0	0	569	139,645
Voluntary	4	311 mainly Catholic	0	0			4	311
Grammar (Voluntary) Under R.C. Management					31	22,661	31	22,661
Grammar (Voluntary) Non-R.C. Management					25	17,731	25	17,731

65.5% had no Roman Catholic pupils at all. (30) It may be added that a more recent study of four areas in Northern Ireland carried out by Dunn et al. in 1983-4, Schools Together?, confirmed 'that the number of children attending schools of the other community is negligible. There is, it seems, a genuinely segregated system.' (31) The Schools Apart? study also demonstrated a similar pattern of segregation in the employment of teachers. Only 29 out of 1,521 secondary (intermediate) teachers studied were employed in schools of a different religion than their own. 9 out of 480 grammar school teachers and 3 out of 750 primary teachers were employed in schools of a different religion. (32)

We turn now to higher education, and the Churches' contribution to this sector, leaving out reference to theological education for intending clergy. Northern Ireland has been served by two universities, Queen's University, Belfast, and the New University of Ulster, now the University of Ulster. Queen's University began in 1845 as Queen's College one of three such colleges in Belfast, Cork and Galway. It became part of the Queen's University in Ireland in 1850 and became independent in 1908 by the passing of the Irish Universities Act. In its early years, Queen's College was regarded with disapproval by the Roman Catholic hierarchy, and it came under an episcopal ban. This was withdrawn when it became a University and, 'as a symbol of goodwill, the university instituted a department of scholastic philosophy with a Catholic priest in charge'. (33) The New University was set up in 1968 as a result of the recommendations made by the Lockwood Report, which also recommended the closure of Magee University College in Londonderry. This College began its life in 1865 as a Presbyterian institution, with the help of a bequest from Mrs Martha Maria Magee. In 1951, Magee became a University College which provided undergraduate studies from which students could transfer to Trinity College, Dublin, or to Queen's University, Belfast, to complete their degree courses. Because of strong local pressure, the recommendation to close Magee College was overturned, and the College became an integral part of the New University. Its work expanded when in 1984 it became one of the four locations of the University of Ulster, formed by the merger of the New University and the Ulster Polytechnic. Like Queen's University, the University of Ulster is non-denominational. In its Faculty of Education at

Coleraine, students can take units of study in Religious Education as part of their degree course which provides them with an understanding of the religion and of the Religious Education of 'the other side', and which equips them for teaching religion in schools of their own tradition.

The training of teachers for primary schools in Northern Ireland took place in the early years of this century in St. Mary's College, Belfast, and in four Roman Catholic colleges and two Protestant colleges in the south of Ireland. St. Mary's trained women, and in 1925 an arrangement was made for Roman Catholic men to be trained in St. Mary's College, Strawberry Hill, Middlesex. This arrangement was ended in 1945 when men were admitted to St. Mary's College, Belfast. Two years later St. Mary's College established a separate campus for men which in 1961 became St. Joseph's College, Trench House, Belfast. In 1932, Stranmillis College was opened in Belfast to train men and women for teaching in controlled primary schools. In its inception, Stranmillis College was a secular, non-denominational institution, but during the period 1930-2, the three main Protestant churches negotiated one place for each church on the committee of management, so that the college came to have a Protestant church connection similar to that in the controlled school. In the beginning, Religious Education classes were taken by Protestant clergy called 'Visiting Chaplains', who lectured students of their own denomination, but in the 1960s this system was replaced by full-time college staff who were responsible for the education of both intending primary and specialist secondary Religious Education teachers. The appointment of college staff to a Department of Religious Studies first took place in 1962.

In 1982, the British Government decided to implement the Chilver Interim Report which took the view that it was preferable for teacher education in Northern Ireland to be located in religiously mixed and multi-disciplinary institutions of higher education and it recommended the amalgamation of St. Mary's and St. Joseph's Colleges with Stranmillis College on the Stranmillis site. In this Belfast Centre for Teacher Education, the voluntary college was promised a distinctive denominational ethos and a separate legal and administrative existence. In the face of considerable opposition, the Government did not proceed with the merger, but the Church authorities decided to merge the two Church Colleges and this took place in 1985 on the St. Mary's site and with St. Mary's name. It should be noted that despite the failure of the merger, there continues to be a measure of co-operation between Stranmillis College and St. Mary's College. The Departments of Religious Studies in the Colleges work together in the planning of syllabuses and examinations and they are represented on a Board of Religious Studies under the Queen's University Faculty of Education.

In this brief historical outline of educational provision in Northern Ireland we have seen how nineteenth century elementary school education continued in the early years of the twentieth century and how it was renewed and expanded following the establishment of the state of Northern Ireland in 1921. We have also seen how in the years following the 1947 Act universal secondary education was achieved. In this outline we have observed how two parallel school systems continued to exist and to develop. The Catholic system of voluntary schools, now mostly maintained, was owned and managed by the Catholic Church, staffed by Catholic teachers who had trained in a Church college, attended by Catholic pupils and largely financed by the state. Alongside the Catholic school system and in so many ways its mirror image, the Protestant/controlled school system developed, owned by Area Boards or Governors on which sat transferors' representatives, largely staffed by Stranmillis College trained Protestant teachers, attended by Protestant pupils and now entirely (or almost entirely) paid for by the state. When the two parallel school systems are compared, it is clear that the Catholic Church made greater sacrifices and thus has retained greater control over its schools. As Graham has observed, 'the Protestant Churches have nothing like the same control, but then neither do they have the same financial responsibilities'. (34) Talk of sacrifices must take our minds away from the rather dry, historical and legalistic account of education contained in this chapter. It must remind us of the dedication of teachers and the financial sacrifice of parents over the past two centuries. It must make us aware of the concern of education for the full development of persons in this life and for an education in religion which deals sensitively with what transcends this life. According to the 1947 Act 'it shall be the duty of the local education authority for every area, so far as their powers extend to contribute towards the spiritual, moral, mental and physical development of the community'. (35) It was to achieve this aim that Churches, clergy, laity, teachers, civil servants and politicians worked, argued, fought and co-operated, and it will be by their achievement of this aim that they will in the end be judged.

This account of the churches and educational provision in Northern Ireland is the story of a great achievement. It tells of the success of a co-operative partnership between the churches and the state which was responsible for building, equipping and staffing a modern school system. But it would be misleading to finish the story at this point, because it is also the story of a serious failure. For twenty years now, since 1968 when the present 'troubles' began, members of the two communities in Northern Ireland have waged civil war with each other, with a ferocity and a cruelty which could never have been predicted or imagined. According to a report in The Times in 1983, the previous fourteen years of the troubles cost £11 billion at 1982 prices to the exchequers of Britain and the Irish Republic. Those years saw violence which caused death to more than 2,300 people and injury to more than 24,000. Economic recession and adverse publicity combined to cause the loss of an estimated 39,000 jobs between 1970 and 1980. (36) The point which is being made is simply that those responsible for such destruction and savagery, those people of violence whose bodies lie in premature graves or who are serving sentences in prison or who continue their campaign of hatred, intimidation and murder, have all been through the school system in one or other of its forms. They have lived in the distinctive ethos of the maintained school or the controlled school. They have received Catholic catechesis or Protestant bible teaching for eleven or twelve or more years, but despite this they have failed to learn basic human values such as respect for others, reverence for human life, or tolerance of political or religious beliefs they do not themselves hold. Brought up in one tradition of Christian faith or the other, they do not exhibit the spirit of Christian love and forgiveness. It does not really meet the criticism to say that only a small minority of pupils is involved or to argue that the situation would be even worse if it were not for the restraining influence of schools and teachers. Catholic and Protestant educators have succeeded in building impressive institutions which have the fabric, the physical structure and the facade of a humanising education but which, for whatever reasons, failed to contribute as they should towards the spiritual, moral and mental development of their pupils, and the community in which these pupils live.

Before we try to answer questions about the role which the Churches might pursue in such a divided and violent society, it is important to examine what has been written recently about inter-community conflict and ignorance in Northern Ireland. A Belfast child psychiatrist, Dr Morris Fraser describes what the environment is like for a Belfast working-class child. It

> means a decaying terrace house, a high flat or a concrete housing estate with less than one third of the Government-recommended playing space. He will mix, play, and be educated exclusively with his own religious group, and may never see a child of the 'other' group, except across a barricade. His home area is divided from other areas by armed sentries and steel barriers ... His home is overcrowded, his father has a high chance of being unemployed, and poverty may be acute. He is brought up with a fear and hatred of members of the other religion that will last him all his life. (37)

Fraser paints a dismal picture of mutual antagonism compounded by poverty and unemployment, which must in part reflect the Belfast urban environment. However, an important study by Murray (38) of two primary schools confirms at least some of the features of intercommunity relationships described by Fraser.

Murray commented that 'in view of the widespread general interest in segregated schooling and its ramifications, it is quite amazing that so little qualitative information is available. In fact no research has attempted to isolate the specific influence of the school'. (39) Because of this absence of research, Murray decided to carry out a participant observation study of two primary schools serving the same country town in the northern part of Northern Ireland. He found that in these schools 'all the teachers expressed a total ignorance of what went on in "the other type of school".' (40) This led him to identify 'the kernel of the problem of Northern Ireland. At an educational level, in keeping with other sections of society, both sides judge each other across a gulf of ignorance. Arising from this ignorance come the negative responses of suspicion and antipathy.' (41) This was expressed in a written comment by one Protestant child at 'Rathlin' Controlled School. 'I don't know anything about "St Judes" except that they train terrorists there.' (42)

It was Murray's opinion that shared activity such as competitive sport 'may actually accentuate the very differences and divisions which it was designed to ameliorate', (43) and he recorded the grim observation of a small Roman Catholic girl made to him at a match with the other school, 'the Protestants are winning five nil'. (44)

One other important issue was raised by Murray but not pursued very far by him, namely the relationship between schools and their surrounding culture. Since schools in Northern Ireland are either Catholic or Protestant, 'it is not unreasonable therefore to expect that each type of school will reflect the cultural aspirations of each religious group as a whole'. (45) Murray concluded that

> at the level of religion and culture, the influence of the school seems to have been grossly exaggerated. Commentators have tended to assume that segregated schools create differences in society rather than reflect them. (46)

> The two main cultures in Northern Ireland are mutually exclusive because of the contrary political aspirations of both. However, it is also true that exclusiveness and intolerance are exacerbated by a mutual ignorance which schools do little to redress. (47)

Bearing in mind, then, the complexity of the relationship between school and society in Northern Ireland, we turn our attention to the basic question, what should be and in practical terms what might be the role of the school in such a divided society? Should or could the churches contribute towards conflict resolution through the schools they own, the schools in which they have control or at least an influence in management and curriculum? These questions were brought to the attention of educators in Northern Ireland in 1973 in an important paper by Skilbeck, then director of the Education Centre of the New University of Ulster. In his paper, Skilbeck argued that schools can adopt one of four hypothetical strategies in response to social change.

> First, schools may swim with the tide by identifying basic trends and going with rather than resisting them. Second, schools may identify particular elements in the past, and seek to preserve them. Third, schools may

carry on their work largely ignorant of or indifferent to what is happening in other key sections of the culture. Fourth, schools may look forward, trying to anticipate situations in the future, assessing them for their educational significance, and influencing them through the various limited means at their disposal. (48)

Skilbeck argued that only the second strategy, conservationism, and the fourth, reconstructionism, withstood strict scrutiny, and while he recognised the attendant problems, he regarded reconstructionism as the most fruitful strategy to explore.

When we look at the argument about reconstruction in Northern Ireland, we find some disagreement. Many educators would take issue with Skilbeck and would maintain that with the best will in the world schools cannot solve society's problems. Certainly society today in Northern Ireland is plural and any diagnosis and recommended treatment of social malaise is unlikely to be shared by many citizens. Reconstructionism also appears to demand too much of its change agents, the members of the teaching profession, who are given a role of considerable sophistication and complexity. Indeed, Pritchard argues that 'since the available research on internal school reforms indicates that teachers are unenthusiastic innovators it would seem unreasonable, in the face of discouraging findings, to cast teachers in the role of catalysts of change, destined to transform the whole of their society'. (49) Committed as they are to democratic procedures, reconstructionists cannot use force or intimidation, and their efforts, thinks Pritchard, seem doomed to fail and place democratic values in danger. In its submission to the New Ireland Forum on 'The Catholic School System in Northern Irleand', the Roman Catholic hierarchy took a similar negative view of reconstructionism. The hierarchy argued that 'there is a virtual consensus among theorists of education that the "reconstructionist" view of education, i.e. the view that schools should be principal agents of cultural or social change is invalid', (50) and they quote the work of Salters (51) and Russell (52) in support.

The hierarchy is particularly concerned to support the argument that an attempt to reconstruct society through the medium of integrated schools is not a viable proposition, and we may well accept its argument. However there are other forms of reconstructionism of a less controversial and less radical kind, which are none the less attempts to contribute to a rebuilding of society through the means of education, and to this 'softer' version of reconstructionism the hierarchy is clearly committed. A committee on ecumenical co-operation in schools has been set up in the diocese of Down and Connor, which unfortunately finds it hard to identify Protestants with whom to co-operate. It may be noted in passing that Protestant teachers and schools can find themselves under pressure not to engage in such ecumenical activity. National catechetical programmes take seriously the ecumenical dimension in Religious Education, though it is hard to accept that the Orthodox Church is the best example of a different Christian tradition for study by Irish pupils. (53) In 1982 an ambitious programme of co-operation between the Church Colleges of Education and Stranmillis College was agreed by the Northern Hierarchy and the Board of Governors of Stranmillis College. This was described as 'an historical ecumenical initiative designed to promote greater understanding and co-operation between teachers in training, while at the same time respecting the separate existence and distinctive ethos of the Catholic college of education and the state college of education. The aim of the initiative is that teachers will be inspired, by their experience in the college of education of a strong commitment to the theory and practice of ecumenism, to promote in their schools greater understanding and respect between the two communities and more co-operation in education. The detailed implementation of this exciting policy is being planned by an intercollegiate working group; some of the ideas being pursued include joint Field Trips; inter-Church Bible Study Groups; a Course in Ecumenism in the B.Ed. degree; joint courses in Peace Education; Common Seminars in History to explore each other's politico-religious traditions; joint Seminars for School Principals from the maintained and controlled sectors; pooling of choral and orchestral resources; combined sporting activities.' (54) Unfortunately four years later in 1986 little progress appears to have been made in this important attempt to embody realistic reconstructionist aims in teacher education in the Belfast colleges of education. Nothing seems to have happened.

It would be wrong to make too much of the apparent failure of this initiative by the northern bishops of the Roman Catholic church and Stranmillis College since there have been other failings, most notably an important report entitled <u>Violence in Ireland</u> produced by a working party set up by the Catholic hierarchy and the Irish Council of Churches. This report outlined a programme of action and education which the Churches might take together. The Working Party was

> in agreement that the Churches should promote pilot schemes and research projects to find effective ways of bringing together Protestant and Catholic young people at school level. Such schemes could include exchanges of teachers between Catholic and Protestant schools (particularly in sensitive areas of the curriculum, such as history, civics, Irish language and culture, history of the Churches in Ireland and in the promotion of joint projects and field work in relevant subjects). Shared Sixth Form Colleges have been suggested. Common nursery schools in suitable areas could be developed. This would give mothers opportunities of meeting which it would otherwise be difficult to bring about. Debates, cultural and folk-cultural exhibitions and other extra-curricular activities can often usefully be shared. Games and athletics are also areas for sharing and this can be further developed. The different traditions in regard to games which have tended to characterise the two communities will need diversification so as to increase sharing. The teaching of Religion in schools of both traditions must have explicitly and deliberately an ecumenical dimension. The stereotypes which each community may have inherited regarding the religious beliefs and practices of the other must be firmly rejected and replaced by exact and sympathetic understanding. It will often be desirable to invite representatives of the other traditions to come to the school to talk about their own tradition. (55)

The Working Party further recommended the establishment of a joint Committee to consider in detail the implementation of these suggestions. The Churches were asked for their responses to the report, and some replied, but nothing came of it. According to Gallagher and Worrall

> there was no indication that any of the Churches, or their representatives on school committees and Education and Library Boards, were either concerned or

convinced enough to do anything about the report's recommendations. None of them had started to think about the suggested pilot schemes or research projects. The shared nursery schools and sixth form colleges were no longer on any agenda. Everybody's business had become nobody's business. (56)

During the 1970s and the 1980s there has been a rapid growth of programmes, projects and agencies which are concerned with peace, reconciliation and the reconstruction of society in Northern Ireland. An account of some of them is given by Gallagher, (57) and a more systematic listing is provided by Ellis. (58) We are here concerned with a small number of educational ventures which are social and religious rather than political in their perspective, and we intend to make a brief statement about each and draw some general conclusions. We are aware that there are other ventures which deserve mention but which cannot be included.

1.   The UNESCO (Northern Ireland) Committee runs inter-schools conferences for senior secondary pupils to promote national and international understanding.
2.   The Community Relations Project of Queen's University Institute of Education was initiated by Malone. (59) It drew on and adapted the work of the Schools Council Project on Moral Education in Secondary Schools.
3.   The Christian Education Movement, an offshoot of the British CEM, organises inter-school conferences throughout Northern Ireland, and has recently experimented with residential conferences for pupils from the two traditions at Corrymeela.
4.   The Schools Cultural Studies Project, based in the New University of Ulster from 1974 to 1981, has as its main aim the encouragement of mutual understanding in social relationships among pupils in Northern Ireland. The project produced, among other things, a five year course leading to the Certificate of Secondary Education. Its work is now supported by a professional association of teachers, the Association of Teachers of Cultural and Social Studies. Courses are available in the University of Ulster for students in teacher training and for teachers in-post to learn about and become involved in the work of the project. (60)
5.   The Religion in Ireland Project was also based in the New University of Ulster and extended in two phases, from

1974-7 and from 1979-81. In 1984 five units of teaching material for secondary pupils was published by Gill and Macmillan under the title Irish Christianity (61) together with a short guide for teachers which attempted to provide a rationale for the reconstructionist approach to Religious Education. (62, 63)

6.   Teaching Religion in Northern Ireland was a follow up to Religion in Ireland and like its predecessor it was based in the Faculty of Education of the University of Ulster, from 1984-6. Its aim was to provide Catholic and Protestant teachers of Religious Education in secondary schools with the opportunity to experiment with discussion in the classroom and to meet with and learn from each other in the process. (64)

7.   A Joint Peace Education Programme was developed during the period 1978-86 by the Irish Council of Churches and the Irish Commission for Justice and Peace. This programme has encouraged teachers 'to take up some of the issues and skills in the field of conflict resolution and education for mutual understanding and peace'. (65) Its most substantial material is Free to Be for 8/9-12 year old children and Looking at Churches and Worship in Ireland for 10-12 year old children and it is based in a Peace Education Resources Centre in Belfast.

8.   The Area Board Advisers in Religious Education have produced a discussion document entitled Religious Education and Mutual Understanding based on the deliberations of a religiously mixed conference of secondary Religious Education teachers held in 1984. (66) This document defined aims and objectives in education for mutual understanding, and explored reasons for inactivity on the part of teachers. Area Board advisers are also able to give practical help to schools by making funds available from the Department of Education which facilitate co-operative activities between schools of the two traditions.

9.   Arising from the Schools Together? project, a three year project called School Links was initiated by Dunn in 1986 which aims at encouraging cross-religious co-operation and contact between schools in the Western Education and Library Board, and at monitoring the enterprise carefully. (67)

10. The most recent development is in the field of history. The European Studies (Ireland and Great Britain) project under the direction of Dr Roger Austin of the University of Ulster will cost £1 million and last for 6 years. Its aim is to

'breakdown embattled perspectives, allowing pupils to see themselves as European citizens with common perspectives'. (68)

Looking at this list of endeavours a number of generalisations may be made. Firstly, the thinking behind several, particularly the Schools Cultural Studies Project and the Religion in Ireland Project, was strongly influenced by the seminal ideas of Malcolm Skilbeck and his advocacy of the reconstructionist view of education. His argument was echoed by Murray that 'schools can, and should, provide the milieux for social reconstruction. Confrontation of the value positions of pupils and teachers may initially seem an intimidating venture. It is however a nettle which can and must be grasped.' (69) Even groups like the Roman Catholic hierarchy, which attacked reconstructionism when used to support integrated education, implicitly accepted a less threatening form of reconstructionist philosophy based on the distinctive nature of the Catholic school and its positive role in society. Secondly, a number of the projects were deeply indebted to the general support and financial backing of the Northern Ireland Department of Education (DENI). This was certainly true of the Christian Education Movement, the Schools Cultural Studies Project, Religion in Ireland, Teaching Religion in Northern Ireland, the Joint Peace Education Programme, the School Links Project, and the European Studies Project. This official support by DENI began in the 1970s and was given a strong impetus in an official circular issued in 1982, 'The improvement of community relations: the contribution of schools'. (70) The second and third paragraphs of the circular make the position of DENI clear with regard to its responsibility for formulating and sponsoring policies for the improvement of community relations:

2.   Our educational system has clearly a vital role to play in the task of fostering improved relationships between the two communities in Northern Ireland. Every teacher, every school manager, Board member and trustee, and every educational administrator within the system has a responsibility for helping children to learn to understand and respect each other, and their differing customs and traditions, and of preparing them to live together in harmony in adult life.
3.   The Department wishes to emphasise that it is not

questioning the right to insist on forms of education in schools which amount to segregation. It considers, however, that this right is coupled with an inescapable duty to ensure that effective measures are taken to ensure that children do not grow up in ignorance, fear or even hatred of those from whom they are educationally segregated.

This policy has been instrumental in initiating and supporting many projects in addition to those mentioned earlier, and has led to the setting up of a special committee of the Northern Ireland Council for Educational Development (NICED) concerned with Encouraging Mutual Understanding (EMU). Thirdly, a number of the projects have had the support of the universities in Northern Ireland and of lecturers in education in these universities. John Malone's project was based in Queen's University while the Social Studies Project, the two Religious Education Projects, the School Links Project and the European Studies Project have been or are linked with the University at Coleraine. It seems that education staff have seen the need and found the time and resources to become involved in reconstructionist projects. As university lecturers they have also enjoyed the independence sometimes necessary for such involvement. Fourthly, the main churches have not been officially involved in the projects as initiators, nor have they carried major responsibility for any of the projects. They have often been kept informed of the progress of projects, as in the case of Teaching Religion in Northern Ireland, or have been consulted on policy matters, as in the Peace Education Project and the School Links Project, but they have not led the way in the manner one might have expected of those who own schools or are deeply involved in school curriculum and management. This is reflected in the 1985 annual report of the State Education Committee of the Presbyterian Church which welcomed Irish Christianity and Looking at Churches and Worship in Ireland and other projects and made this comment:

Our Board was invited to meet officials of the Department of Education to discuss ways by which Churches, school management committees or schools themselves could support these projects. We have felt that, while we are sympathetic and supportive, it is for education authorities to pioneer developments in this particular area. (71)

The Church of Ireland handbook for transferors' representatives does not go so far as to encourage sympathy or support for efforts to encourage mutual understanding. (72) It simply ignores any idea that school managers or governors have any such concern. The DENI circular 1982/21, with its talk of every manager, board member and trustee having a responsibility for helping children to learn to understand and respect each other, is not mentioned and transferors' representatives appear to be given a narrowly denominational brief. This attitude must remind us of the conclusion reached by Gallagher and Worrall that the recommendations to the churches made by the report Violence in Ireland had fallen on deaf ears and had become nobody's business, as far as they were concerned.

In this account of the churches and educational provision in Northern Ireland we have seen how in the nineteenth century the national schools system, intended to be integrated, effectively became denominationalised. After partition a fresh attempt to integrate schools failed and the present dual system of maintained (Catholic) and controlled (Protestant) schools was born. This development of an effective modern system of education, which provided schooling from 5-16 years for all pupils and in which churches and state were partners, is a story of a great success of which the people of Northern Ireland must be proud. But it is also a story of a great failure because the churches were unable to defuse the potentially explosive situation created at partition and in the centuries of Irish history prior to partition, and today they still fail to educate the pupils in their schools for peace and reconciliation. What Eric Gallagher says of the Churches in general applies in particular to the Churches in their contribution to the provision of education.

> The Churches have preached the Gospel but for the most part would not seem to have come to terms with the need to be agents of reconciliation. Except for an occasional foray into the area of appealing for peace or denouncing this or that act of brutality, or for directing or authorising some of their committees to produce reasoned statements, no Church has really geared itself to a peace-achieving operation. They may well for good reason, or reasons that seem good to themselves,

consider that such an operation is not really their business. (73)

Sister Patricia Murray reminds us that education for peace 'means having a vision of a future world where all human beings will experience their dignity as persons and feel at home'. (74) The Churches should have this vision and express it in their schools. Unfortunately they do not, and therein lies their failure.

NOTES

1.   J.J. Campbell, 'Primary and Secondary Education' in Ulster Since 1800- second series edited by T.W. Moody, and J.C. Beckett, (BBC, London, 1957), pp. 182-3.
2.   Quoted in: Government of Northern Ireland, Ministry of Education: Public Education in Northern Ireland (HMSO, Belfast, 1964), p. 5.
3.   J.J. Campbell, op. cit. pp. 185-6.
4.   S. O'Buachalla, 'Church and State in Irish Education in this Century' (European Journal of Education Vol. 20, No. 4, 1985) p. 352.
5.   Public Education in Northern Ireland, op. cit. p. 6.
6.   W. Corkey, Episode in the history of Protestant Ulster 1923-1947 (Privately printed, n.d.).
7.   J.F. Fulton, 'Some reflections on Catholic schools in Northern Ireland' in R. Bell, G. Fowler and K. Little (eds.): Education in Great Britain and Ireland (Routledge and Kegan Paul 1973), pp. 157-65.
8.   J.F. Fulton, 'The debate on denominational and integrated schooling in Ireland, a sociological critique of the dominant Roman Catholic position 1970-1978' Research Bulletin (Institute for Study of Worship and Religious Architecture, University of Birmingham, 1979) pp. 84-101.
9.   M.B. Sutherland, 'Education in Northern Ireland' in R. Bell, G. Fowler and K. Little (eds.) op. cit. pp. 19-25.
10.   M.B. Sutherland 'Progress and Problems in Education in Northern Ireland, 1952-1982', British Journal of Educational Studies, XXX, 1, 1982, pp. 136-49.
11.   J. Darby, Conflict in Northern Ireland, (Gill and Macmillan, Dublin, 1976).
12.   D.H. Akenson, Education and Enmity, (David and Charles, 1973).

13.   S.   Farren,   Unionist-Protestant   reaction   to educational reform in Northern Ireland 1923-1930. History of Education, 14, 3, 1985, pp. 227-36.

14.   S.   Farren,   Nationalist-Catholic   reaction   to educational reform in Northern Ireland, 1920-1930. History of Education, 15, 1, 1986, pp. 19-30.

15.   D.H. Akenson, op. cit. p. 64.

16.   For an account of County schools see J. Greer, 'The County School in Northern Ireland', (The Northern Teacher, Vol. 14, No. 1, 1983), pp. 6-11.

17.   Government of Northern Ireland Local Education Authorities and Voluntary Schools, (HMSO, Belfast, 1967), p. 9.

18.   D. Murray 'Schools and Conflict' in J. Darby (ed.) Northern Ireland: The Background to the Conflict, (Appletree Press, Belfast, 1983) p. 142.

19.   Education (Northern Ireland) Act, 1978, chapter 13.

20.   E.   Graham,   'Religion   and   Education - the Constitutional Problem', Northern Ireland Legal Quarterly, Vol. 33, No. 1, p. 30, 1982. Sadly, Graham, a lecturer in law at Queen's University, Belfast, was killed by the IRA in the autumn of 1982.

21.   Ibid. p. 34.

22.   Ibid., p. 35.

23.   Education Act (Northern Ireland), 1947, chapter 3, 24, (3).

24.   The Education and Libraries (Northern Ireland) Order, 1972, Article 17, (2).

25.   Education Act (Northern Ireland), 1947, Chapter 3, 21 (5), see also J.E. Greer, and W. Brown, 'The Inspection of Religious Education in N.I. schools', (The Northern Teacher, Vol. 13, No. 4, 1981) pp. 3-7.

26.   For an account of Religious Education syllabuses see J.E. Greer, 'Ireland: Northern' in J.M. Sutcliffe (ed.) A Dictionary of Religious Education, (S.C.M. Press and Christian Education Movement, 1984), pp. 177-80.

27.   Figures have been provided by the Statistics Branch of the Department of Education for Northern Ireland.

28.   For an account of independent schools see S.E. McAuley, 'A critical examination of the Independent Christian Schools Movement with particular reference to Northern Ireland'. Dissertation submitted in partial completion of the regulations for the Honours Degree in

Social Administration of the University of Ulster, 1986.

29.   ACT-LETT, News from All Children Together, Vol. 1, No. 1, 1977.

30.   J. Darby et al., Education and Community in Northern Ireland: Schools Apart? (New University of Ulster, Coleraine, 1977), p. 27.

31.   S. Dunn, J. Darby and K. Mullan, Schools Together? Centre for the Study of Conflict, University of Ulster, (1984), p. 38.

32.   J. Darby et al., op. cit. p. 28.

33.   T.W. Moody, 'Higher Education', in Ulster since 1800 (Second Series) edited by T.W. Moody and J.C. Beckett (B.B.C. London, 1957), p. 202.

34.   E. Graham, op. cit., p. 43.

35.   Education Act (Northern Ireland), 1947, Chapters 3, 4.

36.   Report on The New Ireland Forum, The Times, November 4th, 1983.

37.   For an investigation of the cross community perceptions of Catholic and Protestant adolescents see J.E. Greer 'Viewing "the Other Side" in Northern Ireland', (Journal for the Scientific Study of Religion, Vol. 24, No. 3, 1985), pp. 275-92.

38.   D. Murray, A Comparative Study of the Culture and Character of Protestant and Catholic Primary Schools in Northern Ireland, D.Phil. Thesis, New University of Ulster, 1982.

39.   D. Murray, 'Schools and Conflict' in Darby, J. (ed.) Northern Ireland: The Background to the Conflict, (Appletree Press, Belfast, 1983), p. 144.

40.   D. Murray, op. cit., p. 241, 1982.

41.   Ibid., p. 303.

42.   Ibid., p. 255.

43.   Ibid., p. 311.

44.   Ibid., p. 291.

45.   D. Murray, op. cit., 1983, p. 145.

46.   Ibid, p. 149.

47.   D. Murray 'Educational Segregation: "Rite" or Wrong?' in P. Clancy et al., (eds) Ireland: A Sociological Profile, Institute of Public Administration, Dublin, (1986), p. 262.

48.   M. Skilbeck (1973) 'The School and Cultural Development', (The Northern Teacher, Winter issue, 1973), pp. 14-15.

49.   R.M.O. Pritchard, (1975-6) 'Reconstructionism -

Strategy for a Brighter Future?' (The Northern Teacher, Vol. 12, No. 1, 1975/6), p. 7.

50.   The Irish Hierarchy 'The Catholic School System in Northern Ireland', Submission to the New Ireland Forum, 1983, p. 4.

51.   J. Salters, Attitudes towards Society in Protestant and Roman Catholic Schoolchildren in Belfast, (Queen's University, M.Ed. thesis, 1970).

52.   J. Russell, 'The Sources of Conflict' (The Northern Teacher, Vol. 11, No. 3, 1974/5), pp. 3-11.

53.   R. Brady, Teacher guide, The Christian Way II, (Veritas, 1981, pp. 51-7).

54.   The Irish Hierarchy, op. cit. p. 9.

55.   Violence in Ireland, (Christian Journals, Belfast, and Veritas, Dublin, 1976), pp. 86-7

56.   E. Gallagher and S. Worrall, Christians in Ulster 1968-1980, O.U.P., Oxford, 1982), p. 171.

57.   E. Gallagher 'Ecumenism in Northern Ireland' in Ecumenism in Ireland: Experiments and Achievements, 1968-80, Irish Catholic Bishops' Conference and the Irish Council of Churches, 1981.

58.   I.M. Ellis (ed.) Peace and Reconciliation Projects in Ireland, (Co-operation North, Belfast and Dublin, 1984).

59.   J. Malone, 'Schools and Community Relations', (The Northern Teacher, Winter Issue, 1973) pp. 19-30.

60.   Robinson, A. The Schools Cultural Studies Project: A Contribution to Peace in Northern Ireland, Director's Report, 1981.

61.   J.E. Greer and E.P. McElhinney, Irish Christianity: Five Units for Secondary Pupils, Gill and Macmillan, 1984.

62.   J.E. Greer and E.P. McElhinney, Irish Christianity: A Guide for Teachers, Gill and Macmillan, 1984.

63.   J.E. Greer and E.P. McElhinney, 'The Project on Religion in Ireland: an Experiment in Reconstruction', (Lumen Vitae, Vol. XXXIX, No. 3, 1984), pp. 331-42.

64.   E.P. McElhinney, J.E. Harris and J.E. Greer, Classroom Discussion: an internal evaluation, Teaching Religion in Northern Ireland, 1986.

65.   Teaching Peace n.d.: a leaflet describing resources for education in peace and understanding, Irish Council of Churches, Belfast and the Irish Commission for Justice and Peace, Dublin.

66.   Religious Education and Mutual Understanding.

Joint Area Boards Religious Educational Advisers, 1984.

67.   An outline proposal is contained in S. Dunn et al. (1984) op. cit. pp. 46-8.

68.   A. Hills (1986) 'Across the great divide', The Guardian, August 26th issue.

69.   D. Murray (1982) op. cit. p. 301.

70.   Department of Education, The Improvement of community relations: The contribution of schools, (Circular 1982/21).

71.   Report of the State Education Committee (1985). Annual Reports to the General Assembly of the Presbyterian Church in Ireland, p. 224.

72.   A Church of Ireland Transferor or Representative's Handbook, Northern Ireland Committee of the General Synod Board of Education, 1986.

73.   E. Gallagher, 'Ecumenism in Northern Ireland', in Ecumenism in Ireland. Irish Catholic Bishops' Conference and the Irish Council of Churches, 1981, p. 33.

74.   P. Murray, 'Education for Peace' in Ellis, I.M. (ed.) Peace and Reconciliation Projects in Ireland, (1984, Co-operation North, Belfast and Dublin), p. 11.

Chapter Nine

THE CHURCHES AND EDUCATIONAL PROVISION IN SCOTLAND

T.A. FitzPatrick

BEGINNINGS

In Scotland in the 19th Century there was an advanced and distinctive educational tradition which could be traced back to the Reformation. ... The belief that Scottish Education was peculiarly 'democratic' and that it helped to sustain certain correspondingly democratic features of Scottish life, formed a powerful historical myth, using that word to indicate something not false, but an idealisation and distillation of a complex reality, a belief which influences history by interacting with other forces and pressures, ruling out some developments as inconsistent with the national tradition, and shaping the form in which institutions inherited from the past are allowed to change.

Thus Anderson (1) introduces his study of education in Victorian Scotland. He is not alone in seeing in the religious reforms of the 16th century the Fons et Origo of a Scottish educational system. Osborne (2) and others are happy to look no further back than to the year 1600 for a point-de-d-part.

Not everyone however shares this foreshortened view. While it is undoubtedly true that the proposals contained in the Book of Discipline of 1560 constitute the first comprehensive embodiment of the social and intellectual principles which effectively established the Scottish system and gave it its distinctive quality, it is also the case that Knox and his fellow Reformers, far from having to break fresh ground, already had a substantial basis for the structure they sought to establish, the foundations of which

160

had been laid centuries before. 'There is a historic period which ... may be taken as a commencement - the settlement of Columba in Iona. Iona may be regarded as the foundation on which the fabric of Scottish learning and education has been built.' (3)

Thereafter there arose in Scotland monasteries which followed the Irish pattern, centres of learning in which young people were able to receive some general education which nevertheless was related to the life of the Church. 'The Church was at once the great agent of progress and civilisation, and the repository of learning.' (4) There followed half a millenium in which schools grew up in association with these monasteries. By the time of the Lateran Council (1179) which decreed that each cathedral should provide a teacher 'for the local clergy and the poor', 11 dioceses had been established in Scotland. It is arguable that the concept described as 'democratic' which was to take so firm a hold on the Scottish consciousness is rooted in the teachings of the early Church, which emphasised the dignity and worth of every person.

From the Lateran Council until the Reformation - a time which equals the period from the Reformation until the present day - Scotland came more and more under European and Roman influences. Several Religious Orders came into the country, the Cistercians to Melrose, Benedictines to Kelso, Augustinians to Jedburgh and Dominicans to Glasgow, and this influx led to the revival of some old monasteries and the foundation of new ones. Gradually much of the country was mapped out into parishes. This was the period, too, which saw the rise of the burghs, many of which were associated with ecclesiastical foundations. There is documentary evidence of the rise of specific schools linked with these centres. (5)

Grammar schools developed in association with cathedrals or monasteries, and in due time in some parishes schools were set up which offered at least the rudiments of religion and literacy to a section of the population, under ecclesiastical supervision. Mackintosh lists 62 pre-Reformation schools, among them one at Abernethy founded around 1100, and others at St. Andrews in 1120, Dunfermline in 1124, Kelso in 1128, Perth in 1160, Lanark in 1180 and Linlithgow in 1187. (6) After the coming of the Dominicans about the middle of the 13th century, the content of the curriculum offered began to expand to include secular arts and sciences. The extent of Dominican influence is shown by the fact that the grammar schools in Aberdeen, Edinburgh, St. Andrews and Ayr all stood on the grounds of Dominican foundations, and that the first Congregation of Glasgow University was held in a Chapter House of the Black Friars. (7) Most of the grammar schools conducted in or near monasteries taught 'the poor' free, and the poor formed a large section of the population of mediaeval Scotland.

Burghs grew up around cathedrals, abbeys or castles. It is probable that by the end of the 15th century there was a grammar school in every town of any size in Scotland, i.e. in Edinburgh, Dundee, Aberdeen, Perth, Haddington, St. Andrews, Cupar-Fife, Montrose, Stirling, Ayr and Glasgow, and that for a long time control of these remained in the hands of ecclesiastics. 'The six Johns, when they wrote in the Book of Discipline, were building on a foundation with which they were already familiar.' (8) Scotland's first University, St. Andrews, was founded in 1411. Among its early graduates was William Turnbull, who in 1451 as Bishop of Glasgow was instrumental in establishing that city's university. Only Edinburgh University (1583) of Scotland's ancient educational institutions is a post-Reformation foundation. Their very existence implies a supporting educational sub-structure.

> When a University was being founded, the existence of a grammar school to act as a feeder was a sine qua non ... The (Glasgow) chancellor's grammar school had been in existence 'from time immemorial' ... There is no doubt that from the beginning the grammar school provided the literary training for the students, and of this we have evidence from 1452. (9)

That having been said, however, there can be no doubt that the modern Scottish educational system took its shape from the structure envisaged in the First Book of Discipline, and that the prime agency in its subsequent evolution was the Church of Scotland. There is a clear link between the ethos of Calvinism and the Scottish respect for intellectuality and individual achievement which has informed the system ever since. (10)

The Reformers advocated a system which would be open to all and which would cater for every stage from elementary school to university. Its three parts, consisting of parish schools in the rural areas, burgh schools in the towns, and the Universities, would form a structure to be established by law, supported by public funds and supervised by the authorities of Church and State. In it parish schoolmasters, teachers in burgh schools and professors in universities would all in a sense be public officials. Important elements were the notions that the system would put religious education and the elements of literacy within reach of the whole population; that poverty would be no barrier to talent; and that the school would be a place where all social classes would rub shoulders with one another. These proposals have given rise, so it is argued, to a distinctive educational tradition which attaches value to education as a general social good, advocates equality of opportunity for all pupils, and is biased in favour of academic learning and in attachment to the democratic ideal.

The ideas of the Reformers were not at once put into effect, and an educational system founded on their proposals did not come substantially into being until the 18th century, under the stimulus of the Education Act of 1696, one of the final measures passed by the last independent Scottish Parliament before the Union. The aim of this Act was to provide a school in every parish. With some amendments it remained the basis of Scottish educational legislation until 1872. (11) By the structure thus imposed, the heritors, who were the substantial landlords of each parish, were obliged to maintain a school open to boys and girls alike, and to appoint a salaried schoolmaster; funds were to be provided by a rate on landed property; day-to-day supervision was to be exercised by the local minister, and the presbyteries were to inspect the schools and test the teachers' religious and scholarly qualifications. Teachers would be expected to teach the Shorter Catechism, but their main business would be to give instruction to all on reading and writing; parish schoolmasters however were also expected to be able to teach Latin, so that they could if necessary prepare boys for University entrance. Education would be neither free nor compulsory, but in principle at least would be within reach of all.

The parish-school legislation did not apply in towns, which by custom were expected to maintain a burgh school. Only in the largest towns did these give an education of a mainly secondary type, and this under-development of secondary education encouraged what was perhaps the most distinctive feature of the Scottish system, namely a direct relationship between the parish schools and the Universities.

Functions which in other countries were the business of secondary schools were in Scotland performed by the parish schools and the Universities themselves, who assisted by admitting boys at 15 years of age, or even younger. (12)

NINETEENTH CENTURY EXPANSION

The parochial tradition was suited to a rural society, especially one where communications were difficult and the country generally poor and thinly populated; but with the advance of industrialisation and urbanisation in the 19th century the structure was no longer appropriate. Scotland's urban population rose from about one-fifth at the beginning of the century to almost three-fifths at its close, but even more significant was the enormous and rapid increase in the total population. This was most evident in the West Central Lowlands, where Glasgow's population jumped from around 77,000 to about 350,000 in the first half of the century. (13)

The stimulation to social life consequent upon increased industrial and commercial activity moved the growing urban middle class to press for change in the traditional school system, and from about 1820 onwards the burgh schools became the focus of that pressure, directed towards the improvement of secondary education. At the same time many rural and small town communities survived. These helped to preserve the democratic tradition, so that in the longer run a political settlement was reached which kept secondary education relatively open and accessible to the mass of the population. (14)

It need hardly be said that these developments did not apply to the Roman Catholic body, which towards the end of the 18th century was reaching its nadir in the post-Reformation period. By 1800 there were in Scotland some 30,000 Catholics, grouped in surviving pockets of the ancient faith in the north-east around Buchan, the principal stronghold, with smaller groups in the West Highlands and Islands and in remote parts of the south-west. No formal provision of Catholic education existed, save for two schools, one on the island of Barra and one in Invergarry. (15) By 1827 however the Catholic population had more than doubled, to 70,000; by mid-century it had more than doubled again, to 146,000, largely as a result of Irish immigration after the disastrous potato famines of the 1840s; and yet again by 1878, to 333,000. By the beginning of the 20th

164

century the total was nearing the half-million mark, by which time Catholics constituted around 10% of the whole population of Scotland. (16)

As the Catholic community grew, the provision of schools became a practical proposition in the more populous centres. (17) In 1817 a Catholic Schools Society was formed in Glasgow, and through its activities the rudiments of education began to be provided for Catholic children. 'By 1825 there were four schools giving instruction in day and evening classes to 1400 pupils whose ages ranged from 6 to 20.' (18)

State intervention in education was introduced by the Privy Council in 1833 for England and Wales, and applied to Scotland some two years later. At first it took the form of Grants-in-aid, which were paid only to approved agencies acting for the voluntary bodies concerned, mainly the Churches. The provision was extended in 1847, when Catholic interests were first represented by a Poor Schools Committee which looked after the interests of the Catholic community of the whole of the United Kingdom. (19) The Scottish Roman Catholic Hierarchy was not restored until 1878, and Scotland therefore had representation on the Poor Schools Committee. Because of the very poor level of educational provision for Catholic children in Scotland at the time - not surprising in view of the dire poverty and extraordinary social expansion which was then the lot of the Catholic community - and also because of the restrictions on building grants, few Scottish Catholic schools qualified for grants before 1872.

After 1847 schools could obtain government financial aid through the operation of the pupil-teacher system, and Catholic schools like the others benefited from this development. Besides, the enactments of 1847 encouraged religious education in state-aided schools, and in fact made it a condition for the reception of any aid at all. Thereafter, efforts to improve the Catholic sector greatly increased, notably through the work of some Religious Teaching Orders. The Sisters of Mercy and the Franciscan Sisters came to Glasgow in 1846, the Good Shepherd Sisters in 1851 and the Sisters of Charity in 1860. The Marist Brothers, the first Order of men to settle in Scotland after the Reformation, arrived in 1858, and the Jesuits and Vincentians in 1859. As a result of all efforts the Education Commission (Scotland) was able in 1866 to enumerate in the Catholic sector 16 parochial, 3 upper and 4 private schools.

Important also for the religious schools was the denominational system of inspection which gave the Bishops some control over the appointment of Inspectors of Schools. This was vital to the development of the nascent Catholic schools sector, which could not have matched the educational standards then being achieved in the more advanced and long-standing burgh and parochial schools.

With increasing State interest in education, changes were inevitable, and in the run-up to the Education Act of 1872 the power of the voluntary agencies was slowly eroded. In 1862 a Revised Code abrogated the denominational inspectorate, and recommended that aid should be based on the individual examination of pupils. In 1869 a Bill was introduced to establish a non-denominational system of education, with no provision for voluntary schools, which however was returned by the Lords and amended. In 1870 the Education Act for England and Wales was passed. Voluntary schools could continue to receive certain grants, but building grants would be withdrawn; School Boards, funded by local rates, would be empowered to build schools and compel attendance of children from 5 to 13 years of age; in these schools 'No catechism or religious formulary distinctive to any particular denomination' was to be taught. Two years later a corresponding Act for Scotland introduced compulsory education. Elected School Boards were to be set up in every parish and burgh, to provide schools, levy rates for their erection and maintenance, and enforce the attendance of all children between 5 and 13. Inspected Voluntary Schools so desiring could transfer to the School Boards, and a Scotch Education Department, located however in Westminster, would be set up to exercise control over the Boards. No grants for building purposes would be made after the passing of the Act. The continuation of use and wont in the matter of religious instruction was sanctioned, and parents would have the right to withdraw their children from any such instruction of which they disapproved. No grants would be given in respect of religious education, and the Inspectorate would have no authority to examine in religious subjects.

The Act of 1872 was part of a continuous process designed to wrest control of education away from the Churches, weaken their influence and so promote a secular society. (20) In 1861 the Church of Scotland had given up to the Universities its right to examine prospective teachers.

Candidates for teaching in the parochial schools of the

Kirk, instead of signing the Confession of Faith, as had been the practice since 1560, signed a declaration couched in negative terms whereby they promised not to teach any opinion contrary to the doctrines of the Shorter Catechism. In this declaration the teacher's own belief or commitment found no place. The Act of 1872 completed the work begun in 1861. Religious education was not compulsory. It made explicit the principle that religious and secular teaching were things apart, and that the former should occupy second place and not interfere with or interrupt secular instruction. The conscience clause was the only consideration paid to religious teaching, which the Act neither commended nor forbade, but merely permitted the continuance of the custom. (21)

After 1872 therefore the position in Scotland differed from the English case, where denominational instruction was expressly excluded from maintained schools. In Scotland the Boards were free to approve of Catholic or Protestant instruction in the schools; but in practice a Protestant system of education was created.

With negligible exceptions the School Boards of Scotland resolved to provide Religious Instruction in all their schools at the cost of the rates in a form acceptable to the Protestant Churches generally, but refused to make corresponding provision for the Catholic minority among their ratepayers. (22)

Scottish Catholics petitioned against the Bill, unsuccessfully, and along with other voluntary bodies, notably the Episcopalians, decided not to transfer their schools into the national system.

1872–1918

For almost half a century after 1872 the Catholic schools remained outside the mainstream of national educational development. This was a period during which the newly-established Scotch Education Department transformed the educational scene, particularly at primary level. The curriculum expanded to include the physical, emotional and vocational aptitudes of pupils. By the turn of the century a well-articulated system was emerging, based on a primary sector catering for children up to about 12 years of age, with a post-primary structure, entry into which was controlled by a qualifying examination, organised into three fairly clearly defined sectors, Supplementary, Higher Grade and Secondary - Supplementary for children who expected to leave school without seeking further education; Higher Grade for those planning to remain at school until 16; and Secondary for those preparing for the Leaving Certificate and University entrance examinations at about 18 years of age. (23)

Because the first aim of the 1872 Act had been to establish a national system of primary education, all forms of higher education were at first allowed to continue as before. Secondary education remained largely the province of schools outside the public system; some, the private schools, were modelled on the English Public Schools and some were endowed. The former included institutions such as Loretto, Glenalmond and Glasgow Academy, the latter such well-known 'Hospitals' as George Heriot's, Hutcheson's and Morgan Academy. These, originally intended to provide the rudiments of education for indigent children, in the course of time had become secondary schools for middle-class pupils. The Endowed Institutions Acts of 1878 and 1882 (24) dealt in all with 158 of these schools. 72 were closed at once, 47 were transferred to School Boards and 34 were left with their own governing bodies. The 1882 Act made inspection compulsory in these 'Higher Class' schools.

The raising of primary standards inevitably had repercussions at secondary level. In 1892 the SED disbursed sixty thousand pounds for the extension of secondary schooling. 35 Secondary Education Committees were established, one for each county, one for each of the five large burghs and one for the very large parish of Govan. This marked the beginning of a move towards larger administrative units. Around this time too there was a rapid expansion in the provision of secondary education for girls. St. Leonard's, the first Scottish boarding institution for girls on the lines of an English Public School, opened in 1877, offering full secondary courses in all the main academic subjects except science. Day schools for girls also appeared. In Glasgow the Franciscan Sisters and the Sisters of Mercy had opened convent schools with some boarders about the middle of the century, and other private schools followed - Westbourne in 1877 and Notre Dame in 1894. 1892 was the year in which the Scottish Universities opened their doors to women. (25) A crucial development was the institution of a Leaving Certificate under the control of the Universities. The examiners may have had a twofold objective - to give secondary schools an idea of the standards required for entry into the Colleges, and provide an objective for girls who were debarred by virtue of their sex from entry into University courses.

These developments are indicative of the growing strength of the national system, and of the increasing control being exercised by the central authority. They also reflect the changes which had taken place during the 19th century in Scottish society, which as a result of increased affluence had become markedly divided along class lines. The bourgeoisie, 'revitalised by the renascent Calvinism at the Disruption of 1843' (26) now held positions of influence, but continued to share with the mass of the people an ideology based on free enterprise on the one hand and on the traditional Scottish virtues of respectability and self-help on the other. By the end of the century however that solidarity was wearing thin, and a slow movement towards a limited radicalism began. In response to the demands of an expanding and increasingly wealthy middle class, a largely separate system of secondary education had emerged, to which the number of academies, high schools, proprietary boarding schools and so on bears witness. A defining characteristic of the bourgeois lifestyle was the drive for social and material advancement, and one main route was through education to one of the professions, notably, in Scotland, the law. This required an educational system which would provide continuity from primary through secondary to the university stage; and, as a corollary, a tight selection process at the crucial points of entry.

Clearly the system which did emerge to meet these criteria maintained to some degree the distinctive Scottish tradition, as exemplified in the parochial schools system. There too, continuity from primary school to university was seen to be essential; and the acceptance by all sections of society of the 'free enterprise' approach might be seen to be a function of what has been described as its 'democratic' character, albeit in this context the term 'democratic' requires to be specially defined. (27) Despite the fact that the aims being pursued belong to 'this' rather than to 'the other' world, the cement which provided the cohesion of society derived from a common religious outlook as much as from growing affluence. Indeed, in the Scottish mind these were interdependent.

Perhaps not surprisingly, the Catholic secondary system developed in a somewhat similar fashion. The first prospectus of St. Aloysius College in Glasgow, dated September 12, 1859, states that 'the object of this College is to afford a Religious, Literary and Commercial Education to the Catholic Middle Classes of Glasgow'; (28) and the Marist Brothers, who could be said to have shown a 'preferential option for the poor' when they took over the direction of the parochial school of St. Mungo's parish in the Townhead district of Glasgow, at the same time opened a fee-paying school which operated in the first instance in the Brothers' own house. Likewise the Franciscan Sisters opened their doors to boarding pupils at a very early stage in their school's history, and the Sisters of Mercy also aimed to provide a 'Middle Class' school. (29) Nevertheless the targets being set by the Scotch Education Department were still beyond the range of the nascent Catholic sector. Its first priority had to be the provision of primary schools adequately staffed by fully qualified teachers before it could hope to expand at the post-primary level; and therein lay a fundamental dilemma, in that upgrading and expansion at secondary level was essential if a well-qualified teaching force were to be produced. The majority of Catholic teachers at that time were products of the pupil-teacher system, or were untrained. A minority only had received College training at Hammersmith or Mount Pleasant in Liverpool. In 1894 a Training College for women was opened at Dowanhill in Glasgow under the direction of the Sisters of Notre Dame, and this brought some relief. Progress however was slow, and if the Orders themselves had not borne the burden of Catholic secondary education at this time the system could not have survived. By 1913-14 in the whole of Scotland, 'of 99,400 Catholic pupils, 9,000 were taught in supplementary classes, but only 1,278 were receiving higher education. These were taught in 14 schools, 12 of which were conducted by Religious Orders.' (30)

From the Slough of Despond into which they were in danger of sinking, the Catholic schools were rescued by the Education (Scotland) Act of 1918, passed ten days after the Armistice which ended the Great War. The Act set up a framework for progressive advances at every level of the formal educational structure. Into this the Catholic schools were transferred, and with its support the system flourished, particularly its secondary sector.

Central to the Act was a concept of secondary education for all, to be provided at differing levels suited to the capacities of pupils. Supplementary classes would disappear, and secondary schools would be classified as Junior or Senior Secondary. The county was substituted for the parish as the administrative unit, and authority in education was given to 'Ad Hoc' committees elected for the purpose. Their powers and their relation to the Department, renamed Scottish, were established. The Act laid down a minimum salary scale for teachers, and made it lawful for an Authority to give financial assistance to young people qualified to attend a secondary school, university, training college or central institution. In many of its aspects it extended to the secondary sector 'the distinctive Scottish tradition' in education, including adherence to the concept of secondary education for all, and the provision of financial aid whereby the continuity of educational progress from the primary stage through to university could become a reality for a greatly expanded proportion of the population. However the definition of secondary education written into the Act, namely that it should be open to all those who showed themselves 'fit to profit from it' made it easy to absorb the pre-existing private secondary sector into the State system, and for it to preserve therein its selective character.

For the denominational schools the major issue was whether or not to transfer into the national system. The religious character of any school transferring could be preserved (a) by the continuance of use and wont in the matter of Religious Instruction, (b) by the denominational body having a measure of control over school staff through the right to approve of any candidate 'as to religious belief and character', and (c) through the appointment of a Religious Supervisor for each school. Teachers would of course have to meet the State's requirements in the matter of professional qualifications, and their appointment would be in the hands of the Ad Hoc Authority. (31)

The Act made possible the evolution of a system of denominational education under State control, supported by public funds. The Catholic Authorities decided to transfer their schools, and when the Act became effective from May 1919, 226 Catholic as well as other voluntary schools came into the control of the Ad Hoc authorities.

A new era of opportunity opened for the Catholic

community. There was an immediate upsurge in the demand for secondary places in Catholic schools, and a perceptible if temporary improvement in the vital area of supply of teachers. However, if the potential benefits of the Act were to be fully realised, a conglomeration of massive and interlocking problems had to be resolved. The Catholic schools, the vast majority of which were primary establishments, were in many cases grossly overcrowded, ill-equipped and antiquated; there was a shortage of well-qualified teachers, particularly of men; and in addition there was a gross imbalance between the primary and secondary sectors. In effect a new educational system had to be established, one which would conform to the requirements of the State and at the same time satisfy the Church in respect of the religious education now to be given at the secondary level to a much wider spectrum of the Catholic community than ever before. Although within that community there was a growing awareness of the material and social benefits that could follow from the raising of its educational standards, and of the fact that the financial provisions of the Act brought these aspirations closer to realisation, there remained a distrust in some quarters of State control in the educational system, seen by some as the harbinger of a secular and materialist society. The concept of education that held sway in the Catholic community was essentially that of the parochial schools, in which the spiritual formation of children lay at the heart of the exercise. Whatever its merits - and they were many - that system had suffered many distortions, partly through the practice of early leaving endemic in the community and partly as a consequence of material deprivation and lack of resources. It was designed for pupils who would leave school without any preparation for higher education. The schools were an essential part of the parochial structure, and through them instruction in the Catholic faith designed to last for a lifetime was given once and for all. What was taught was not expected to give their alumni the equipment for reflection on the meaning of their religion. Within the system there had developed a special relationship between the clergy and the teachers, whose moral authority to teach derived essentially from the ecclesiastical authority which, pre-1918 was also the paymaster. The parochial schools, therefore, offered a totally inappropriate model for the kind of secondary institutions which could be expected to develop after 1918.

172

BETWEEN THE WARS

The educational revolution set in train by the 1918 Act had to take place during a period of stress in the economic, political and cultural life of the nation. Throughout the 'twenties there was never less than 14% of the insured labour force of Scotland out of work, and in the West Central belt in the 'thirties unemployment averaged 25%. (32) World trade virtually collapsed, and with it went what was left of the prosperity of the Clyde docks and ship-building industry. Because of the high concentration of the Catholic community in the industrial areas and its disproportionate representation in the ranks of the unskilled and semi-skilled, the impact on it was particularly severe. The shared sufferings of 1914-18 had helped to unite the nation, but in spite of problems of poverty, unemployment, housing and education the Irish question remained the most emotive political issue in the west of Scotland, and sectarian tension was never very far below the surface. After 1922, deep disillusionment with the Liberal Party developed, and in the aftermath of war the influence of the Labour Party steadily increased.

Formally, Scotland was still a religious country. The Church of Scotland Act of 1921 permitted an established Presbyterian Church to remain, and in the inter-war period the Presbyterian Church was more united than it had been for over a century. (33) By 1930 the Church of Scotland claimed about 26% of the population as its adherents, while Catholics with 11.2% now slightly outnumbered Anglicans in the country. In subsequent years the decline in membership of the Kirk continued, while the Catholic Church steadily grew in strength. The extent to which this change in the religious balance was affected by emigration is difficult to gauge. From 1871 till 1976 net emigration from Scotland exceeded 2 million, reaching a peak in the 1921-30 decade. It has been estimated that the Great Depression resulted in some 128,000 Catholics leaving Scotland for America, Canada, Australia and New Zealand. (34)

According to educational historian James Scotland, the 1918 Act was comparatively unsuccessful, on account of the hard times which followed the Great War. Financial stringency meant that many praiseworthy schemes did not come into effect. The Act provided for the raising of the school leaving age to 15, but in the upshot this did not happen until after World War 2. Similarly the proposal for compulsory further education was a casualty, and free secondary education was not introduced until 1945. (35) Harvie charts a relative decline in Scottish education.

> Although Scotland continued to receive about 14% of British educational expenditure, her relative performance declined. She had 18% of secondary pupils in 1913, 15.3% in 1938 ... The day of the all-ability local school was ending ... the new secondary schools ... divided into 'Junior' and 'Senior' secondaries ... created a serious social gulf in the larger towns ... The number of full-time students at the four universities fell from 10,400 in 1924 to 9,900 in 1937, while English universities registered a rise of nearly 19%. (36)

Paradoxically the Catholic community gained in status during the same period. 'The period between 1918 and 1939 was one of growing activity in all directions ... a new degree of social mobility was being experienced by the Scottish-Irish community.' (37) The financial incentives of the 1918 Act for pupils to remain at school brought a sustained rise in the rolls of Catholic secondary schools. Parents were relieved of a financial burden they had carried since 1872, and teachers found themselves in an undreamt-of position of security and affluence. A new spirit of confidence began to grow in the community. Whereas in 1920 the number of Catholic students in all faculties of Glasgow University was very small, by 1930 numbers had increased to such an extent that a chaplaincy for Catholic students was set up and the first post-Reformation Catholic chaplain installed. Altogether a new dimension of social life was brought to the Catholic community, and while it could perhaps be said that something of the ghetto mentality lingered on, there was manifested also a consciousness of the richess and power of its Christian heritage. The conviction grew that the community had a specific contribution to make to the cultural and social life of society at large.

Overall, clerical dominance of Catholic social life diminished. It was in this context that there emerged a new political ideal. Distributism was an attempt to find a middle way between Liberalism and Socialism, both of which had come under the strictures of the Vatican. It looked for a solution to contemporary problems of political and economic organisation which would reject equally the fashionable alternatives of Capitalism or Communism. It stood for the individual in an increasingly collectivist age, insisted that industrial organisation should be based on principles of profit-sharing and co-ownership, and was an early advocate of industrial democracy half a century ahead of its time. (38)

The revolutionary changes in education which were to mark the post-war scene were foreshadowed in the immediate pre-war period. Early in 1939 a revised Day Schools (Scotland) Code abandoned the practice of defining secondary education in terms of types of school, substituting instead the natural divisions of an educational course. 'At last secondary education was recognised (as) ... a stage in the schooling of every child, not a particular kind of education to be provided for some but not for all.' Progress was interrupted by the war, but 'even before the guns were silent, Parliament had passed an Education Act transcending in its scope even the enlightened provisions of the new Code.' (39) The Education Acts of 1944 in England and 1945 in Scotland made education compulsory for children between the ages of 5 and 15; all were required to have a number of years of secondary education in their school career, to be provided out of the public purse; and education authorities had to make provision for the further education of those who had left school.

AFTER 1945

The most urgent problem arising from the 1945 Act, in the view of the Advisory Council on Education, was 'to evolve a new type of schooling that will suit the many as well as the old fitted the few.' (40)

Easier said than done. The raising of the leaving age added 60,000 pupils to the school roll, with a consequent demand for increased accommodation and for teachers, who were already in short supply. Difficulties were aggravated by the dramatic rise in the birth-rate that characterised the immediate post-war years, the effects of which continued to be felt in the secondary schools into the 1960s. An Emergency Training Scheme to recruit and train additional teachers was set up as a stop-gap measure, but for the longer term a more radical solution was needed. The Regulations for the Training of Teachers were revised and three new Colleges of Education were instituted; but before the benefits could be felt in the schools, unrest in the teaching profession had grown to such a pitch that in 1961 teachers in Glasgow took strike action for the first time in their history.

Beyond the logistical problems lay difficulties of an altogether different order. The traditional Scottish course of secondary education, designed to provide a broad general education with a distinct academic bias, could not meet the needs of the great majority of the new secondary population brought into being by the Act. Conservatism among teachers trained in the traditional manner offered a substantial obstacle to the changes that were required. Furthermore, teachers had long followed a conventional curriculum regarded as appropriate for the bulk of their pupils. Now every subject was put under scrutiny. No subject-matter or method however hallowed by experience was exempt, and elements which for decades had occupied an unchallenged place at the core of the curriculum began to crumble and disappear. The classical tradition went into decline, with the result that the capacity of pupils to benefit from their Christian heritage in the languages and literatures of European civilisation was substantially diminished. In the sciences, vast and rapid change was initiated by an upheaval in the teaching of Mathematics, and continued by the introduction of a wide range of concepts needed to enable pupils to move confidently in the world outside the school. The frequent re-drawing of the world map added to the demands on educators. Over all, with the spread of television it became evident that the model of the school as a sheltered environment quietly discharging its function unaffected by the moral and spiritual ferment of the outside world no longer applied.

Living standards rose. The dependence of the nation at war on its pool of female labour continued in time of peace, and womenfolk were able more and more to take up gainful employment outside the home. A new lifestyle emerged. The experience of the post-war generations differed so radically from that of their parents that communication became more than ordinarily difficult, and the gap between them widened to their mutual loss and bewilderment. Adolescent affluence, unscrupulously exploited, and fuelled by a revolution in modes of communication, stimulated youthful sub-cultures, while parental authority, vitiated by the uncertainties of a society no longer sure of its moral bases, was no match for the conformism demanded by the peer-groups of the young. The result was a permissive society, marked by confusion rather than by any positive understanding of what could or could not be permitted.

From the mid-'fifties onwards, the consequences of this moral decadence became more apparent in the forms of broken homes, vandalism, single-parent families and increases in divorce, abortion, drug addiction, crime, alcoholism and mental illness. These symptoms were manifest mainly in the major cities, where the social continuum was further distorted by the advent of numbers of Commonwealth citizens from parts of Africa, the Indian sub-continent and the West Indies, drawn in to meet the demand for labour in those more menial but necessary tasks no longer attractive to the increasingly affluent indigenous population. It was noticeable that the acceptance of Commonwealth immigrants into Scotland took place with a relative absence of the kind of disturbances that affected conurbations elsewhere in the United Kingdom. This may have been due in part at least to the accessibility of good quality education, particularly at secondary level, to immigrants able to cope with language difficulties, as well as to its egalitarian and democratic tradition.

For a quarter of a century after 1945 the Scottish system of secondary education was reorganised along lines consonant with the Act of 1945. A far-reaching and often agonising revolution took place, in which the accepted functions and objectives of secondary education were subjected to fierce reappraisal in the light of two fundamental principles – one, that it is a natural right of all children to receive an education so ordered as to allow them to develop to their full potential; and two, 'that a liberal state ... will seek to ensure through education that the creative energies of a new generation are used to direct the forces of change along lines which are socially desirable and in general accord with the nation's traditions and practices'. (41) A number of organisational patterns were tried out, and in the upshot the all-through six-year comprehensive school became the most generally accepted model.

Within this general approach were hidden a number of assumptions about the nature of secondary education, and also about the roles of the school and its power to influence the lives of its pupils and the society in which they live. Whereas natural justice would concede the right of all children to an appropriate education, it does not necessarily follow that this would be best achieved by sending all of them to the same kind of school. The problems of educating physically or mentally handicapped children, or the very highly gifted, point up this issue in the most obvious way. Then, there is enshrined in the second principle an assumption that the rights of the state are superior to those of the parents, and for that matter to those of the children themselves. There is a further assumption of a real consistency between the principles themselves, and yet concealed within them are those conflicting forces which tend to polarise all educational effort, towards the development of the individual person on the one hand and towards meeting the needs of the community on the other.

In the application of these principles, selection procedures for the transfer of pupils from the primary to the secondary stage were abolished; the curriculum expanded the better to meet the needs of individuals, and the pastoral role of the school in social education was more fully recognised.

These developments tended to exacerbate the tensions being felt throughout the secondary sector. More teachers were required to meet the enlarged spectrum of curricular demand, and the skills and attitudes demanded of them shifted from emphasis on mastery of subject content to the development of those capacities which ease inter-personal relationships. It is probably true to say that the Catholic sector adjusted more easily to the changed pattern than did the national system as a whole. Catering as it had done in the inter-war period for only a small proportion of the Catholic population, its clamant need had been for a major expansion at secondary level, in schools whose character would be determined by their commitment to Christian outlook and practice rather than by their organisational structure. Besides, it seemed to many in the Catholic sector that the demands of social justice were more likely to be met by a comprehensive rather than by a selective system, and that the latter ran the risk of supporting divisions within the community which would conflict with the Christian view of the value of every individual.

For secondary education in general a range of problems arose from the need constantly to revise curricula in response to pressures outside the school. The practical consequences of meeting within a short space of time the challenges presented, for example, by the 'new' mathematics, the re-structuring of the sciences, or the introduction of new subjects at school level were in themselves enormous. They were compounded by the decline of the classical tradition, for which no complete substitute has yet emerged, with implications for the teaching of language and literature and for religious education, and also by a revolution in physical, aesthetic and technical education as well as in the general area of communications. In addition the Catholic sector had to adjust to another kind of pressure that had its source in the insights of the Second Vatican Council (42) and which had profound implications for all aspects of Christian education.

A crisis in moral and religious education occurred throughout the whole system, reaching its height towards the end of the 'sixties. Reflecting the malaise of contemporary society, it evoked radical responses from both civil and ecclesiastical authorities. The first initiative took the form of a revision of the management structure in schools, which improved the career prospects and therefore the morale of teachers and at the same time met the needs of management in comprehensive schools, some of which had grown to mammoth proportions; the second was the introduction of a system of Guidance, defined as 'the taking of that personal interest in pupils which makes it possible to assist them in making choices or decisions.' (43) The Catholic sector supported these initiatives, particularly in fostering the guidance innovation, and in addition the ecclesiastical authorities adopted a policy of appointing full-time chaplains to secondary schools. A new category of Organiser of Religious Education was created in some dioceses, followed by the setting up of catechetical centres through which the work of chaplains could be co-ordinated and resources made available to teachers. At another level, a Catholic Education Commission was instituted to advise the Scottish Bishops in all educational matters, and the training in religious education of Catholic teachers was overhauled at both pre- and in-service levels. (44)

The changed view of secondary education promulgated by the 1945 Act brought closer collaboration between Church and State in the educational field. In the opinion of the Advisory Council

the chief end of education is to foster the full and harmonious development of individuals ... in accordance with their own nature ... and their nature is social ... one of the major functions of the school is to pass on the moral and social inheritance and to direct ... young people towards the good life. (45)

179

The view of the Vatican Council was that

> every man ... has an inalienable right to an education
> corresponding to his proper destiny and suited to his
> native talents, his sex, his cultural background and his
> ancestral heritage ... young people have a right to be
> encouraged to weigh moral values with an upright
> conscience and to embrace them by personal choice.
> (46)

Church and State agree in recognising the dignity of
persons, the social dimension in education, the importance
of moral values and the cultural inheritance of groups.

Nevertheless this philosophical convergence leaves a
number of profound questions unanswered. Are Church and
State agreed on what constitutes the good life? Does the
development of the individual ever conflict with the
common good? Is it possible to have full regard for 'cultural
background and ancestral heritage' in a multi-cultural
society? Is the 'full and harmonious development of
individuals' a practical possibility in a modern urbanised
society? When can it be said to have been achieved in any
particular instance? Who can give it? By education do
Church and State mean the same thing? Is schooling the
same thing as education? Can an education given under
compulsion ever be a true education? Who will teach the
teachers? and by what authority may one individual claim
the right or power to influence the spiritual and moral
formation of another? Can a teacher properly serve two
masters? These questions, and there must be many more to
be asked in the rapidly changing environment of modern
global society, point to the spiritual and intellectual tension
which faces the western world.

Whatever answers might be given, it is clear that the
schools by themselves cannot bring about the changes in
direction and attitudes that are required. A concentrated
effort by the whole community, involving political, social
and spiritual leaders as well as educators will be needed; but
it is also clear that a special burden will rest on the
teaching body, especially those involved at the secondary
level, if any practical outcome is to be achieved.
Traditionally the Catholic schools accepted responsibility
for the moral and spiritual guidance of their pupils, as well
as for their intellectual development, and in so doing they
benefited from the presence of religious Teaching Orders

who have now almost completely vanished from the schools. The task was lightened also by the unity of the Catholic community in belief and practice. Before World War Two, the State schools were in somewhat similar case, in that the Home-School-Church triangle was still in position, although beginning to be shaken at each of its vertices. As the educational service expanded in the 'fifties and 'sixties, strains began to show in both sectors. Religious education was a major casualty. It is fair to say that it was a demographic factor, namely a dramatic decrease in the birth-rate sustained over a long period, which brought a measure of stability to the situation.

Throughout the period of expansion the Catholic sector in particular strove to maintain concern for moral and religious formation. This concern was shared by many throughout the national system, but what emerged was rather a recognition of the problem than a solution to it. One submission to the Millar Committee (47) noted that 'No society has yet solved the problem of how to teach morality without religion', which suggests that that is precisely what the originator of this comment would have liked to do, while the Headmasters Association of Scotland felt that 'Moral education without reference to religious belief would be arid, depersonalised and ineffective.' Both statements are lukewarm in their approach to religion and to the importance and necessity of religious education in schools.

Something more profound and galvanising is needed; and whatever that something is, the business of conveying its import to the rising generations will rest on the shoulders of the teachers, who will have to be convinced before they can become committed. The key to advance therefore lies in the intellectual, spiritual and moral formation of the teachers themselves.

In spite of the fact that teacher-pupil ratios are more favourable - from the teacher's point of view - now more than ever, there is widespread disaffection among the teaching body. This seems to stem partly from the general lack of appreciation, as the teachers see it, of the difficulties of the educator's task, partly from frustration arising from their subjugation to the directives of several masters, and partly from the erosion of confidence in traditional approaches to the spiritual and moral formation of young people. The motivation which formerly derived from the generally accepted 'Protestant Ethic' no longer applies in a community in which high levels of unemployment especially among the young look likely to persist for years to come. Added now are the complex issues of education in a society evidently pluralistic.

In the past, Scotland experienced ethnic and cultural division, most obviously through the presence of a Gaelic-speaking minority. Diversification came with the advent of Irish, Jewish, Italian, Polish and other immigrants, and now in these latter days of others of Asian, African or West Indian origin, among them adherents of a broad spectrum of world religions. Educational policies designed to respond to the rights and needs of this multi-cultural and multi-racial population as yet have not emerged, either from regional or national government sources, although it is fair to say that at both levels serious analysis of the problems involved has already begun. In that process the present ethos of Scottish education, seen in some quarters as monocultural and ethnocentric, is being subjected to criticism of a kind not previously encountered. The issues involved point up the interdependence of secular and religious education in a special way, and demand the involvement of the Churches in the search for solutions of universal application. In this pursuit they may have to face up to a dilemma which affects not only the Christian Churches but indeed most world religions, namely the incompatibility between traditional beliefs and the modern scientific outlook. (48)

Within the traditions of the two educational masters, civil and religious, lie elements of a viable educational philosophy for a multi-cultural society, based on deep respect for the individuality and integrity of all human beings, and dedication to the pursuit of justice. There remains the practical matter of how these traditional attitudes are to be preserved and made effective. Perhaps the profound observation of Stravinksy in another context is worth noting:

> The word TRADITION now seems to mean 'that which resembles the past' ... In fact traditional work may not resemble the past at all, and especially not the immediate past ... Tradition ... is not simply handed down fathers to sons, but undergoes a life process: it is born, grows, matures, declines and is reborn. (49)

Scotland

NOTES AND REFERENCES

1.   R.D. Anderson, Education and Opportunity in Victorian Scotland. (Oxford, 1983).
2.   G.S. Osborne: Scottish and English Schools. (Pittsburgh, 1967).
3.   J. Grant: History of Burgh Schools in Scotland. (Collins, 1876), p. 2.
4.   Ibid: See also F. McGrath: Education in Ancient and Mediaeval Ireland. (Dublin, 1979).
5.   M. Mackintosh: Education in Scotland Yesterday and Today. (Gibson, 1962), p. 20.
6.   J. Scotland: History of Scottish Education (Vol. 1) p. 7.
7.   Ibid.
8.   J. Durkan: William Turnbull, Bishop of Glasgow. (Scot. Cath. Historical Committee, 1951), p. 45.
9.   R.D. Anderson: Op. cit. pp. 24-6.
10.   Ibid., p. 3.
11.   Ibid.
12.   Ibid.
13.   J.E. Handley: The Irish in Scotland, 1798-1845. (Cork, 1943).
14.   Anderson, op. cit., p. 6.
15.   Bro. Kenneth: Catholic Schools in Scotland 1872-1972. (C.E.C., 1972).
16.   J. Darragh: 'Catholic Population of Scotland' in Innes Review, IV I (1953), p. 58.
17.   Bro. Kenneth, op. cit.
18.   Handley, op. cit., pp. 279-81.
19.   Sister M. Skinnider: Catholic Elementary Education in Glasgow 1818-1918. (S.C.R.E. No. 54).
20.   T.A. FitzPatrick: Catholic Secondary Education in S.W. Scotland 1922-1972. (Ph.D. thesis University of Glasgow, 1983), p. 103.
21.   T.A. FitzPatrick: Catholic Secondary Education in S.W. Scotland before 1972. (Aberdeen University Press, 1986), p.31.
22.   J. Struthers: SED/ED/14/129.
23.   N.A. Wade: Post-primary Education in the Primary Schools of Scotland 1872-1936. (S.C.R.E.), p. 105.
24.   J. Scotland: Op. cit. Vol. 2, p. 64.
25.   T.A. FitzPatrick, Op. cit. p. 171.
26.   H.M. Paterson: 'Incubus and Ideology', in Scottish Culture and Scottish Education, p. 201.

27.   M. Mackintosh: Op. cit. p. 9.
28.   T.A. FitzPatrick: Op. cit. p. 28.
29.   Ibid., p. 26.
30.   Ibid., p. 32.
31.   Ibid., pp. 43 et seq.
32.   S.G. Checkland: The Upas Tree (University of Glasgow Press, 1976), p. 35.
33.   C. Harvie: No Gods and Precious Few Heroes. (Arnold, 1981), p. 82.
34.   T.A. FitzPatrick: Op. cit. p. 85.
35.   J. Scotland: Op. cit. Vol. 2, p. 6.
36.   C. Harvie: Op. cit. p. 78.
37.   A. Ross: Innes Review, XXIX, p. 43.
38.   T.A. FitzPatrick, Ibid., p. 88.
39.   Advisory Council Report on Secondary Education. Cmnd 7005.
40.   Ibid.
41.   Ibid.
42.   Gravissimum Educationis. Declaration on Christian Education. Documents of Vatican II pp. 639-40.
43.   Guidance in Scottish Secondary Schools (HMSO), pp. 3-4.
44.   T.A. FitzPatrick: Op. cit. p. 141.
45.   Report on Secondary Education, 48, 50, 90.
46.   Declaration on Christian Education. Loc. cit.
47.   Moral and Religious Education in Scottish Schools, 3.11.
48.   R. Pannikar, Tablet, 18 Oct. 1986.
49.   I. Stravinsky, in Shawe-Taylor, D. and Buckle, R. Stravinsky.

Chapter Ten

THE CHURCHES AND EDUCATIONAL PROVISION IN ENGLAND AND WALES

Bernadette O'Keeffe (1)

In 1986 Church of England and Roman Catholic schools accounted for almost one third (32.6%) of all maintained schools in England. Church of England schools provided for 17.5% of all primary school pupils. At secondary level, 4.4% of pupils attended a Church of England secondary school. Roman Catholic schools provided for 9.7% of all primary pupils and 9.0% of secondary school pupils. The comparative statistics for Wales show that Church of Wales schools accounted for 7% of primary pupils and for 1.9% of secondary pupils. Roman Catholic schools in Wales accounted for 5.8% of primary pupils and for 5.4% of secondary pupils.

While the State has a major share in providing a national system of education today, the initiatives during the early eighteenth and nineteenth centuries came from the Churches in establishing schools for children of the poor who had no opportunity to receive even the most elementary education. It can be said that the first stone was laid for developing a partnership between the Churches and the State in 1833 when the State made its first contribution towards education by assisting the National Society and the Foreign Schools Society with a grant of £20,000 to help maintain their schools. When, in 1847, the Roman Catholic Church established the Catholic Poor School Committee, it too became entitled to receive grants from the State to help maintain existing Catholic schools.

Throughout the nineteenth century the Churches set about establishing a national network of schools through the efforts of voluntary societies. When, in 1870, the Forster Act was passed, the State adopted a strategy of building

Board schools in areas where the Churches had been unable to make adequate provision for the growing school population. The Act was designed 'to complete the voluntary system and to fill up gaps'. In addition, it gave schools founded by Church voluntary bodies financial support by means of grants-in-aid. Thus, these schools became an integral part of the national system of education.

The Education Act of 1902 established what has come to be known as the 'dual system'. The Act required the new Local Education Authorities to assist voluntary schools from the rates. When the 1936 Education Act was passed the partnership between the Churches and the State had developed to the point where Local Education Authorities were empowered to extend financial aid to the Churches to assist financially in the building of voluntary secondary schools. Thus, as the State schools developed, Church schools developed along parallel lines and, after the 1944 Education Act, they became the voluntary schools of today.

As a result of the 1944 Education Act which envisaged the provision of education for all children, voluntary schools could choose one of two statuses: that of an 'aided' or that of a 'controlled' status. This choice was designed to enable voluntary-aided schools to retain their existing independence provided they could satisfy the Minister that, within a limited period of time, they could meet half the expenditure required to bring the school up to a specified standard, and to carry out necessary external repairs to the school buildings. Those voluntary schools that were unable to find the capital sum needed to bring their premises up to standard, or were prepared to accept reduced independence, opted for a 'controlled' status and, in doing so, were freed from all financial responsibility.

Voluntary aided schools required the financial support of the Churches. The Churches were responsible for meeting half the cost of any improvements, external repairs, and the provision of new school buildings. The initial grant aid of 50% was subsequently raised to 75% in 1959; 80% in 1967; 85% in 1975. The Local Education Authority became responsible for all other running expenses of aided schools.

The day-to-day control of an aided school became the responsibility of the Governors. The Churches retained the right to appoint two thirds of the school Governors, the remaining one third being appointed by the Local Education Authority. Governors of an aided school had the responsibility for pupil admissions and staff appointments.

The Act also enabled aided schools to provide denominational religious instruction and denominational worship.

A voluntary <u>controlled</u> status resulted in reduced rights for the Churches but, at the same time, they were freed of all financial obligation. The Churches retained the right to appoint one third of the governing body while the Local Education Authority appointed the remaining two thirds of Governors. Denominational religious instruction was to be given not more than twice a week to those children whose parents requested it. Any other religious instruction had to be based on an 'agreed syllabus'. The Local Education Authority became responsible for financing the voluntary controlled school, its admission policies and staff appointments, except in the case of 'reserved teachers' who were appointed for the purposes of giving religious instruction.

The 1944 Act also provided for the <u>special agreement</u> school. These schools emerged from proposals made by the State and the Churches under the 1936 Act, whereby the Local Education Authority contributed from 50/70% of the initial cost. Special agreement schools, though giving the voluntary bodies less control of the appointment of teachers than aided status allows, are conducted in substantially the same way as voluntary aided schools.

Where the Churches had decided to register their schools as voluntary aided they faced massive financial commitments. Writing about the concerns of Catholics, Beck remarked:

> The passing of the 1944 Education Act was accepted by the majority of Catholics in this country with mixed feelings, varying from alarm at the financial implications of the new measures to a certain morose dismay that we were not sufficiently organised to make the best use of additional opportunities offered by new legislation and the new conceptions of education. (2)

There were considerable differences of opinion between the Churches and each responded very differently to the possibilities offered by the Education Act. The Church of England adopted a strategy of allowing decisions to be made on a local level concerning the status of voluntary schools. The net result of decisions taken at that time is that, in 1986, over half the schools provided by the Church of

England in England and Wales have a controlled status.

The Roman Catholic Church was not prepared to surrender its relative independence for the comparative security of financial support from the State. The Roman Catholic Church adopted a unified national policy of voluntary aided schools. (Earlier agreements resulted in a small number of special agreement schools.) In addition, extensive building programmes were undertaken to provide a whole system of secondary schools.

Today these features of the 'dual system' allow for diversity of response from both Churches and from the State as partners in education.

The overall purpose of the 1944 Education Act was to construct a viable system of education in which the Churches became partners in a publicly funded system. The construction of this system was, however, fraught with difficulties characterised by divisive religious rivalry, sectional interests, and general antagonism. Murphy referred to the 1944 settlement as 'the end of "passionate intensity"' after decades of opposing forces. (3) As Fletcher points out:

> It was a point of arrival and a point of departure in the fullest sense - accomplishing a consolidation of all that had been achieved in the making of the educational system so far, but also reconstructing this in the light of the new addition of a comprehensive system of education. (4)

Having traced briefly the historical background of the developing partnership between the Churches and the State in public education we now turn to look at policy statements relating to Church of England and Roman Catholic schools.

When, in 1811, the Church of England (acting under the auspices of the National Society) established schools for the children of the poor, it identified twin objectives for these schools. First, it set out to provide children with numeracy and literacy skills in preparation for work. Second, it sought to provide education in the Christian religion in all its schools. The first annual report of the National Society states its intentions for schools in the following words: 'to educate the poor in suitable learning, works of industry and the principles of the Christian religion, according to the established Church'. (5)

The principle of the unity of education was at the heart

of these endeavours and there was, therefore, to be no divorce between religious and secular education. Today, policy statements of the Church of England continue to stress the Church's general concern in education as being to educate the nation's children, and its domestic concern as being to provide for the needs of the worshipping community.

In a recent Green Paper for discussion published by the National Society there is confirmation that the undifferentiated twin aims historically applied to its schools by the Church of England must continue to be applied today. In discussing a strategy for Church schools with voluntary aided status, the paper states that 'both service to the general education of the nation and education in the Christian faith are important aspirations'.

Beales, writing about the pioneers of Catholic education for children of the poor links its origins with a body of Catholic laity and clergy who established charities in London 'for educating and (later) clothing and (still later) apprenticing poor Catholic children, and this at least sixteen years before the penal laws were relaxed at all.' The total of the charity schools that resulted was, by 1800, only 10, most of them in London. These became the Catholic Charities in 1811 and the Catholic Poor School Committee in 1847. (6)

The aims of the Catholic Church in providing Catholic schools were clearly stated. The policy of the bishops was to provide a Catholic school for every Catholic child to be taught by Catholic teachers. The schools were established on a parochial basis, and closely linked with the life of the parish. They were instructed to accept only Catholic children and to employ only Catholic teachers. The Church's educational policy was supported by a code of Canon Law: 'Catholic children must not attend non-Catholic schools, neutral or mixed schools, those opened to non-Catholics. (7)

However, the thinking of the Roman Catholic Church has moderated somewhat. The Declaration on Christian Education issued by the Vatican Council in 1965 called on the Roman Catholic Church to share with others the challenges that have arisen from the changes in modern society:

so it is that, while the Catholic school fittingly adjusts itself to the circumstances of advancing times, it is educating students to promote effectively the welfare of an earthly city, and preparing them to serve the advancement of the reign of God. (8)

Traditionally, the Catholic Church pursued isolationist policies in the field of education. In a recent report on Catholic education, the Bishops of England and Wales describe the approach of Catholic education as tending towards 'separatism' from its secular counterpart. They note that the 1944 Education Act did much to foster a sense of common interests, and a stronger concept of partnership. (9)

In 1978 the Bishops' Conference in England and Wales provided a statement on Catholic education confirming their full commitment to education which they saw as 'the unswerving policy of the bishops to provide and preserve Catholic schools whenever possible'. The bishops spoke of Catholic schools as an extension of the home, providing 'a positive service to the wider community in teaching and upholding our Christian standards and values'. In addition, 'they reminded parents to educate their children in the knowledge and practice of "the Christian faith".' (10)

It is clear from the policy statements reviewed here that there is a fundamental difference in how the Church of England and the Roman Catholic Church see their provision for education and the role of their schools. The Church of England continues to stress its general and domestic concerns, its responsibility to the nation's children and its responsibility to the worshipping community. The Roman Catholic Church sees its schools primarily in domestic terms, providing for the needs of the Catholic community.

While policy statements provide important insights into the role of the Church schools, they may nevertheless give only a partial picture. It is necessary to consider the question of how far policy statements are reflected in practice. One major area is that of pupil admissions. Drawing on research carried out in a sample of Church of England schools, we turn now to examine to what extent the twin aims outlined above are reflected in admissions policies in Church of England schools with a voluntary aided status. (11) It is through voluntary aided schools that the Churches exercise their greater influence. While variations do exist in admissions policies for these schools they are, however, weighted in favour of a religious criterion: that of religious affiliation. The majority of schools in the study gave first priority to children from Anglican homes and second priority to children from other Christian traditions. Other criteria listed include medical factors, special needs, and requests for church school education. As a means of assessing the extent of Church connections, some schools require applications to be supported by a letter from the Minister or Vicar whilst others interview pupils and, in some cases, parents as well.

In popular, over-subscribed schools admissions criteria are strictly adhered to. When the research was undertaken 82% of the secondary schools were over-subscribed. In 44% of Church secondary schools all places were filled with children from Christian backgrounds. In two of these schools all the pupils were members of the Anglican church. The remaining schools admitted pupils belonging to other Christian traditions, other faiths, and some of no professed faith.

While admissions policies for Church primary schools with a voluntary aided status have some of the same features as secondary schools regarding their admissions policies, they differ in important ways. A smaller percentage of Church primary schools stress Church-related criteria as a top priority for admission. This partly explains the finding that only 10% of the sample filled all their school places with children from Christian backgrounds. Primary schools place a greater emphasis on serving the needs of the local community.

One of the effects of the 1944 Education Act is that the all-age elementary parish schools in many instances became primary schools, and this has led to greater Church of England provision at primary level. The disproportionate number of primary to secondary schools has resulted in a situation where parents who want their children to attend a Church of England school are frequently presented with the fact that the Church of England voluntary aided secondary school is predominantly, if not entirely, Christian in its intake.

The historic aims of Church schools are called into question when popular over-subscribed schools restrict their pupil intake to Christians only. The message is Christian education for Christian children. In this sense the schools become 'denominational' because service to the nation is no longer the first priority. The priority is towards the worshipping community. Admissions policies that exclude sections of the community inform those sections that Church schools do not 'belong' to them. Some of the implications and effects of these policies will be developed later.

191

Today Catholics continue to see their primary responsibility as being to the Catholic community and, therefore, give priority to Catholic children in their school admissions policies. The Catholic Church has pursued a programme for planning and building sufficient numbers of Catholic schools to provide for Catholic children. Statistics on baptisms are used to forecast the likely figures for future school places. This has not always been possible to project accurately and, from time to time, there has been a shortage of school places. In the late 1950s and for the first half of 1960 there was considerable demand for places in Catholic schools. After 1966 the baptismal rate fell to below 130,000, and continued to decline into the 1970s. (12)

Statistics collected by the Catholic Education Council also revealed that one third of all baptised Catholic children were not attending Catholic schools. How far this was due to unsatisfied demand for school places and how far to the fact that non-practising Catholic parents do not want a Catholic school education for their children is difficult to quantify. (13)

Nevertheless, it would be wrong to assume that Catholic schools are concerned only with Catholic pupils. Statistics compiled by the Catholic Education Council show an increase in the number of non-Catholic pupils entering Catholic primary and secondary schools. In 1970 non-Catholic pupils accounted for 1% of all pupils in Catholic primary schools and for 2.1% of all secondary school pupils. In 1986 the percentage of non-Catholic pupils had risen to 9.4% in primary schools and 8.7% in secondary schools. (14)

The features of the dual system outlined earlier facilitate Church schools with a voluntary aided status to retain their relative independence. In addition to the right of governing bodies to develop their own admissions policies, another major area of autonomy concerns staff appointments. This independence enables voluntary aided schools to fulfil the provisions of their Trust Deeds and thus perpetuate the wishes of their founders.

It was evident from discussions with school Governors and Head Teachers that governing bodies of Church of England voluntary aided schools appoint teachers who are equipped to continue the tradition entrusted to them. In general, Governors appointing staff give first preference to applicants who are members of the Church of England and, secondly, to those who belong to other Christian traditions. In many instances, when Governors advertise a teaching post they specify 'a communicant of the Church of England preferred' or 'member of the Christian faith preferred'.

Head teachers provided details of the percentage of teachers who are members of the Church of England. In just under half of the secondary schools in the study, over 50% of the teachers were members of the Church of England. Ths figure is slightly higher in primary schools, at 51%.

In 71% of secondary and 81% of primary schools Christian teachers accounted for over 70% of the teaching staff. There was a noticeable absence of any significant number of teachers who were members of other faiths, and one of the main reasons given for this is that schools receive very few applications from teachers of other faiths. Clearly, the stipulation 'Christian preferred' acts as a sufficient deterrent.

Primary Head teachers discussed a major difficulty envisaged in the employment of teachers of other faiths - religious education. They expressed their doubts as to whether Hindu, Sikh or Muslim teachers would have either the knowledge or the wish to teach the Christian faith which, in the majority of primary schools, is integrated.

The Catholic church has also pursued a policy of appointing Catholic teachers to teach in its schools. The percentage of non-Catholic teachers in primary schools has remained constant during the 1970s and 1980s, accounting for almost 9% of all teachers. Over the same period there has been a gradual increase at secondary school level. The percentage of non-Catholic teachers teaching in Catholic schools has increased from 26.4% in 1960 to 36.5% in 1986. (15)

The Bishops of England and Wales in a memorandum on the appointment of teachers stress that the Catholic school must be staffed with 'good and well qualified Catholic teachers'. Where there is no suitable Catholic applicant then 'Governors and Managers' will naturally seek to appoint a teacher whose faith and quality and standards come nearest to the ideal'. Furthermore, the memorandum highlights the important role of teachers in so far as the faith, practice and standards of teachers all play an important part in preserving the Catholic character and environment of schools. (16) Considerable emphasis is placed on the relationship between faith and living:

> The extent to which the Christian message is transmitted through education depends to a very great

193

extent on the teachers. The integration of culture and
faith is mediated by the other integration of faith and
life in the person of the teacher. (17)

It is evident that the underlying policies adopted in staff
appointment procedures attempt to maintain continuity with
the Trust Deed by giving expression to the Founders'
intentions in the preservation of the Christian character and
distinctive ethos of Catholic schools.

The independence afforded to voluntary aided Church
schools enables them not only to fulfil the provisions of
their Trust Deeds but also to develop distinctiveness in the
curriculum and ethos of the school.

The concept of ethos is indeed complex, and notoriously
difficult to define. Rutter talks of ethos as 'the values,
attitudes and behaviours which are characteristic of the
school as a whole'. (18) Dancy, using the shorter Oxford
Dictionary's definition of 'ethos' as 'the prevalent' tone or
sentiment of a people or community', observes that the word
'prevalent' implies that 'the tone is more powerful than
other competing "tones" and will go on being so ...'
Furthermore, he points out that the word 'prevalent' 'holds
sway in the sense of being shared by either most members of
the community or the most powerful or influential or some
weighted mixture of the two'. (19)

The distinctive elements of a Church school ethos
originate from at least four different sources. First, the
Trust Deeds; second, the expectations of parents; third, the
pupil intake which varies according to the schools' selective
admissions policies; fourth, the characteristics of the
institution itself, the formal structure of the school, its
policies, procedures, curriculum and staff.

We have seen that one way in which Church schools
endeavour to fulfil the wishes of their Founders is by means
of their staffing policies and pupil admissions policies. The
expectations of parents also have an impact on the school
ethos. A sample of 139 parents provided reasons for
choosing a Church of England secondary school for their
children. (20) Their replies fell into four main categories:
those wanting a Church of England education; those wanting
a Christian education; those who had chosen the school for
its academic standing; those who had chosen it for its good
discipline. Other reasons given for choice of school (under
7% in each category) included proximity to the school, its
size, whether it was mixed or single-sex, whether the child

had friends at the school, its caring atmosphere, parental links with the school, primary school links, and 'nice kids'. Choices made on the grounds of Church of England or Christian education offered by the school accounted for just under half (48%), making this the top priority of parents in selecting a Church school. Its academic reputation was a main consideration for just under one quarter (23%) of the sample. Good discipline was the main concern of 7% of parents.

Parents attached a great deal of importance to religious education in Church schools. Their expectations in this regard can be grouped under four main headings: a commitment to Christianity; a knowledge and understanding of Christianity; a broad religious understanding, including different world religions; the school's commitment to provide moral standards for living. Parents who hoped their children would be committed Christians (27%) expected the school to 'strengthen Christian commitment' and to make Christianity 'a way of life and not something that is confined to Church attendance'.

For these parents the role of the Church school had an important part to play in maintaining and reinforcing home values and in encouraging pupils to attend Church and Sunday school and participate as members of the worshipping community. The Church school offers an opportunity for developing the links between home, school and Church. As the authors of the Durham Report point out, 'The Church school can become an educational community which brings into explicit focus the shared assumptions of parents and teachers, the link with the Church exemplifying the beliefs about the purpose of education which underlie the school's activity'. (21)

Religious education was seen by parents (29%) as making a major contribution towards enabling children to increase their knowledge and understanding of Christianity. While some parents did not claim to be committed Christians, they nevertheless hoped that the Church school would contribute to the child's understanding of Christianity. A small percentage of parents (16%) looked to religious education classes to provide a broad understanding of religion which would not be confined to the study of Christianity.

Just under a third (31%) of parents looked to the Church school, and in particular to religious education classes, to provide moral standards for living. Replies suggest that, for parents, religious and moral education are closely allied: 'R.E. will give him basic standards for life' ... 'I hope it teaches her respect for others'. By implication, parents consider the content of religious education will be concerned with morality. They spoke of a lack of morality in society and in general looked to religious education to fill this moral vacuum. Clearly parents have clear expectations and perceptions of Church schools and ascribe to them distinctive features which cannot be guaranteed in County schools.

The secular concepts of education exist within temporal and finite boundaries. Their variety of purposes range from Hirst's and Peters' models of education as initiation into 'worthwhile areas of knowledge' to aims of education which include moral purposes: as Mary Warnock notes: '... education is concerned with the right raising of children, and with the provision for them of a good future and here if anywhere moral values appear to be inextricably involved.' (22) Their ultimate meaning revolves around man's relationship with man. Church schools on the other hand take as their starting point their relationship with God. For the Christian, man's relationship with man is mediated through the primary relationship of man to God. The significance of the religious experience as seen through secular eyes is generally in relationship to perceived cultural manifestations. On the other hand, the religious dimension for Christians is significant in its own right because it points to the actuality of that reality which exists outside time and space.

Flynn stresses the unique contribution of Catholic education in the following way:

> The unique contribution of the Catholic school to any system of education is that it stands as a community of faith founded on belief in God and faith in Jesus Christ, and is involved in full personal development of youth. As well as basing its values, ideals and practices on the gospel, it provides opportunities for its members to celebrate their faith in Jesus Christ. (23)

Through school worship Church schools affirm uncompromisingly the religious and spiritual dimension to life. They provide a context where all children can become aware of a spiritual interpretation to life. Schools are frequently involved in liturgical activity as a worshipping community. Through acts of worship the Church school can be 'a beacon signalling the transcendent, by the development of awe, mystery and wonder'. (24)

For the majority of primary head teachers, their school is an extension of the local parish church and their school activities reflect this link. The local incumbent is a frequent visitor and he is seen as having an important pastoral role in the school. Secondary head teachers see their schools as active Christian communities and maintain strong links with the local church. Church visits find a regular place in the life of the school, holy communion services are held regularly, and the clergy frequently lead school assemblies.

In schools where the pupil intake is entirely Christian, Christian worship, sacramental life and participation in Church services fits the Durham Report's definition that 'Christian worship ... refers to offerings in corporate gatherings of prayer and praise to God through Christ.' (25) There is a recognition of shared values, beliefs and a unity of intention. Worship in church schools articulates a system of meaning and prevents it being lost from sight. An extra dimension is added to school worship where the pupil population is diverse. School worship for non-Christian children provides the opportunity for them to understand Christian worship in an informed way through religious language, concepts and symbols.

Church schools provide the opportunity for children to become aware of their Christian heritage and to understand the Christian faith and values through school worship and religious education. The contribution of Christian staff and the close links with the local Church are key factors in enabling this to happen. The cornerstone of religious education is the Christian faith. It starts from 'the fundamental acceptance of the "givenness" of the Christian religion as a fact of history and, so Christians believe, as God's self-disclosure within history. From this starting point, pupils are encouraged to explore Christian beliefs and practices of other religions, critically, openly and creatively, in ways suitable to their personal development.' (26)

The facility for governors to appoint Christian staff to teach religious education provides the opportunity for Christian nurture. A context is thus provided in which Christian nurture is offered by Christians 'in order to strengthen the Christian faith and develop Christian character.'

Church schools continue to exist in the 1980s because they are valued for a number of reasons: they provide a continuing Christian presence within the maintained sector of education and they are a visible expression of the Churches' involvement in education; they are also an expression of the religious freedom of parents; they provide within the maintained sector an element of variety by supplying a religious and specifically Christian option to secular humanistic values. Finally, Church schools have particular responsibilities with regard to school worship and religious education.

The distinctive features of Church schools are also sources of tension for the Churches in their contribution to education. There are increasing pressures being brought to bear. Today Church schools are at the centre of a wide-ranging debate. Their place in the dual system is being increasingly challenged by educationalists, pressure groups, and politicians. Among Christians there is a lack of consensus concerning the role of Church schools. Educational cuts, falling pupil rolls, school closures and amalgamations have brought many aspects of the dual system into much sharper focus. The presence of a culturally and religiously diverse pupil population raises important questions and challenges for Church schools. This is particularly the case where schools are situated in areas where different cultural and religious groups form the majority.

The Socialist Education Association (an affiliated educational Association of the Labour Party) in a discussion document raises a number of fundamental questions concerning the Churches' provision in education. (27) This document reflects the variety of views to be found in the Labour Party ranging from those who support and value Church schools to those who oppose them on the basis of their divisive nature. Ways are advocated in which the 'existing problems' can be solved without dismantling the dual system. They suggest that, in view of the State's heavy financial commitment to the voluntary sector, the State should have a greater degree of control over it, in an attempt to establish the 'principles of harmonisation of all schools'. They see the 'principle of harmonisation' as fundamental in protecting the rights and freedoms of minorities. The Labour Party in its policy statement of 1982, Labour's Programme, appears to have endorsed the SEAs commitment to 'seek greater harmonisation between voluntary and County schools.' Furthermore, they pledge a total commitment to the comprehensive principle which they believe is undermined by the differential power accorded to voluntary aided schools. For example, the different admissions policies and procedures operating unilaterally for County and Church schools with a voluntary aided status are seen as working against the realisation of either principle. They summarise what they see as the current situation in the following way:

> In simple terms, it is that the continuing existence of the segregated voluntary school sector will frustrate the achievement of the truly comprehensive system. It means that equal educational opportunity of all children will always be threatened, and that there can never be genuine parity between schools.

One area which receives a great deal of attention in the discussion document and in a second discussion document published in 1986 is admissions procedures adopted by Church voluntary aided schools. (28) These are seen as a means of preserving 'a privileged selective intake' and a skewed social or racial intake as well. They contend that, despite comprehensive reorganisation, some Church schools abuse their power and continue to select on the basis of academic attainment.

Where Church schools use a single criterion - religious affiliation - this criterion can produce inequalities resulting from differential access and a preponderance of white middle-class children. This is particularly the case in popular, over-subscribed schools which operate large catchment areas. Research carried out in a sample of London schools found that, while in principle Church schools observe the banding arrangements devised by the Local Education Authority to ensure a pupil intake across the ability range, a significant number of Church of England schools attracted a higher percentage of high attaining pupils when their pupil intake was compared with the local County schools. Furthermore, the research found that in the same sample of London schools a higher percentage of County schools had a higher proportion of pupils receiving free school meals; a higher percentage of pupils from single-parent families (although the percentage differences are small); a smaller percentage of pupils with parents in non-manual occupations, and a higher incidence of parental unemployment than their matching Church of England secondary schools. (29)

These research findings lend support to those who accuse Church schools of 'hidden selection'. There is no doubt that there are attendant difficulties where social discrimination accompanies a religious criterion. This has led to a greater recognition of 'institutionalised selection'. In other words, forms of selection may result in ways that are unintended but the very procedures employed will ensure that they do. Therefore, the disparity between 'intent' and 'effect' becomes very marked.

In the SEA's second discussion document it is argued that the way the dual system operates in providing different rights for voluntary schools, 'institutionalised' selection by attainment, class and race in the comprehensive system, it risks making all these forms of selection harder to eradicate than would be the case if all schools and all individuals had equal rights within the educational system. The question is then posed: 'Are so many differences worth the risk, especially when most have nothing to do with religious freedom?' (30)

A narrowly interpreted 'denominational' policy has also been attacked on the basis of racial discrimination. A group of Christians committed to racial justice voiced their concern over admissions policies in the following way:

> Some Church schools emphasise their Christian basis and thereby ... exclude, in practice, children of other faiths, thus becoming unrepresentative of their neighbourhood. Thus in some areas Church schools have become white enclaves using religion as a means of discrimination. (31)

A joint working party which was set up to look at Catholic education in a multi-cultural society makes a similar point when it notes that an 'all white' Catholic school in a racially mixed neighbourhood 'can, unless great care is taken to foster links with the local community, stand out as a symbol of racial segregation contradicting the good work which may be attempted within the school itself'. (32)

When statistics relating to the ethnic backgrounds of pupils in a sample of Church of England primary and secondary schools with a voluntary aided status were compared with local County schools, important facts emerged. (33) First, there was seen to be a greater degree

200

of diversity in County schools in terms of the nationalities of their pupils. In other words, at secondary level, ethnic minorities were, in the main, concentrated in County schools. The degree of concentration was greatest among Asian pupils. However, the backgrounds of pupils in Church primary schools were more likely to resemble the diversity to be found in County schools.

Second, in many areas, admissions policies for Church secondary schools had the effect of restricting the possibility of cultural and religious diversity within the school environment. While these schools made provision for the diversity among Christian children from different cultural and racial groups, there was less opportunity for children to interact with children belonging to different faiths and cultures. Consequently, the educational experience for these pupils was, in this respect, narrow.

Third, popular over-subscribed schools operating a narrowly interpreted 'denominational' policy in areas where there was a large concentration of Asian families had the effect of reinforcing divisions along religious lines within the local community. Headteachers spoke of their obligation to the large number of parishes who supported them financially. This invariably resulted in accommodating 'one's own flock' at the expense of children living in the local neighbourhood. This constitutes a pattern of provision which antagonises those who had hoped for 'equality of opportunity', 'parity of prestige', 'ease of transfer', and a pupil intake which would reflect a cross-section of groups and social classes in the neighbourhood which the comprehensive principle sought to achieve.

The criticisms levelled at Church schools and their admissions policies raise serious challenges for Church provision in education. Can Church schools be sure that 'institutional selection' is not resulting in 'institutional racism'? This question is particularly relevant in view of the fact that Gibson, among others, believes schools are '... one of the pillars of institutional racism'. (34) The Swann Report defined 'institutional racism' as

> ... the way in which a range of long-established systems, practices and procedures both within education and the wider society were originally conceived and devised to meet the needs and aspirations of a relatively homogeneous society, and can now be seen not only to fail to take account of the

> multi-racial nature of Britian today but may also ignore
> or even actively work against the interests of ethnic
> minority groups. (35)

The Swann Report draws attention to the fact that practices
which were well intentioned, not racist in 'intent', can in a
changed context be seen as 'racist in effect' by denying
ethnic minority groups the 'equality of access' to the range
of opportunities available to the majority community.

A complex inter-relationship exists between the
Churches' provision in education through their Church
schools, the requests of Christian parents, and the need to
respond to religious and cultural diversity. They are
challenged to find ways of adjusting to changing
circumstances and at the same time continuing to maintain
the central Christian tradition which the Church schools
have contributed to education.

In a report on the Catholic Church's commitment to the
black community, an advisory group stresses that the
Catholic Church's mission should be one that provides 'a
multi-ethnic/multi-racial education'. Central to this
approach are the concepts of rights, responsibilities and
social justice. It believes that there are certain factors that
inhibit Catholic schools from adopting such an approach to
education. For the advisory group, a major area of concern
is 'the endemic nature of institutional and individual racism'.
It points to 'the widespread resistance to a genuine
reflection on and lack of willingness to change rules,
practices, procedures and attitudes that may discriminate
against certain children.' (36) Furthermore, it stresses the
urgent need for Catholic schools to address themselves to
the area of admissions policies in an attempt to eliminate
racist practices. The recommendation is that a multi-ethnic
and anti-racist approach must inform decisions when
formulating policies for Catholic schools on admissions
criteria.

Church schools with a predominantly 'white' Christian
pupil intake face particular challenges in preparing pupils
for a religiously and culturally diverse society. Where
Church schools are seen as an extension of the local Church
there is an inherent danger that these schools will not see
the need of introducing positive aspects of the various
cultures and religions which reflect contemporary society
into the school curriculum. Research evidence available
shows that while many church schools have developed

multicultural programmes a significant number of schools continue to see these programmes as irrelevant. (37) These schools do not acknowledge or accept the view that multicultural education, including anti-racist teaching, have relevance for all children and that these programmes have the potential to provide an appropriate education for a multicultural society. Governors and head teachers believe that a Christian ethos is sufficient. The emphasis is on continuity and the preservation and transmission of the dominant values of the school culture. It is not to deny that schools will not be concerned with maintaining continuity but it is the balance that is struck between continuity and responding to change that is crucial.

A homogeneous school culture which varies little in values and practices is more likely to strive for continuity. But where the school population is heterogeneous in the sense of being ethnically, religiously and culturally diverse, schools must choose between making provisions for those variations or ignore them. A traditional curriculum with a mono-cultural, ethnocentric character does not reflect the reality of British society today.

The Church of England as a partner in education affirms that, in seeking to take seriously its mission to the nation's children, it must uphold a system of education in which all children are helped to realise their full potential and, at the same time, all pupils are prepared for life in a culturally and religiously diverse society. The Archbishop of Canterbury's recent Commission on urban priority areas emphasises that all schools have an important role to play 'in encouraging personal attainment and building up self-esteem'. (38)

The Commission identified serious grievances amongst Asian parents concerning religious assemblies, uniform, physical education and dietary needs. It pointed out that Church schools are now challenged 'to find ways in which Muslim parents can feel their children are receiving an education sensitive to their traditions and their faith'.

The problem for Church schools, today, therefore, is twofold. On the one hand there remains the need to bear witness to a Christian way of life and, on the other hand, there is the question of how to respond positively to the challenges presented to Christians by pupils of other faiths. Furthermore, there is a pressing need for those involved in Church school education to explore theologically the question of school worship in a community of mixed beliefs.

The Church school is uniquely placed to treat the faith dimension seriously. It provides an acknowledgement of 'other worldly' values and concerns; it allows for a religious option as a basis for living.

NOTES

1.   In this chapter I concentrate on the provision of the Church of England, the Church in Wales, and the Roman Catholic Church in the maintained sector.

2.   G.A. Beck: Progress Report, p. 12. The Catholic Education Handbook, 1962/63 edition, Catholic Education Council.

3.   J. Murphy: Church, State and Schools in Britain: 1800-1970 (Routledge 1971).

4.   R. Fletcher: Education in Society: the Promethean Fire, A New Essay in the Sociology of Education, (London, Penguin Books, 1984), p. 188.

5.   National Society Annual Report 1811/1813, p. 7.

6.   A.C.F Beales 'The Tradition in English Catholic Education, (The Catholic Education Handbook 1962/63 edition, Catholic Education Council), p. 9.

7.   P. Jebb, (ed.), Religious Education, (Darton, Longman and Todd, 1968), p. 268.

8.   W.M. Abbot (ed.): The Documents of Vatican II, Declaration on Christian Education, (Gravissimum Educationis), Introduction p. 646.

9.   D. Konstant: Signposts and Homecomings, A Report to the Bishops of England and Wales, (St Paul Publications, 1981), p. 3.

10.   Statement by the Bishops of England and Wales on Catholic Schools, 1978.

11.   Permission to use my research findings has been granted by Falmer Press. The research findings were first published in Faith, Culture and the Dual System: a Comparative Study of Church and County Schools, (Falmer Press, 1986).

12.   R. Cunningham, Tablet, 1975.

13.   R. Cunningham, The Present and Future Situation in Catholic Education - some aspects.

14.   Statistics provided by the Catholic Education Council.

15.   Ibid.

16.   Memorandum on the Appointment of Teachers,

the Bishops of England and Wales Education Commission, 11 February, 1986.

17.   Signposts and Homecomings, p. 104.

18.   M. Rutter et al. have made an important contribution in this area. Fifteen Thousand Hours: Secondary Schools and their effects on Children, (Open Books, 1971).

19.   J. Dancy, Perspectives 1 in RUTTER Research p. 29-37, (University of Exeter School of Education).

20.   O'Keeffe, op. cit. pp. 59-66.

21.   The Fourth R, The Durham Report on Religious Education, (National Society, SPCK, 1972), p. 114.

22.   Mary Warnock, Schools of Thought, (Faber, 1977), p. 41.

23.   M. Flynn Some Catholic Schools in Action, (Sydney, Catholic Education Office, 1975).

24.   A Future in Partnership, (National Society, 1984), p. 71.

25.   The Fourth R, op. cit., p. 134.

26.   The Work of the London Diocesan Board of Education, December, 1975, p. 14.

27.   The Dual System of Voluntary and County Schools, Socialist Education Association, 1983.

28.   All Faiths in All Schools, Socialist Education Association, 1986.

29.   Faith, Culture and the Dual System, Chapter 4.

30.   Op. cit., p. 14.

31.   Issues in the 80s, Christians against Racism and Facism.

32.   Learning from Diversity, p. 29. Report of the Working Party on Catholic Education in a Multi-racial, Multi-cultural Society, (Catholic Media Office, 1984).

33.   B. O'Keeffe, op. cit. pp. 40-4.

34.   A. Gibson, The Unequal Struggle, (London Centre for Educational Studies, 1986).

35.   Education for All, p. 28, The Report of the Committee of Inquiry into the Education of Children from Ethnic Minority Groups (The Swann Report), Cmnd 9453, London, HMSO 1985.

36.   With you in Spirit? p. 20, the Report of Cardinal Hume's Advisory Group on the Catholic Church's Commitment to the Black Community, 1986.

37.   B. O'Keeffe, op. cit. See also Learning from Diversity.

38.   Faith in the City. The Report of the Archbishop

of Canterbury's Commission on Urban Priority Areas. (Church House Publishing, 1985), p. 294.

Chapter Eleven

THE CHURCHES AND THE TRAINING OF TEACHERS IN ENGLAND AND WALES

John D. Gay

INTRODUCTION

An assessment of the churches' role in teacher education in England and Wales must take full account of the different principles motivating the three main religious groups in this area of education. The Roman Catholic Church has always been clear that the task of its colleges is to train Catholic teachers for Catholic schools and this principle has dominated its thought and actions. The Church of England, as the established church, has operated on a more complex and changing set of interrelated principles and motives which have been closely linked with the national development of an educational system in this country. The Free Churches, or as they were known at the height of the controversies over who should control education in the nineteenth and early twentieth centuries the Nonconformists, have never really wished to provide their own educational system, but saw the development of a state system as the most effective way of countering the power of the Church of England.

HISTORICAL DEVELOPMENT

The English teacher training college, in the form we have come to know it, was very much a product of the 1840s. Before that however, there were systematic attempts by the church to undertake some form of training for teachers in its schools. The Society for Promoting Christian Knowledge (SPCK), founded in 1699, established a number of charity schools to provide religious instruction among the poor. Lack of funds in the eighteenth century forced SPCK to abandon the foundation of a training college, but it kept alive the idea of teacher training which was done largely through the apprenticeship method.

The beginning of systematic teacher training in the early nineteenth century was closely allied to the establishment and development of the school system (see Dent, 1977). This system had two main initiators, Joseph Lancaster who attempted to develop a non-denominational style and Andrew Bell who was determined to create an Anglican pattern of education. As early as 1808 Bell was concerned with the training of teachers and established a scheme for a school at Bishop Auckland which would have attached to it a training centre. Bell's scheme attracted much support and culminated in 1811 in the foundation of the 'National Society for Promoting the Education of the Poor in the Principles of the Established Church throughout England and Wales'. At Bell's insistence the National Society adopted a serious line on teacher training and in 1812 opened a school in central London, Baldwin's Gardens, which became the Society's main training centre. Other centres were developed in schools throughout the country. Prior to the 1840s there were no training colleges in the accepted sense of the word and most teachers were trained in centres attached to schools.

The 1840s saw the development of new residential institutions for the training of teachers. Although these institutions took over many of the features of the old centres, they were founded on the residential principle and so were in practice the first of the teacher training colleges. The reasons behind the development of the colleges were complex but the fundamental cause was a political battle between the Church of England and the state for control over the emerging educational system. If the schools were to be largely church schools the training of teachers should similarly be in the hands of the church. Indeed, this link between the control of the school system and the provision of teachers was one that dominated much of the subsequent discussion on who should be responsible for teacher training. In the 1830s the issue had been decided, at least for the immediate future, largely in favour of the Church of England. Plans discussed during the 1830s for the foundation of a state controlled 'normal school' for training elementary school teachers were eventually shelved in 1839. Both the Anglicans and the Nonconformists objected to the role that the other was likely to play in the area of religious instruction in the normal school. As a result of this the government agreed that a grant of £10,000 which had been voted in 1835 for government of normal schools should be divided equally between the two voluntary societies, the National Society and the British and Foreign Society. This placed on both societies an urgent obligation to provide for teacher training.

Whether the churches were right to prevent the state from entering the educational arena is a debatable point. Rose (1981, p. 1) argues that although the churches were wanting fundamental educational reform in the 1830s their divisions and antagonisms stemmed progress and resulted in the dual system of schools and colleges which he describes as 'a precarious, uneasy and divisive arrangement'. Bitter antagonism there certainly was between the Nonconformists and the established church over the provision of education but there was no guarantee that the government's scheme for a unitary national system would have been any more successful than the dual provision arrangements. Following defeat of the government on this issue it was then up to the churches to take initiatives in the teacher training area. The Archbishop of Canterbury, as President of the National Society, exhorted diocesan bishops to investigate ways in which training institutions might be established under the direction of the church for training teachers to teach children of the poor in church schools in the dioceses.

The Secretary of the Committee of Council on Education, Sir James Kay-Shuttleworth as he was later known, on the collapse of the normal school plan, obtained government grants for the building of colleges. With a friend, he founded his own college at St John's in Battersea in 1840. Although the influence of Kay-Shuttleworth on the future pattern of teacher training is generally acknowledged, Dent (1977) argues that his reputation for creating the residential pattern as the norm is perhaps over-emphasised. Dent believes that Kay-Shuttleworth's main influence was to underscore the primacy of religion in the whole training and teaching enterprise.

Kay-Shuttleworth shared both the Nonconformist and the Church of England view that elementary teachers were first and foremost Christian missionaries. Of the other influences on the emerging college scene the greatest importance undoubtedly attaches to St Mark's, Chelsea,

founded in 1841 and which was led for twenty-three years by
the Reverend Derwent Coleridge, son of the famous poet.
Although he shared many of Kay-Shuttleworth's ideals,
including the need for a tight Christian residential
community, he believed that the prime aim was to develop
cultured all-rounders:

> to this end Coleridge erected for his college elegant
> buildings, and created within them a community life
> designed to inspire and refine. Central to his concept
> was the college chapel whose architectural beauty he
> enhanced by services of great dignity embellished by
> music of rare quality (Dent, 1977, p. 14).

Foundation dates of colleges always need treating with
some caution for it is often not clear at what precise point
in time a college came into being and there is considerable
difference of interpretation in some of the histories.
McGregor (1981, p. 28) lists Chester and Exeter as the first
two Anglican colleges with Chichester coming a close third
'all three date their foundations from 1839 and actually
began to train teachers early in 1840. Durham, York and
Winchester have all been credited with 1839 foundation
dates, but did not admit students until late 1840 or early
1841'. By 1945 the Minutes of the Committee of Council list
twenty Anglican colleges in England and Wales which had
admitted their first students. There was also the Home and
Colonial and Borough Road colleges and the National
Society's central school in Westminster. By 1850 the number
had reached around thirty (1) the overwhelming majority of
which were associated with the Church of England. The
Roman Catholics had opened the College of St Mary's in
Hammersmith in 1850. In the same year the Methodists
opened Westminster College and two years later the two
small Congregational colleges in London merged to form
Homerton College in Cambridge which was supported also
by the Baptists and Wesleyans. All but Llandaff were
residential and apart from Borough Road and the Home and
Colonial none exceeded seventy-five in student numbers.

Prior to the 1870 Education Act many Roman Catholics
were trained in Church of England colleges and also Church
of England students were admitted to British Society
training institutions. Thus although institutions had clear
denominational labels, in practice the student bodies were
frequently much broader in their composition. The 1860s

was a time of hardship for the colleges and many were hit by the reduction of government grants. Interestingly it was the women's colleges which suffered less as they were cheaper to run and there was a strong demand for women teachers as they were paid less than men.

With the passing of the 1870 Education Act there was a growing need for more teachers and the churches did what they could to meet this challenge: during the following decade the Church of England opened three further colleges and the Roman Catholics one. However the churches could barely meet the needs of their own schools let alone those of the new Board schools and the gradual decline of the Church of England's dominant position in teacher education can be dated from this time. Between 1870 and 1876 the school population virtually doubled and the efforts of the churches and other voluntary bodies were clearly insufficient. As a result of the Cross Commission's investigation into the training of teachers, state training colleges run in association with universities were proposed. There was to be no religious instruction in these colleges and they were to be on a non-residential basis and so the seminary ideal of teacher training was effectively challenged. By 1900 the universities were training one third of all teachers in sixteen colleges and so the dual system was extended into teacher training. At this time, of the residential teacher training places, 69% were in Church of England colleges, 6% in Roman Catholic colleges and the other 25% in colleges which admitted Nonconformists. The new day training colleges did in fact extend the opportunities available to Nonconformists to become teachers although of course these colleges also admitted Anglicans and this had the effect of reducing the places for others (Murphy, 1971, pp. 88 and 89).

The second challenge to the churches came in 1902 when the local education authorities entered the teacher training sphere as a consequence of the 1902 Education Act and by 1914 the local education authorities had established twenty of their own colleges. A further challenge came in 1908 when the church colleges were obliged to take up to half their students on merit irrespective of any religious background. Many churchmen disliked this as it was felt that properly Anglican colleges were essential for the Christian future of the country. This regulation had little effect on the Roman Catholic colleges for few non-Roman Catholics wished to attend such colleges.

Perhaps the most serious challenge, however, to the churches came during the two World Wars and the intervening period when the colleges were having to grapple with financial survival (for a fuller account of this see Boyd, 1984 and Lofthouse, 1983). Throughout this period closures were an ever present possibility and in 1938 the Church of England did in fact close three women's colleges at Truro, Peterborough and Brighton. At the outbreak of war in 1939 many of the colleges had obsolete buildings that were in urgent need of repair or replacement and virtually all of the colleges were facing financial difficulties. There was relatively little central government help for them. Most of the church colleges remained enclosed, single sex and small with less than 200 students.

The immediate post-war years were characterised by rapid expansion in the overall teacher training area but within this general expansion there was a major shift in balance from church to state. In 1945 the government gave grants of 50% to all existing voluntary colleges for improvements and extensions of their accommodation and facilities but nothing at all was available for the building of new colleges. Thus between 1946 and 1948 nineteen new local education authority colleges were built and overall between 1939 and 1951, while the number of voluntary colleges declined from sixty-three to fifty-six, the number of local education authority colleges increased from twenty-eight to seventy-six.

At the end of the Second World War the Church of England, centrally through its Church Assembly, decided to make a commitment to the future of its colleges. It was hoped that this commitment would encourage a more corporate feeling among the colleges and that they would abandon their earlier individualistic modes of operating. However, as Boyd (1984, p. 62) notes, the Church of England colleges' Board of Supervision did not have the same authority as the Catholic Education Council to engage in strategic planning and the individualistic mode was to continue.

Gedge (1974 and 1981) traces the post-war growth of the Anglican college system and relates it clearly to forces both in church and state which influenced developments, for development it was. An internal Anglican report in 1958 was very optimistic about the future and argued that the colleges were of great importance to the church as they provided Anglican teachers for schools, influenced parishes through their Christian teacher products and gave the church a key role in an expanding area of higher education. The following year the Church of England extended three of its colleges and provided for a new college in Canterbury which was opened in 1961. Between 1958 and 1961 the Anglican colleges had added nearly 3,000 places to their existing 5,000 and in 1960 there was a plan to double this number, although the enthusiasm for such rapid growth was beginning to wane in the church's central councils. Although there was agreement in 1962 to build a new college at Lancaster, some had doubts about the wisdom of such a venture. In 1963 the government announced that it wished to extend its teacher training numbers from 50,000 to 80,000 by 1970 and at this point the Church Assembly decided it was not willing to provide any further central funds for college extension. If colleges wished to expand any further they would have to raise their own funds. This was precisely what many did and between 1963 and 1970 the number of students in the twenty-seven Anglican colleges doubled to 19,000 representing a numerical high point for the colleges.

The 1960s was a crucial time for the colleges. The freedom and permissiveness characteristic of that decade so coloured educational thinking and action that the church colleges felt obliged to modify their own images in order to stay within the mainstream of higher education. The tightly regulated forms of communal life had to be slackened and the religious dimension increasingly phased down (see Gay, 1979, pp. 8-13). If anyone was tempted by all this to question the continuing raison d'être of the colleges they were quickly silenced by the overwhelming manpower needs and the Herculean efforts of the colleges to produce more teachers for the hard pressed schools which more than justified their existence.

The harsher climate of the 1970s brought changes on several fronts. First, monotechnics became suspect on educational, professional and administrative planning grounds. There was a growing feeling, highlighted by the James Report, that teachers ought to be educated within mainstream higher education and alongside students of other subjects. This, it was believed, would raise the level of academic education and also give students a wider perspective on life through the greater range of contacts available to them. In planning terms, larger, diversified institutions would be able to cope with the ebbs and flows of the teacher training requirements. As a result, many colleges embarked on large scale diversification programmes as colleges of <u>higher</u> education and some achieved considerable success.

A second and related change was the rapid decline in the need for new teachers from the colleges. Several factors contributed to this, the most significant being falling pupil numbers in schools and a continuing bleak economic climate. Furthermore, there was a shift in emphasis away from the professional degree which the colleges were equipped to provide, towards an academic qualification topped up with a professional diploma. The resourcing of higher education led to further question marks over the colleges. Even if small institutions could be justified on other grounds, there was a strong feeling that in terms of acceptably quantifiable factors small was expensive.

The consequence of all these contextual changes was a severe reduction in the number of Anglican institutions in the 1970s. At the beginning of the decade there were twenty-five such colleges in England and two in Wales. By the end of the decade the number had dropped to twelve in England and one in Wales and of these thirteen only nine were fully autonomous and free-standing colleges of higher education, two were federated with other voluntary colleges, one with a local education authority college and the fourth all but disappeared in a much larger college which may in the near future become a polytechnic. Of the remaining fourteen colleges, four were closed outright, eight were amalgamated with secular institutions and have in effect disappeared as church colleges and two were merged with other Anglican colleges. The work of these closed colleges continues at a much reduced level and in slightly different areas through the Church College Trusts which were formed as a result of the sale of the institutions.

The historical context affecting the Church of England was also the one in which the Roman Catholic church has had to operate. However, the principles upon which the Roman Catholic church based its teacher training activities were markedly different. The Roman Catholic church has always seen a clear and tight manpower link between the functions of its colleges and the needs of its schools. The dominant purpose of the Catholic colleges has been to train Catholic teachers in a Catholic environment to teach Catholic pupils in Catholic schools. Despite the diversified courses of recent years, the raison d'être of its colleges remains as it always has been.

It was not just the principles behind the Roman Catholic involvement in teacher education that were different: the structures also showed little similarity with the Church of England's. There was little direct diocesan initiative but instead local needs were met either through the Catholic Education Council or by one of the Religious Orders. As colleges were expensive both to found and to maintain, the resources of the largely immigrant nineteenth century Catholic communities could barely stretch to cover the colleges and so it was to the independent Religious Orders that many looked for help. The role of the Religious Orders was crucial in the development of the Catholic college system and without their initiative and resources the history of Catholic teacher education would have looked very different (Battersby, 1950 and Kennedy, 1977).

The foundations of the Catholic colleges fall conveniently into three sections. There were the five nineteenth century foundations in Liverpool, London and Hastings (although this college only survived a few years), a group of six colleges founded in the first decade of this century and a further seven colleges founded after the Second World War of which five were established during the height of the need for teachers in the 1960s. During this latter period the number of teacher training students in the Catholic colleges grew from 4,500 in 1963 to 11,000 in 1970. It was estimated that of these students only 15% were non-Catholic.

Of the original sixteen Catholic colleges which were in existence at the beginning of the 1970s only eight survived the decade. Since then, St Mary's, Fenham has closed and the college in Manchester will close in the near future. Thus of the sixteen colleges only six will go through into the future and of these only three, St Mary's Strawberry Hill, Trinity and All Saints Leeds, and La Sainte Union Southampton will remain as free standing Catholic colleges. Of the other three, Digby Stuart is a federal college in the Roehampton Institute in which staff are appointed by the Institute and then assigned to a college. The Liverpool college of Christ's and Notre Dame is in a federation of two with an Anglican college and here both the religious dimension of the institute and the Catholic dimension of the college is stronger. Although at this stage Newman College in Birmingham is autonomous, it is working in growing association with Westhill College. Despite the broadening of the mission of the Catholic colleges by the advent of diversified degree programmes in the colleges, the purposes of the teacher education courses remain similar to those operating in the past, namely to provide Catholic teachers for Catholic schools. The balance of management in the colleges remains roughly as before, a mixed economy between the Catholic Education Council and the Religious Orders.

The role of the Free Churches is somewhat different to that of the Anglican and Roman Catholic churches in that historically, as has been shown, they were aligned with a movement to establish state involvement in education. However, the Wesleyans did have a number of schools, especially in the north west, and so there was a certain manpower impetus behind the foundation of the two Methodist colleges of Westminster in 1852 and of Southlands some twenty years later, both in London. The former moved to Oxford in 1959 and the latter is now a federal college within the Roehampton Institute. The Congregational connection with Homerton is now only an historical one. Westhill, founded by a consortium of Free Churches in 1907, has survived the ravages of the 1970s and is now in an interesting academic association with the Roman Catholic Newman College.

THE PRESENT STRUCTURE AND NATURE OF THE CHURCH COLLEGES

Each of the three main denominational groups has a co-ordinating structure for its colleges. In the case of the Roman Catholic church this is the Catholic Education Council which has been able to exercise something of a strategic planning role for its colleges although this role has been somewhat weakened by the power of the independent Religious Orders. The Church of England's central Board of Education operates at a less direct level, historically explained by the decentralised nature of the Church of England, although its influence and advice has been strong. The Methodist church also has a structure within its education department for its two colleges. Both Catholic and Anglican principals meet regularly on a separate basis and the Association of Voluntary Colleges brings together principals and governors on an ecumenical basis. The move to bring all non-university sector higher education under one umbrella through the National Advisory Body (NAB) has encouraged the voluntary colleges into a closer association with the local education authority colleges. This has been achieved through the device of the Voluntary Sector Consultative Council (VSCC) which links into the NAB structures but at the same time enables the colleges to maintain something of their independent status and close link with the DES as direct grant institutions.

The extent to which relatively small institutions can remain autonomous and free-standing is a subject of some current debate. All colleges have been encouraged to look at associations with other institutions at a local level although there is inevitably some concern as to whether such associations might weaken the church relatedness of the colleges. Particularly within the Anglican group there has been a recurrent theme of some style of closer federation among the colleges at a national level, although to date nothing very definite has emerged.

One of the major difficulties in attempting to assess the future potential of the church college sector is the relative lack of research information and evidence about the colleges themselves. When the Anglican college sector was being restructured in the mid 1970s as a consequence of the closures, mergers and federations, those in the system were very conscious of this slender research base. As the dust began to settle, the author undertook a research study on the colleges and the resultant report (Gay, 1979) highlighted the lack of contemporary research evidence about the British scene and much of its work on college processes had to draw from American sources such as the Carnegie Commission. Discussion of this report encouraged action to be taken on assembling evidence on the English scene and eventually a major new initiative was launched in 1981 looking at the future role and validity of the Anglican college system. The Church Colleges Research Project, as it came to be known, was undertaken by Culham, an independent research institute founded out of the closure of an old church college with the role of investigating the issues surrounding the church's involvement in statutory education.

To what extent are the results of this work of interest beyond the Anglican colleges? A pre-publication presentation of the results was given at the residential meeting of the principals of the Association of Voluntary Colleges in March 1986 which was attended by Roman Catholic and Free Church principals and members of their sponsoring organisations. The emergent consensus was that while inevitably the details reflected the particular composition of the Anglican colleges, the general results and conclusions were extremely pertinent to the situations and needs of the other colleges. This was echoed by McClelland (1986) in a review of the report in The Tablet, the Roman Catholic weekly journal, when he concluded 'one suspects that some of the major issues thus presented are not exclusively problems for the Church of England'. In the light of this feeling that the results are of more generalisable interest to the other colleges, and given the relative lack of other evidence about the present nature of the colleges, it is proposed to summarise and amplify some of the results and their implications.

The research project was designed as a policy-oriented one and took as its central question 'what justifications can validly be put forward for the retention of the Anglican colleges in the 1980s and beyond?' The approaches adopted are set out in some detail in the Final Report and Interim Papers (Gay et al., 1986). Is there a future for the Anglican colleges? The very fact that the question could be seriously posed underlines the possibility that there might not be a future for them. Throughout its history the church has taken initiatives in many fields which it has subsequently handed over to be run by others. As has been illustrated earlier, the Anglican and Roman Catholic churches established training institutions in order to provide teachers for their growing number of day schools. But only the Roman Catholic church still retains a straightforward manpower link: the Church of England has moved away from such a link very substantially and the Free Church colleges never really had it there as a dominant motivator in the first place. Might not, therefore, teacher education be another of the fields that the church hands over to secular agencies? Answers differ, but inevitably and understandably there is major pressure for the colleges to continue.

One key element in the survival of the remaining church colleges must be their ability to demonstrate that they are comparable to similar sizes and styles of institution on issues such as academic and professional quality and value for money. There are already many agencies concerned with assessing these elements such as the validating bodies, the DES and HM Inspectorate. The Culham project focused squarely on the nature and characteristics of the Anglican colleges as church colleges.

The original distinctiveness of the church colleges lay in their foundation. Although secular institutions may contain many devout Christian staff and students, and many have thriving chaplaincies, it is in the church colleges that this religious dimension has been institutionalised. The extent to which the charter elements of the colleges continue to have visible and practical effects on their day-to-day life and work is a fundamental question and this was the one that the Culham project has attempted to investigate.

It was recognised that the research question could not be answered solely in empirical terms: any discussion about the future validity of the colleges involves a theological component as well. Consequently, as part of the research a theological critique group was formed in order to develop work in this area and its initial results were published in Gay and Francis (1985). What became rapidly apparent was that there appeared to be little development within either the Anglican colleges or the Roman Catholic and Free Church colleges of a coherent and sustained theology of education. Indeed, among a substantial number of college staff there was a grave suspicion of any theological attempts to influence the curriclum and nearly a third of them felt there was no place for the application of Christian insights in the curriculum. It is likely that the general educational philosophy prevalent in this country at present, as exemplified by exponents such as Paul Hirst, is so entrenched in the colleges that alternative world views become difficult to sustain. Waddington (1984) strongly criticises the colleges for accepting and using in an uncritical way in their teacher education courses the neo-marxist type of sociology of education which has been so successfully marketed through agencies such as the Open University. He asks why the Anglican colleges have not undertaken a theological critique of this work.

Whatever the reasons for staff reluctance to acknowledge the possibility that Christian insights might have relevance outside of the conventional religious domain, the fact that the reluctance exists is a major constraint on the ability of the colleges to develop a distinctive contribution based on their Christian foundations to teacher education in the future. It is hoped that the highlighting of this finding in the report will encourage the colleges to give serious attention to this and perhaps develop a critique on an ecumenical basis.

Although the report could find little evidence of

explicit theological critique of the work and contribution of the colleges, nevertheless at a more implicit level there was a very powerful and practical theological critique contained in the replies given in the questionnaires by large numbers of theologically competent lay people, clergy and bishops. In considering their answers to a variety of questions, they used a theological yardstick as one of their measures. Although one must be cautious about putting too much emphasis on it, the fact that the large majority of bishops, clergy and laity in the General Synod felt there was a continuing validity for the church colleges is inevitably in part a theological statement.

Eleven of the thirteen remaining Anglican colleges in England and Wales were included in the empirical study. It was decided to adopt a cross-sectional approach to the work and in all the views and perceptions of over 7,500 people were sought. These included all members of the General Synod of the Church of England, head teachers of church aided schools, head teachers of the colleges' teaching practice schools, the staff and students of the colleges themselves and a number of other significant groups. Much of the work was done using questionnaires and overall a very satisfactory response rate of 69% was obtained. The questionnaires were supplemented by interviews, visits and other methods. As a result of the research, a detailed picture has emerged of the Anglican colleges as they are at present.

All the colleges are small institutions as compared with universities or polytechnics; they range in size from about 600 to about 1,700 students. The larger ones tend to retain smaller community units within them, generally based on what, before amalgamation, were independent colleges. Each has a good proportion of student accommodation on site offering residence for at least the first year students and in many cases for some second and third year students as well.

Whilst originally all the colleges were founded for the education and training of teachers, most have diversified over the last twenty years by providing training for other caring services beside teaching and more generally by offering degree courses in a range of subjects mostly on the arts side. The proportion of full-time students following first degree courses other than the BEd degree varies greatly from college to college but overall is about 50%. All the colleges additionally have a substantial programme of in-service training for teachers, mostly part-time, which in some cases takes up as much as a fifth of the total teaching load. The education and training of teachers, therefore, represents the major workload and concern of the colleges in quantitative terms.

Students drawn to the colleges tend to be predominantly female, well over twice as many women as men, and middle class, over half of them being from social groups one or two. For most of their families the present generation represents their first experience of higher education. The great majority are aged twenty or less when they come to college. The academic level of undergraduate students on entry is fairly modest, although as far as can be judged from other recent research this is no different from other students entering polytechnics and colleges of higher education in general, but much lower than university entrants. All the colleges recruit nationally and most show little obvious regional bias. While half the students are engaged in degrees other than BEd, about four-fifths of them in their first year in college are considering teaching either as their chosen profession or as one of the options to which they are giving serious thought.

In their responses to questionnaires the first year students showed themselves as somewhat immature and lacking in confidence: nearly three-quarters had some anxieties about coping with their course and about two-thirds felt some concern about homesickness, whilst almost as many were worried about failing to make friends in college. For such students the security of a relatively small, resident society is important, and it is significant that many of them specifically linked the friendliness of the college with its size. The colleges certainly seem to be providing a supportive environment in which such students can develop.

The third year student group was very similar in most respects to the first year students - for example in the proportion of women students, the age pattern, the proportion who came straight from school to college and the numbers following BA and BEd courses. PGCE students are rather a different group from either of the undergraduate groups in the survey. The sexes are rather more evenly balanced, more are older and they appear to be more able academically - their A level qualifications are much higher and the levels of their degree are comparable with those of PGCE students in university departments of education.

The colleges share a number of features which mark

221

them out as Christian institutions. The nature of their foundations is, in most cases, obvious from their name and it is made clear in the prospectuses. The chapel is in nearly all cases a feature and in some a central feature of their complex of buildings. While in many ways the colleges appear to be more secular institutions than they were thirty or forty years ago, this may be more a difference in the degree of outward observance than of actuality: there is some evidence that even in the past the students in church colleges were frequently not people with very profound beliefs.

The level of religious commitment of staff and students remains high in comparison with similar groups of people in other walks of life. Three-quarters of the students describe themselves as members of one of the main Christian denominations, not far short of one in three say they attend church services regularly 'most weeks' and a slightly lower proportion overall describe themselves as having 'strong' or 'total' commitment to Christianity (22% of the first year, 30% of the third year and 34% of the PGCE students). Well over half profess at least 'moderate' commitment to Christianity. The same is true, to an even greater extent, of the academic staff. Again three-quarters describe themselves as members of the Anglican, Roman Catholic or Free Churches, 44% claim 'strong' or 'total' commitment to Christianity and a further 24% 'moderate' commitment. 41% attend church services weekly and a further 13% at least once a month. Only one in five describe themselves as having no commitment to Christianity and a mere 1% as being hostile.

A major part of the research was to identify those objectives to which various groups thought the colleges ought to be assigning priority. Where the expectations of all or most of the different groups consulted tend to converge it is possible to assert with some confidence that these are essential characteristics of the church colleges. From the responses to this section of the inquiry, three major expectations emerge. The first is that the great majority see the colleges' role as being pre-eminently concerned with their traditional task of educating teachers. All groups see teacher education - the original raison d'être of church colleges - as of prime importance. This finding is perhaps not surprising considering that the bulk of the work in most colleges, when their heavy involvement in in-service training is included, is in the teacher education field. Their education departments, in almost every case, are substantial in size when compared with those in universities and polytechnics and collectively their contribution to the national requirement for trained teachers is large and indispensible. It is no wonder, therefore, that this is seen as their major role. They could survive without much of their diversified work: they could barely do so without their involvement in the education of teachers.

The second major expectation to emerge is that the colleges should be recognisably Christian institutions with worship at their centre and a concern to create communities based on Christian principles and to communicate Christian values. Considering the poor press that worship often receives, it is interesting to note the almost universal importance attached to a worshipping dimension of college life by groups both within and outside of the colleges.

The third major expectation to emerge is that the colleges should have an important role in religious education and also in relating Christian insights to their curriculum. This expectation is shared by all the outside church-based groups, but not so much by the college groups themselves. In both of these areas major mismatches of expectation arise.

Given the importance of the manpower issue in the past, it is interesting to note that the training of teachers for Anglican schools is among the objectives least frequently identified by the groups within the colleges with about a third of the staff, students and heads of teaching practice schools feeling it should be given no priority whatsoever. The role of the Anglican colleges is thus seen to be very different from that of the Roman Catholic colleges in this aspect. Even the heads of Anglican aided schools, who might be expected to take a particular interest in the products of church colleges, do not expect this to be a major part of the colleges' role.

Over the years the colleges have undoubtedly become more secular although caution needs to be exercised in any interpretations of the situation. It would appear that more recently the process of secularisation may have been checked and in some cases reversed. Some colleges have begun to reaffirm their Christian foundation more strongly and sought to fulfil a more specific Christian role in higher education. The fact that the majority of interested groups both within and outside the colleges believe they should have such a role may well reinforce such a tendency. While the principal justification for church colleges, as for any institution of higher education, is that they are fully effective places providing higher education of quality, the fact that they are attempting to do this within a Christian context is a further and unique qualification that should not be lightly discarded.

Although there is this major expectation that the Anglican colleges should be recognisably Christian institutions with worship at their centre and a genuine concern to create Christian communities and to communicate Christian values it is much more difficult to show whether they are in fact distinctive, especially when the possibility of direct comparison with other secular colleges was not available to us. This study of the Anglican colleges shows them as having marked individuality, but they also appear to have many characteristics in common, some of which set them apart from most other colleges. They are mostly fairly small, have a substantial residential element and a major involvement in teacher education although these are all characteristics shared by many other institutions. What initially appears to differentiate them from most other colleges is the nature of their foundation and the expectation that they should display certain Christian qualities and fulfil a Christian role.

In order to judge whether the colleges are distinctive in fact and not simply in the expectations people have of them, five particular aspects of the study were drawn upon. These are firstly the basic characteristics of the colleges themselves; secondly, the degree to which various objectives relating to the priorities of the colleges are being pursued; thirdly, the extent to which the objectives are being successfully achieved; fourthly, responses of various groups to a number of questions directly raising the issue of college distinctiveness; and fifthly, the subjective impressions of the colleges by members of the research team as a result of their visits to them.

It was concluded that no one of the characteristics discussed is in any way unique to the Anglican colleges. Thus, one could point to a polytechnic with an active and effective chaplaincy working among its students, or to an LEA college with a Christian principal and a high proportion of Christians among its staff whose beliefs and attitudes influence the ethos of the college. In few other institutions, however, is the range of characteristics identified combined within a single institution. The Anglican colleges do share a group of characteristics sufficiently marked for them to be seen as a coherent group standing, to some extent, apart from other higher education institutions and not simply as a random collection of individual colleges. Moreover the group of characteristics identified is not a haphazard or accidental occurrence, but one which is purposeful and the outcome of a deliberate policy. It is in respect of the overall profile of these characteristics rather than one or two single factors that the church colleges stand out as distinctive.

The really difficult question to answer is the extent to which the distinctiveness of the colleges affects their impact upon their student population. Although it is not possible to identify special characteristics of former students which can be directly attributed to their time at college, it is likely that institutions with a clear sense of purpose shared by a high proportion of staff and students and with a range of characteristics which cumulatively distinguish them from other colleges of higher education will have an impact on students who spend three or four years in them at an important stage in their developing maturity. The report concludes that this expectation derives some support from the empirical evidence available.

All those taking part in the study were asked whether they thought the church colleges had a future and the overwhelming majority felt they did. Two main reasons for this positive answer emerged. First, was because many felt the colleges are doing a good job and especially they are judged by many to be providing the appropriate context for teacher education which is viewed as their prime purpose. They are seen as the right size and style of community for the students who come to them and for the tasks that they are attempting. The second reason for the strong support is because the colleges are seen as distinctive. Evidence such as the religious commitment of staff and students, college worship, the expectations and perceptions of various groups and the styles of community that the colleges try to create form a cumulative basis for asserting that the colleges are offering a distinctive and valued contribution to British higher education and that this contribution is underpinned by their Christian foundations.

However, there is much in the research study to challenge the colleges particularly in the area of their distinctive role. Their work in religious education, in relating Christian insights to the curriculum and their links with church schools are all areas of potential weakness which need much greater attention. The apparent inability

225

of the colleges to evolve a Christian theology of education and curriculum is serious and this is identified as one of the main issues that the colleges should consider deeply over the next few years when planning their future. Conversely, the church itself is challenged to become more aware of and work more closely with its colleges. A key finding from the project was the considerable lack of awareness of the current situation within the colleges and also of their purposes among crucial groups outside the colleges, such as members of the General Synod, the head teachers of church schools and diocesan directors of education. One reviewer of the report has suggested that the colleges are suffering a crisis of identity and that this crisis is not confined just to the Anglican colleges. The extent to which the church colleges remain recognisably Christian institutions in the future is at this stage an open question. The report both illustrates great weaknesses and sounds notes of warning and yet at the same time points to areas of strength, both potential and actual, and ends on a note of hope.

CONCLUSION

While many individual colleges have been closed, and in recent years all colleges have felt at risk, nevertheless there has been no concerted threat to the sector as a whole. The churches' role in teacher education, through their colleges, looks as if it will remain for some years to come. As long as the churches continue to have institutional involvement in state maintained schooling then it is likely that their colleges will be seen as a necessary part of the teacher education pattern. Although the manpower links between the Church of England's schools and colleges are not strong, nevertheless the fact that 8% of all primary pupils are in Church of England aided schools and 10% in Church of England controlled schools is likely to be sufficient cause for the Church of England to have a continuing opportunity to be involved in teacher education in the years ahead. At a political level it is unlikely that the small Free Church involvement could be completely eliminated unless such a desire was expressed by the Free Churches themselves. In the case of the Roman Catholic church, however, the manpower link is tight and it is difficult to visualise how the Roman Catholic sector of schooling, which educates 10% of the nation's primary

226

children, could be supplied with appropriate teachers without the existence of the Roman Catholic colleges.

Whether the diversification of the colleges into other areas of work has helped either the colleges themselves in the long term or their teacher education role is a debatable point. Certainly the diversified courses have added a new dimension to the colleges but teacher education remains their primary and dominant function. Whilst the churches could continue to have some residual involvement in teacher education without their colleges, such involvement would be a pale reflection of the present position; as in many spheres there tends to be no substitute for an institutional presence. However, institutional involvement in itself is no guarantee that the purposes which institutions are assumed to be fulfilling are in practice being achieved: it is the nature of what goes on in institutions which is crucial. As well as tracing the historical evolution of the churches' institutional presence, this study has attempted to look at what is happening inside one group of colleges. The extent to which the colleges can offer a distinctive contribution to teacher education based on their Christian foundations is likely to determine their long term future.

NOTES

1. The author has experienced considerable difficulty in reconciling the numbers of colleges quoted by different authors at different dates with the lists of colleges in existence according to their foundation dates. There is scope here for further historical investigation on the early history of each college, but such investigation is beyond the brief of this chapter. Hence, in certain instances, use is made of approximate numbers.

APPENDIX

THE CHURCH COLLEGES OF H.E. IN ENGLAND AND WALES IN 1987

Roman Catholic

Christ's and Notre Dame, Liverpool (Liverpool Institute)
De la Salle, Manchester (about to close)
Digby Stuart, London (Roehampton Institute)
La Sainte Union, Southampton
Newman, Birmingham
St Mary's, Strawberry Hill, London
Trinity and All Saints, Leeds

Church of England/Wales

Bishop Grosseteste, Lincoln
Bishop Otter, Chichester (West Sussex Institute)
Christ Church, Canterbury
The College, Chester
King Alfred's, Winchester
Ripon and York St John
St Katharine's, Liverpool (Liverpool Institute)
St Mark and St John, Plymouth
St Martin's, Lancaster
St Paul and St Mary, Cheltenham
Trinity, Carmarthen
Whitelands, London (Roehampton Institute)
(Derbyshire College remains in a special relationship with the Church of England)

Appendix

Methodist

Southlands, London (Roehampton Institute)
Westminster, Oxford

Free Church

Westhill, Birmingham

BIBLIOGRAPHY

Adelman, C. and Gibbs, I. (1979). A Study of Student Choice in the Context of Institutional Change, Bulmershe College, Reading

Alves, C. (1979). The Church Colleges into the 1990s, The College of Ripon and York St John, Occasional Paper No. 2

Ball, C. (1985). Fitness for Purpose: Essays in Higher Education, S.R.H.E., Guildford, Surrey

Battersby, W.J. (1950) 'Educational Work of the Religious Orders of Women' in Beck, G.A. (ed.) The English Catholics 1850-1950, Burns and Oates, London

Bereday, G. and Lauwerys, J. (1966). Church and State in Education, World Yearbook in Education

Berry, M. (1973). Teacher Training Institutions in England and Wales, a Bibliographical Guide to their History, S.R.H.E., Guildford, Surrey

Boyd, M.V. (1984). The Church of England Colleges 1890-1944: an Administrative Study, Educational Administration and History Monograph No. 14, University of Leeds

Bradbury, J.L. (1975). Chester College and the Training of Teachers 1839-1975, Chester College

Catholic Education Council for England and Wales, Annual Reports

Chadwick. O. (1966, 1970). The Victorian Church, Pts. 1 and 2, A. and C. Black

Collier, K.G. (1959). 'Religion in a Church College' in Education for Teaching, November 1959, pp. 28-9

Cruickshank, M. (1963). Church and State in English Education, Macmillan

Bibliography

Dent, H.C. (1977). The Training of Teachers in England and Wales 1800-1975, Hodder and Stoughton

Department of Education and Science (1972). Education: A Framework for Expansion, Cmnd. 5174, H.M.S.O.

Durham Commission (1970). The Fourth R: The Report of the Commission on Religious Education in Schools, S.P.C.K.

Gay, J.D. (1979). The Christian Campus? The Role of the English Churches in Higher Education, Culham College Institute, Abingdon

Gay, J.D. (1981). 'Religious bias in British higher education' in Warren-Piper, D. (ed.), Is Higher Education Fair?, pp. 140-59, S.R.H.E., Guildford, Surrey

Gay, J.D. (1983). Chaplaincy in Church Colleges, Culham Occasional Paper No. 3, Culham College Institute, Abingdon

Gay, J.D. and Francis, L.J. (1985). The Future of the Anglican Colleges: A Preliminary Theological Critique, Interim Paper No. 3, Culham College Institute, Abingdon

Gay, J.D. et al. (1986). The Future of the Anglican Colleges: Final Report of the Church Colleges Research Project, Culham College Institute, Abingdon

Gedge, P.S. (1974). The Role of a Church of England College of Education, M.Ed. Thesis, University of Birmingham

Gedge, P.S. (1981). 'The Church of England Colleges of Education since 1944' in Journal of Educational Administration and History, pp. 33-42

General Synod Board of Education, (1977). The Camberwell Papers, G.S. Misc. 60, Church House, Westminster

General Synod Board of Education, (1980). The Church Colleges of Higher Education: the Financial Involvement of the General Synod, G.S. 417, Church House, Westminster

General Synod Board of Education, (1980). Partners in Understanding: An Account of Church of England Chaplaincy in Higher Education, Church House, Westminster

Gibbs, I. and Harland, J. (1984). The Diversified Colleges: Student and Graduate Experience, A report from the Combined Colleges Research Group, College of Ripon and York St John

Hornsby-Smith, M.P. (1978). Catholic Education: The Unobtrusive Partner, Sheed and Ward, London

Jebb, P. (1968). Religious Education: Drift or Decision?

231

D.L.T., London

Jones-Davies, C. (1986). 'The Anglican Colleges of Higher Education', in Yates, J. (ed.), Faith for the Future, National Society, Westminster

Kennedy, S. (1977). An Examination of Catholic Education and the Work of the Catholic Poor Schools Committee 1800-1888, private publication made available by the Catholic Education Council

Locke, M., Pratt, J. and Burgess, T. (1985). The Colleges of Higher Education 1972 to 1982: The Central Management of Organic Change, Critical Press, Croydon

Lofthouse, M.T. (1983). Teacher Training - the Church Colleges 1890-1944, Ph.D. Thesis, University of Leicester

Lynch, J. (1979). The Reform of Teacher Education in the United Kingdom, S.R.H.E., Guildford, Surrey

McClelland, V.A. (1973). English Roman Catholics and Higher Education 1830-1903, Oxford University Press

McClelland, V.A. (1986). 'A Crisis of Identity', in The Tablet, 14.6.86

McGregor, G.P. (1981). Bishop Otter College and Policy for Teacher Education 1839-1980, Pembridge Press, London

Murphy, J. (1971). Church, State and Schools in Britain, 1800-1970, R.K.P.

Niblett, W.R. (1976). The Church's Colleges of Higher Education, Independent Publication, Church Information Office, Westminster

Powell, R.N. (1978). Tradition and Change in Church of England Teacher Training Colleges 1944-1974, M.Ed. Thesis, University of Manchester

Pye, M. (1977). The Language of the Church in Higher and Further Education: An Account of the Bradwell Consultation, Church House, Westminster

Rich, R.W. (1933). The Training of Teachers in England and Wales during the Nineteenth Century, Cambridge University Press

Robertson, J.S. (1971). 'Voluntary Colleges', in Hewett, S., The Training of Teachers: A Factual Survey, University of London Press, pp. 42-50

Rose, M. (1981). A History of King Alfred's College, Winchester, 1840-1980, Phillimore, Chichester

Seaman, R.D.H. (1978). St Peter's College, Saltley, 1944-1978, St Peter's College, Saltley, Birmingham

Spencer, A.E.C.W. (1971). The Future of Catholic Education

in England and Wales, Catholic Renewal Movement

Thatcher, A. (1986). 'Questions of faith in the light of experience' in Times Higher Education Supplement, 11.4.86, p. 14

Waddington, R. (1984). A Future in Partnership, The National Society, Church House, Westminster

Working Party on Christian Involvement in Higher and Further Education, (1978). Christian Involvement in Higher Education, National Society, Church House, Westminster

Wyatt, J.F. (1977). 'The Idea of "Community" in Institutions of Higher Education' in Studies in Higher Education, pp. 125-35

Wyatt, J.F. (1977). 'Collegiality during a period of rapid change in higher education: an examination of a distinctive feature claimed by a group of colleges of education in the 1960s and 1970s' in Oxford Review of Education, pp. 147-55

Wyatt, J.F. and Gay, J.D. (1984). 'The Educational Effects of Different Sizes and Types of Academic Organisation', in Oxford Review of Education, Vol. 10, No. 2, pp. 211-23

CONTRIBUTORS

Brenda Almond is Director of the Social Values Research Centre and Reader in Philosophy and Education, University of Hull

Alan S. Brown is R.E. (Schools) Officer to the Board of Education of the General Synod of the Church of England

T.A. FitzPatrick is a former Vice-principal of Notre Dame College of Education in Glasgow

John D. Gay is Director of the Culham College Institute for Church Related Education

John E. Greer is Reader in Education, University of Ulster

Edward Hulmes is Professorial Fellow in Theology at the University of Durham and Fellow of the Centre for Theological Inquiry at Princeton in the United States

Philip R. May is Reader in Education, University of Durham

Vincent A. McClelland is Professor of Educational Studies at Hull University and Anatole von Hügel Fellow at St Edmund's College, Cambridge

James O'Connell is Professor of Peace Studies at Bradford University

Bernadette O'Keeffe works at the Centre for Educational Studies, King's College, London (KQC)

234

Contributors

Derek H. Webster is in charge of religious education programmes in the School of Education, University of Hull

INDEX

Agreed Syllabus of Religious
  Education 45, 52, 58, 70-1,
  103-4, 121
  Bedfordshire 72-3
  Berkshire 54
  Birmingham 103
  Bradford 66
  Cambridgeshire 57
  Hertfordshire 66
  Humberside 55
  Warwickshire 53
  West Riding 65
Anderson, R.D. 1860
Aquinas, Saint Thomas 61,
  123, 130
Augustine, Saint 69, 123,
  130

Barclay, O.R. 5
Batson, C.D. 66
Belgium, language teaching
  in 118
Benvenisti, M. 96-7
Bible 5-12 passim, 18, 36, 45
  Genesis 3, 6, 8
  New Testament 107, 125-7
  on role of parents 9-10
  Proverbs 9-10
birth control 39
Blamires, H. 5, 15, 18, 20,
  27

Catholic
  Education Commission 179
  Education Council 35, 192,
  215-16
  Poor School Committee
  185
  Schools Society 165
celibacy 39
Chichester Project 45
church
  Churches Joint Educational
  Policy Committee 47
  Colleges Research Project
  (Culham Project) 217-22,
  224-6
  of Scotland Act 1921 173
  role in education 4-18
  passim, 27, 84-94 passim,
  97, 103, 113, 146, 161, 179,
  196-8, 223, 226
  see also schools, teacher-
  training institutions

Darby, J. 139-41
Dawson, C. 23, 28-9
discipline
  in the home 8-11 passim
Dunn, S. 141
Durham Report on Religious
  Education 195, 197

Christian education in a
pluralist society